"This is **the best book I have read on small-cap stock investing.** It is easy to read and **jam-packed with ideas** on how to successfully navigate this seemingly difficult investment area. It is **required reading for professionals and individual investors alike.** There is more to buying small-cap stocks than meets the eye. This book is **timely** because **we are about to see a major shift** from big-cap stocks that have controlled the market to the small-cap universe."

> THOMAS J. DORSEY
> President
> *Dorsey, Wright & Associates, Inc.*

"*Investing in Small-Cap Stocks* **combines the ideas of Wall Street's top money managers into a practical, comprehensive plan** for the individual investor. From explaining the basics to identifying successful strategies for small-cap investors, *Investing in Small-Cap Stocks* is a **good foundation for investing in one of the most lucrative sectors** of the stock market."

> JIM OBERWEIS, JR.
> Vice President & Portfolio Manager
> *Oberweis Asset Management*

"*Investing in Small-Cap Stocks* provides a broad overview of investing in general and of small-cap stocks in particular. **It should help individual investors get off on the right foot.**"

> LAURA LALLOS
> Senior Analyst
> *Morningstar*

INVESTING IN

Small-Cap
STOCKS

Also available from
THE BLOOMBERG PERSONAL BOOKSHELF

Smarter Insurance Solutions
by Janet Bamford

A Commonsense Guide to Mutual Funds
by Mary Rowland

And from
THE BLOOMBERG PROFESSIONAL LIBRARY

Best Practices for Financial Advisors
by Mary Rowland

*Swap Literacy:
A Comprehensible Guide*
by Elizabeth Ungar, Ph.D.

*An Introduction to
Option-Adjusted Spread Analysis*
(Revised Edition)
by Tom Windas

INVESTING IN

Small-Cap STOCKS

CHRISTOPHER GRAJA AND ELIZABETH UNGAR, Ph.D.

Bloomberg Press

◆

PRINCETON

Books are available for bulk purchases at special discounts. For information, please write: Special Markets Department, Bloomberg Press.

This publication contains the author's opinions and is designed to provide accurate and authoritative information. It is sold with the understanding that the author, publisher, and Bloomberg L.P. are not engaged in rendering legal, accounting, investment-planning, or other professional advice. The reader should seek the services of a qualified professional for such advice; the author, publisher, and Bloomberg L.P. cannot be held responsible for any loss incurred as a result of specific investments by the reader.

First edition published 1997
1 3 5 7 9 10 8 6 4 2

Graja, Christopher, 1966–

    Investing in small-cap stocks / Christopher Graja and Elizabeth Ungar.

        p.   cm.

    Includes bibliographical references and index.

    ISBN 1-57660-012-2 (alk. paper)

    1. Small capitalization stocks. I. Ungar, Elizabeth Merrifield,

1951–   . II. Title.

HG4751.G7   1997   97-7862

332.63' 044—DC21   CIP

Permissions credits continued on page 221.
Chart illustrations by Myra Klockenbrink.
Diamond icon illustration by Natasha Tibbott.

Book design by Don Morris Design

To Jennifer and Claire,

for their love,

friendship,

and encouragement

— C.G.

ACKNOWLEDGMENTS

THIS BOOK HAS BEEN A LOT OF FUN to write, thanks to the support and enthusiasm of countless people. Here's where my coauthor and I get to actually say thanks to a few of them.

From concept through research, writing, and revising, Bill Inman, who manages the magazine and publishing group, has given us his complete support and nearly unlimited resources to produce the best book we could. That task was made easier by the fact that we work for an organization and a boss as well respected as Bloomberg Financial Markets and Mike Bloomberg, whose name opened doors and data banks for us. Among the market professionals who answered our questions, offered ideas, and provided research and charts, we owe a particular debt to Bill Berger, founder of the Berger Funds; Mike Berry at Heartland Advisors; Dan Coker at NatWest Securities; Michael Gerding of Founders Funds; Roger Ibbotson of Ibbotson Associates; Steve Kim at Merrill Lynch; Claudia Mott at Prudential Securities; Bill Nasgovitz of Heartland Advisors; Steve Norwitz at T. Rowe Price; Jim Oberweis Jr. of Oberweis Funds; Satya Pradhuman at Merrill Lynch; Robert Rodriguez of First Pacific

Advisors; Tom Dorsey of Dorsey, Wright & Assoc.; Chuck Royce of Quest Advisory; John Spears of Tweedy, Browne Co.; and Matt Wright at First Investors.

Our colleagues at Bloomberg deserve particular thanks. We're grateful for the help and encouragement given by Mike Tonrey, Roy Thoden, Bill Merk, and the library staff; Jon Heller, Seth Pitkow, John Place, Joe Schmitz, Scott Darvin, and Noel Cook from the Bloomberg Equity group; the Bloomberg Teledata department; Matt Winkler and Tim Quinson of Bloomberg News; and John Aubert, Stuart Bell, Mike Hastings, Fred Mitchell, Erin Sanders, Kevin Foley, and Tom Heebink, able managers all.

We'll be picking up the tab well into the 21st century to repay the Bloomberg Press people for their fine editing and assistance, as well as fellow magazine staffers, for their research, opinions, and suggestions. So thank you, Jared Kieling, John Crutcher, Barbara Diez, Priscilla Treadwell, Matt Goldenberg, Maria Pittore, Bill Hester, Mary Ann McGuigan, and Andy Treinen.

And finally, thanks to our parents, who raised us well.

INTRODUCTION

HIS IS A NO-NONSENSE guide to making money. It's for long-term investors, not speculators, people who want to beat inflation but aren't willing to stake their life's savings on the slim chance of making a killing. And the best way I know to achieve superior returns with reasonable risk is to put part of your savings into stocks having small market capitalizations—companies like the Scotts Co. and Vans, Inc., whose issued shares have market values that are dwarfed by those of IBM and Microsoft.

You probably already know that in the long run, stocks beat out investments like bonds and money markets. You may also have heard that small stocks trounce larger ones. If not, here are a few stats to convince you: According to a study by Chicago-based consultants Ibbotson Associates (whose findings are summarized in the charts on pages 4 through 7), stocks outperformed bonds in every one of the 20-year periods from 1926 to 1995, and in 94 percent of those periods, the smallest stocks did better than larger ones. Twenty years is probably a suitable investment horizon for most working people. But even if you're retired and most of your biggest bills lie behind you, you may well need to keep your savings growing for another 10 years or more. So you should know that Ibbotson also concluded that stocks beat out bonds in 86 percent of the 10-year periods between 1926 and 1995, and the smallest stocks outshone all other investments in 60 percent of those periods.

With comparisons like that, why am I telling you to put just part of your savings in small stocks?

Why not the whole wad? Because, as you probably also know, there's no free lunch. Higher returns come with greater risks. That's the curse of an efficient market.

Investors in U.S. Treasury bills, notes, and bonds may barely beat inflation, but they know if they hold on to their securities till maturity, they'll get their principal back; equity investors can lose their shirts. In addition, the small-cap performance figures quoted above have been averaged over a 70-year period, a process that smooths out some heavy-duty price volatility and variability. During

20-YEAR ROLLING PERIOD RETURNS

TYPE	MAXIMUM VALUE	
	RETURN	YEARS
Small Company Stocks	21.13	1942–61
Large Company Stocks	16.86	1942–61
Long-Term Corporate Bonds	10.58	1976–95
Long-Term Government Bonds	10.45	1976–95
Intermediate-Term Government Bonds	9.85	1974–93
U.S. Treasury Bills	7.72	1972–91
Inflation	6.36	1966–85

certain months, years, even decades, the small-stock group lagged giants like Intel Corp. and Nike. And for the entire period, the triple-digit growth of a few stars pulled up a large number of stocks that went nowhere or failed altogether. Small companies, which often have only a few products and limited reserves against hard times, are particularly vulnerable to recessions, rising interest rates, or the loss of key executives; it takes only a few spooked investors to send their sparsely traded shares down the tube.

In short, small stocks are risky. Pick the wrong

MINIMUM VALUE		TIMES POSITIVE (OUT OF	TIMES HIGHEST
RETURN	YEARS	51 OVERLAPPING 20-YR PERIODS)	RETURNING ASSET
5.74	1929–48	51	48
3.11	1929–48	51	3
1.34	1950–69	51	0
0.69	1950–69	51	0
1.58	1940–59	51	0
0.42	1931–50	51	0
0.07	1926–45	51	0

SOURCE: IBBOTSON ASSOCIATES

one or the wrong time to buy it, and you can kiss part of your nest egg goodbye. "Certainly in any study that you ever read about how small caps have performed, you are going to see that you get that extra return," says Prudential Securities director of small-cap research Claudia Mott. "But it doesn't come without a lot of added risk. And, certainly, the smaller you get in size, the worse the risk tends to get."

The lesson is to be cautious, not afraid. Despite their volatility and principal imperilment, these investments are still your best buffer against what

10-YEAR ROLLING PERIOD RETURNS

| | MAXIMUM VALUE | |
TYPE	RETURN	YEARS
Small Company Stocks	30.38	1975–84
Large Company Stocks	20.06	1949–58
Long-Term Corporate Bonds	16.32	1982–91
Long-Term Government Bonds	15.56	1982–91
Intermediate-Term Government Bonds	13.13	1982–91
U.S. Treasury Bills	9.17	1978–87
Inflation	8.67	1973–82

Bill Wilson, economist at Comerica Bank, has characterized as the real danger facing low-saving Americans: having to spend their underfunded golden years flipping burgers under the Golden Arches. Small stocks have offered better returns over the past 70 years than any investment except loans to new businesses. You need the kind of reward they offer to reach your long-range goals. And you can reduce the risks that go with it by just planning your portfolio properly, doing a bit of homework, and sticking to a few well-thought-out strategies. That's what this book is about.

| MINIMUM VALUE | | TIMES POSITIVE (OUT OF 61 | TIMES HIGHEST |
RETURN	YEARS	OVERLAPPING 10-YR PERIODS)	RETURNING ASSET
-5.70	1929–38	59	35
-0.89	1929–38	59	16
0.98	1947–56	61	6
-0.07	1950–59	60	0
1.25	1947–56	61	2
0.15	1933–42/1934–43	61	1
-2.57	1926–35	55	1

SOURCE: IBBOTSON ASSOCIATES

In the following chapters my coauthor, Elizabeth Ungar, and I will explain how to incorporate the high performance of small stocks into your portfolio without high anxiety. The exact method you choose will depend on what kind of investor you are. You might feel most comfortable, for example, leaving the detailed decisions to a professional. In that case, you would probably do all your small-cap investing through mutual funds. A good fund manager can earn you returns of 15 percent a year. That's after expenses, which can be steep—usually about 1 to 2 percent of the assets you invest. But doing it right yourself isn't cheap, either: One percent of a $100,000 investment is $1,000, which disappears pretty fast when you start buying a souped-up computer and subscribing to a few periodicals. And that doesn't count the time you need to spend.

On the other hand, you might be someone who likes to take matters into your own hands. You should still probably put a large part of your small-cap portfolio into funds. But you might want to devote a small portion to individual stocks, picking and following these yourself or with the help of a broker specializing in the small-cap market.

Whichever route you choose, this book will help you on your way with information, advice, and strategies—all of it supplied by experts in the field and expressed whenever possible in their own words. (One cautionary note: A disadvantage of letting people speak their own minds is that you also allow them to cite their own pet statistics; as a result, the same point made in different places in the book may be bolstered by different data, none necessarily inaccurate, just derived from diverse time periods or sets of securities.)

Each chapter builds on the previous ones. The opening chapter lays the groundwork, presenting definitions and discussions of basic terms and concepts. Chapter 2 addresses mutual funds and how to use them in your small-cap investing. The third discusses how to create and care for a portfolio of small stocks; Chapter 4 presents some strategies to use in picking and weeding out your investments. Finally, following these chapters are an appendix, listing small-cap companies alphabetically and broken down by state, and a "Resources" section, containing the names and phone numbers of regional brokerages as well as sources for further reading and research.

The book is written for a range of readers, from relative market novices to those who, though not professionals, have experience with stocks and perhaps have dabbled in derivatives. Sophisticated investors may want to skip the introductory material and concentrate on the strategies section. Less experienced ones should probably start at the beginning, to ensure they have the background they need at each stage to apply the recommendations and schemes described. They may then decide to stop at the funds chapter but later dip in again to learn more about investing in individual small stocks.

So turn the page or flip to the chapter that interests you most. The one ground rule is to enjoy yourself. Sure, investing, by definition, means giving up something: stuff you won't allow yourself to spend money on right now, time you have to devote to tending your nest egg. But don't let it drive you nuts. A reporter once asked Tom Kite (at the time, golf's all-time money winner) how he dealt with the pressure of a putt on which several hundred thousand dollars were riding. He answered that having the chance to win that much money wasn't a burden; it was the culmination of everything he'd worked for. We all dream of being able to do something to make life better for our families. You should feel good about investing. Just by doing it, you're miles ahead of the rest of the world.

CHRISTOPHER GRAJA

CHAPTER

1

LAYING THE
Foundation

SUCCESSFUL INVESTING has two components. One is finding areas where you have an edge and putting your money there. The other is integrating the investments you make into a diverse portfolio that has been constituted to reflect both your long- and short-term savings goals.

In this chapter, you'll see that the small-cap sector is one area in which an individual investor can find an edge—where, in fact, small players have distinct advantages over large institutions. You'll learn, as well, how small stocks fit into a general investment strategy, both boosting the returns of your portfolio and reducing their variability. Along the way, I'll slip in a few definitions of concepts that you will need to understand in order to apply the tips and advice given in later chapters.

A SMALL CAP IS NOT A BEANIE

"I would tell every individual investor not to spend a whole lot of time analyzing Coca-Cola. If they're going to put their efforts on something and do stock analysis, it should be in the microcap, small-cap area."

—JOHN MARKESE, *president of the American Association of Individual Investors, during a February 1996 episode of "Adam Smith's Money World"*

YOU'VE PROBABLY GOT THE IDEA by now that small-cap companies can be a good investment. But what exactly are they? To understand, you have to know that *cap* is shorthand for *market capitalization,* which refers to the market value of a company's common stock. It is equal to the number of shares outstanding times the price per share. So a small-cap company is one that either has issued only a few shares or trades at a low price in the market. It may not be diminutive by any other measure—sales, assets, staff—

though just about everyone in the field, including me, uses *small stock, small company,* and *small cap* interchangeably.

Microsoft, which has 597.6 million shares outstanding, each priced, as of November 1996, at $150.50, is obviously a large-cap stock; fast-food franchiser Nathan's Famous, with 4.7 million $3 shares, is just as indisputably small. Somewhere in between lies the cutoff—exactly where depends on who's counting and whether the market as a whole has been growing or retrenching. Complicating matters, *non*large stocks are often subdivided into *mid-, small-,* and *microcap.*

The fluidity of the boundaries between all these categories is one reason analysts often refer not to dollar ranges but to *deciles* and *quintiles*—10- and 20-percent segments, respectively, of a universe of stocks ranked according to some criterion, such as market cap. That's a useful solution for academic studies that generalize across periods in which share prices and market size vary considerably. But for you and me, it's easier to talk in concrete dollars. So I settled on the following cutoffs, which more or less reflect the current consensus. When I say "small," I mean any stock with a capitalization less than $1 billion. I'll use

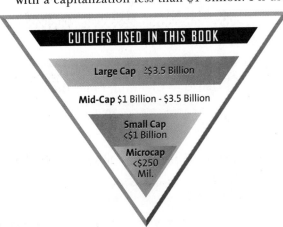

CUTOFFS USED IN THIS BOOK

Large Cap ≥$3.5 Billion

Mid-Cap $1 Billion - $3.5 Billion

Small Cap <$1 Billion

Microcap <$250 Mil.

"micro" only when I need to distinguish the subset of small stocks having caps below $250 million. "Mid-cap" refers to stocks between $1 billion and about $3.5 billion in size; anything above that is "large." *(For a graphic representation of the cutoffs, see the diagram, left.)*

The smaller the cap size of the category, the more companies it contains, a fact captured by the major associated indexes *(illustrated in the chart below).* A stock index provides a measure of the performance of a particular market segment using the combined weighted performances of a group of companies that are considered representative. Weightings are assigned according to various criteria, including capitalization, and members are replaced as their defining characteristics change. The index most commonly used as a proxy for the large-cap universe is the Standard & Poor's 500, which tracks a group of 500 companies that, as of June 1996, had a total market capitalization of more than $5 trillion. The Russell Mid-Cap Index has 800 members, but their combined market cap is only $2 trillion, 40 percent as large as that of the S&P. The cap of the Russell 2000, widely cited as a small-cap benchmark, is $804 billion, 16 percent of the

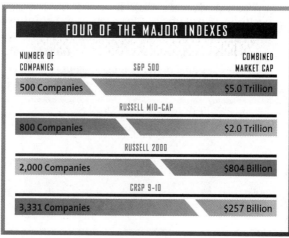

FOUR OF THE MAJOR INDEXES

NUMBER OF COMPANIES	S&P 500	COMBINED MARKET CAP
500 Companies		$5.0 Trillion
	RUSSELL MID-CAP	
800 Companies		$2.0 Trillion
	RUSSELL 2000	
2,000 Companies		$804 Billion
	CRSP 9-10	
3,331 Companies		$257 Billion

SOURCE: PRUDENTIAL SECURITIES INC. DATA AS OF JUNE 1996

S&P's and equal to less than twice the assets under management of mutual fund company Fidelity Investments. The CRSP 9-10 index compiled by the Center for Research in Securities Prices contains 3,331 microcap stocks (in the 9th and 10th deciles) that weigh in at a tiny $257 billion in total market cap.

However you define them, small caps are profitable. According to data compiled by Chicago consulting firm Ibbotson Associates *(displayed in the table below)*, the little guys have outperformed the big ones by an average of 2 percent a year since 1926.

But bear in mind a couple of caveats. First, Ibbotson defined small-cap stocks for its survey as those in the lowest quintile in terms of market cap; in the 1990s, that would produce a cutoff of $155 million, well within my *microcap* category. In fact, it seems that much of the outperformance of the small-cap sector is produced by the very smallest, and riskiest, segment.

Second, the figures cited are averages. In each of the decades studied, a sizable number of small companies not only failed to grow at the rate shown in the chart but actually failed altogether. Of course, those failures mean at least a few other stocks far outstripped the average. To see how variable the results of a small-cap portfolio—even one put together by well-informed experts—can be, consider the one-year results for *Individual Investor* magazine's "Magic 25." This is a portfolio of 25 very small stocks that the magazine's market-savvy editors believe have tremendous growth

RETURNS FOR LARGE AND SMALL CAPS*

	1920s	'30s	'40s	'50s
Small	-4.5	1.38	20.69	16.9
Large	19.9	-.05	9.17	19.35

* "SMALL CAPS" = STOCKS IN THE LOWEST TWO DECILES IN TERMS OF MARKET CAP

potential. According to the table appearing in the January 1997 issue, the portfolio as a whole rose 15.7 percent in 1996. Individual stock performance, however, ranged from a 372 percent gain for Act Networks to a 99.2 percent *loss* for Vista 2000.

Bob Barker—the "Warren Buffett of small-cap stocks," according to "Adam Smith's Money World"—feels the sector's extreme variability can work to investors' benefit. The octogenarian head of the investment firm Barker Lee & Co. pointed out in a February 1996 "Money World" appearance that "if... half your companies are mistakes, and you lose everything in them, and the other half go up between 5 and 10 times, that's all you need." Barker tested this insight by putting together a theoretical portfolio of 20 companies and leaving it alone for five years. At the end of that time, nine stocks had fallen, four of them by 80 to 90 percent. But the portfolio as a whole had an annual compound rate of return of 23 percent, because the winners had risen between 80 and about 1,000 percent.

Barker's point was illustrated in a family story that Bill Sams, manager of the First Pacific Advisors Paramount fund, told at a recent conference sponsored by Morningstar Mutual Funds, the Chicago rating service. "My father bought $700 worth of Frito in the old days," Sams said. "Frito got bought out by Lay's, and then Lay's got bought by Pepsi. That investment turned into more than $6 million. Every other stock he bought lost money, but that one made up for it."

'60s	'70s	'80s	'90s	AVG	$1.00 INVESTED IN 1926
15.53	11.49	15.83	11.47	12.2	$2,843
7.81	5.86	17.55	11.53	10.19	$811

SOURCE: IBBOTSON ASSOCIATES

WHERE'S THE EDGE?

"There was a two-tier market: You had large companies selling at 20 times earnings, and small companies with prospects similar to large companies selling at 12 times earnings. There seemed to be a lot more value in the smaller companies, so I learned that way. And back then there were a lot of small companies not followed by analysts. You could call on somebody and get information that had not been widely published."

— RALPH WANGER, *manager of Acorn Fund, telling* Kiplinger's Personal Finance Magazine *in a February 1995 interview why he started his small-cap fund in the 1970s*

VALUATION VS. COMPANY SIZE & GROWTH RATE

Small and midsize growth companies are cheaper than large growth companies, relative to expected earnings per share.

	AVG. MARKET CAP (S MILLION)	QUINTILE BY MARKET CAP
Large	$ 14,036.89	1
Mid	1,590.05	2
Small	641.37	3
Small	307.14	4
Micro	123.76	5

◆ Sample—1,272 U.S. companies as of December 31, 1996. ◆ P/E based on consensus 12-month forward EPS estimate. ◆ Long-term growth = projected five-year EPS growth rate. ◆ Companies in sam-

NOW THE REALLY IMPORTANT QUESTION: Why are stocks with small market capitalizations particularly good for individual investors like you? The answer: Although things have changed since the early days of Acorn to which Ralph Wanger was referring, you still have a better chance of finding real value in small stocks than in larger ones.

First, as the table below illustrates, the prices at which small companies trade are generally lower in relation to their expected earnings growth than those of larger companies. I'll discuss the price-to-earnings ratio later, in the section on growth and value, but for now, you should know that this measure indicates that the smallest stocks, as a group, deliver the best value.

AVERAGE P/E RATIO				
28.46	21.07	18.69	16.05	13.53
28.08	17.68	15.98	13.66	12.42
23.99	16.78	14.57	11.77	11.89
21.20	16.04	12.49	11.88	12.69
17.69	12.61	11.48	11.04	11.56
1	2	3	4	5

QUINTILE BY LONG-TERM EPS GROWTH

Fastest Expected Growth				Slowest Expected Growth
32.25	21.20	16.05	12.38	7.88

AVERAGE LONG-TERM EPS GROWTH

ple include only those showing positive increasing earnings for 1996, 1997 (projected), and 1998 (projected), with market capitalization in excess of $50 million, and with share price above $5.

SOURCE: T. ROWE PRICE ASSOCIATES, INC.

Second, more good values exist among these companies because so many of the big players give the sector short shrift. It's a matter of economics: Large institutional investors can't earn enough on small stocks to recover their research costs. An institution must know a lot about a company to feel comfortable buying a stake in it. That can take many hours of a researcher's high-priced time and probably an on-site visit. Any purchase the institution makes must have the potential to boost its returns enough to cover these expenses and then some. But to move a $10 billion portfolio requires an investment of at least $100 million. That would amount to 10 percent of a company with a market cap of $1 billion. Many portfolio managers are limited by their mandates to 5 percent stakes. Even those not so limited might find it impossible or imprudent to amass a large number of shares of small-cap companies, which generally trade infrequently, in small blocks, and among a limited number of buyers and sellers.

Brokerages also neglect small stocks, as illustrated in the bar graph *(below)*. Although the 450 U.S. companies with market caps larger than $2.4 billion are covered by an average of 22 analysts each, according to Merrill Lynch, the 2,600 companies between $60 million and $600 million are each followed by about

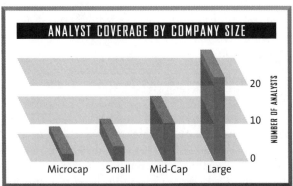

ANALYST COVERAGE BY COMPANY SIZE

NUMBER OF ANALYSTS

20

10

0

Microcap   Small   Mid-Cap   Large

SOURCE: MERRILL LYNCH QUANTITATIVE ANALYSIS, I/B/E/S

three: "the underwriter, the co-underwriter, and usually the third is a total fool," jokes a money manager at a New York–based mutual fund. The even tinier microcap issues average about two analysts each; it's your guess if the dropout is the co-underwriter or the fool.

The reasons for this neglect are again economic. "It does not pay [a broker] to have an analyst research a company where a buy recommendation will not generate orders for hundreds of thousands of shares," investment advisor Tweedy, Browne Co. says in a February 1996 letter to its clients explaining why the firm likes the small sector.

The result: Many fine companies remain undetected, their share prices far below what their intrinsic value would justify. You—or the manager of a mutual fund nimble enough to profit from small-cap research—gain an edge by discovering these gems before other investors can bid them up.

Finding them, moreover, does not take a jeweler's loupe. Again according to Tweedy, smaller companies are often easier to analyze than larger ones: They tend to have fewer products and lower debt levels, since borrowing is more difficult for them.

The relative simplicity of small caps means that the professionals' huge staffs and technical support give them less of an advantage over individuals here than in the large-cap sector. I once asked Peter Kris (managing director of the Van Wagoner funds and no relation to the drummer from Kiss) if an ordinary investor could replicate any part of the strategy followed by star small-stock picker Garrett Van Wagoner. "All of it," he said. "Garrett is just an individual investor who has decided to devote his life to it. He has no analysts and finds that he can uncover new developments before Wall Street analysts [do]."

ALL PART OF A GRAND PLAN

"Two are better than one; because they have a good reward for their labour. / For if they fall, the one will lift up his fellow: but woe to him that is alone when he falleth; for he hath not another to help him up."

— ECCLESIASTES *4:9, 10*

SMALL-CAP STOCKS ARE A crucial investment if you want to get the most value out of your research and grow your wealth faster than inflation eats into it. But crucial as they are, they should still be just one part of a larger, diverse portfolio whose composition is determined by an overarching savings strategy.

The key word here is *diverse*. You never want to put all your eggs in one basket, whether it's one U.S. Treasury bond or a selection of Pacific Rim equities. Only by diversifying can you ensure both the growth you'll need for a prosperous future and protection against the economic and company-specific bumps you'll inevitably hit.

Your portfolio, of course, shouldn't look like your grandfather's (unless you're 75 and he's 110). Different goals, outlooks, and stages of life demand different investment classes in different proportions. The pie charts on pages 26–27 show the asset allocations that experts typically recommend for the main stages of a person's financial life cycle. These are just guidelines. If you need pointers on modifying the mix to suit your particular needs, you should turn to a book such as Burton Malkiel's *A Random Walk Down Wall Street*, or go to www.russell.com, the Web site run by the same folks who compile the Russell 2000 index of small-cap stocks *(see "Resources")*. But whatever your stage in life and specific needs, the same general principle applies: To get good growth with a minimum of risk, you should divide your investments between debt and equity; your equities between large and small stocks; and your small stocks among different size, regional, and style segments.

DEBT AND EQUITY

"By mixing bonds with small stocks, a portfolio can have higher returns yet no greater volatility."
— PETER L. BERNSTEIN, *author of* Against the Gods:
The Remarkable Story of Risk

NO MATTER HOW CAUTIOUS OR aggressive you are as an investor, your portfolio should contain both instruments that conserve principal and those that, in the long run, increase it. The prototypical principal conservators are government debt instruments such as Treasury bonds, bills, and notes; the standard growth producers are equities, or stocks. These two types of securities serve two distinct purposes. Treasuries are best for funding fast-approaching goals, since you know exactly how much money you'll have if you hold them until maturity. They provide a short-term cushion that allows you to put money you don't need immediately into stocks, whose earnings tend to be higher but more variable *(see the graph on page 28)*. Stocks are used to beat inflation and ensure that you have the funds you need to meet expenses in the more-distant future.

Diversifying your investments thus enables you to provide for both imminent needs and far-off goals. It also serves to stabilize the value of your portfolio. Different types of investments tend to prosper in different economic climates, so while one part of a diversified portfolio is taking a breather, another may be coming on strong. Stocks and bonds, for instance, have moved in tandem in the recent period of economic growth with low inflation, but a change in either condition could send them careening in opposite directions. In a low-inflation recession, for

TYPICAL RECOMMENDED ASSET ALLOCATIONS

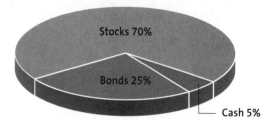

AGE: Mid-Twenties

LIFESTYLE: Fast, aggressive. With a steady stream of earnings, capacity for risk is fairly high. Need discipline of payroll savings to build nest egg

CASH (5%): Money-market fund or short-term-bond fund (average maturity 1 to 1½ years)

BONDS (25%): Zero-coupon Treasury bonds; no-load GNMA fund; or no-load high-grade bond fund

STOCKS (70%): 20% small-company stock fund; 20% growth stock fund; 15% international stock fund; 15% growth and income or "value" fund

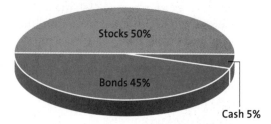

AGE: Mid-Fifties

LIFESTYLE: Many still reeling from college tuitions. No matter what the lifestyle, this age group must start thinking about retirement and the need for income protection

CASH (5%): Money-market fund or short-term-bond fund (average maturity 1 to 1½ years)

BONDS (45%): 10% zero-coupon Treasury bonds; 17½% no-load GNMA fund; 17½% no-load high-grade bond fund

STOCKS (50%): 10% international stock fund; 20% high-income stock fund; 20% growth and income or "value" fund

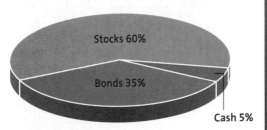

AGE: Late Thirties to Early Forties

LIFESTYLE: Midlife crisis. For childless career couples, capacity for risk is still quite high. Risk options vanishing for those with college tuitions looming

CASH (5%): Money-market fund or short-term-bond fund (average maturity 1 to 1½ years)

BONDS (35%): 10% zero-coupon Treasury bonds; 12½% no-load GNMA fund; 12½% no-load high-grade bond fund

STOCKS (60%): 10% small-company stock fund; 10% growth stock fund; 10% international stock fund; 30% growth and income or "value" fund

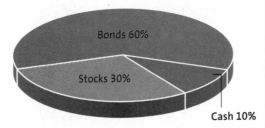

AGE: Late Sixties and Beyond

LIFESTYLE: Enjoying leisure activities but also guarding against major health costs. Little or no capacity for risk

CASH (10%): Money-market fund

BONDS (60%): 20% no-load short- or intermediate-term bond fund; 20% no-load GNMA fund; 20% no-load high-grade bond fund

STOCKS (30%): 15% high-income stock fund; 15% growth and income or "value" fund

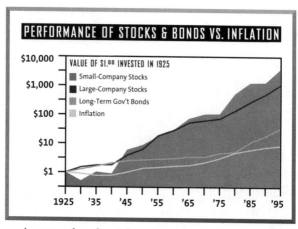

PERFORMANCE OF STOCKS & BONDS VS. INFLATION

VALUE OF $1.⁰⁰ INVESTED IN 1925
- Small-Company Stocks
- Large-Company Stocks
- Long-Term Gov't Bonds
- Inflation

instance, bonds might rally as stocks slump. An opposite reaction could follow an inflationary expansion. By holding both instruments, you position yourself to win either way. That's a lot safer, and cheaper, than trying to time the market, constantly jumping out of one period's losers and into its winners.

LARGE AND SMALL

"I now favor investing in an index that contains a much broader representation of U.S. companies [than the S&P 500], including large numbers of dynamic companies that are likely to be in early stages of their growth cycles."
— BURTON G. MALKIEL, *in* A Random Walk Down Wall Street

IT IS AS IMPORTANT TO diversify your equity holdings as it is to diversify your overall portfolio, and for the same reasons. By investing in both small and large stocks in a variety of industries, you stabilize your returns while also giving them a boost.

Just as equities as a class outpace bonds, the more volatile small stocks outperform slow-but-steadier large ones. This is illustrated in the graph *(right)*. Of

SOURCE: CRSP, THE UNIVERSITY OF CHICAGO, PRUDENTIAL SECURITIES INC.

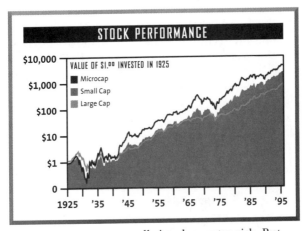

STOCK PERFORMANCE

VALUE OF $1.ᵒᵒ INVESTED IN 1925

- Microcap
- Small Cap
- Large Cap

$10,000
$1,000
$100
$10
$1
0

1925   '35   '45   '55   '65   '75   '85   '95

course, extra return usually involves extra risk. But
time tends to reduce the trade-off. Statistics compiled
by Ibbotson Associates illustrate this point. Ibbotson
studied the 1-, 5-, 10-, 15-, and 20-year returns of government and corporate bonds and large and small
stocks from 1926 through 1995, noting both the maximum and minimum values generated by each security type. The gap between the highest and lowest values decreases steadily as you move from risky small
caps to conservative U.S. Treasury bills, but so does
the size of the greatest gains: the one-year returns of
small caps during this period ranged from 142.87 to
-58.01; U.S. Treasury bills, meanwhile, earned from
14.71 to -0.02 annually. As the holding period length-
ens, differences in variability decline while growth
rates continue to diverge: The maximum and minimum 20-year returns for small stocks were 21.13 and
5.74 percent, respectively, versus 7.72 and 0.42 percent for T-bills.

Given those performance figures, small stocks can
clearly play a specific role in your portfolio: funding
goals that lie in the relatively distant future and that will
require outlays well beyond your current cash reserves
and income. For example, they're suited to saving for

SOURCE: CRSP: THE UNIVERSITY OF CHICAGO. PRUDENTIAL SECURITIES INC.

a far-off retirement or your baby's college tuition.

Adding small caps to your investment mix also provides the second benefit of diversification: stable returns in a variety of environments. Small and large stocks, like equities and bonds, tend to perform best at different times and in response to different economic factors. "It is generally accepted that big-cap and small-cap stocks perform in alternating multiyear cycles," Kenneth Fisher and Joseph Toms, president and senior vice president of Fisher Investments, point out in the book *Small Cap Stocks*. These cycles of under- and overperformance *(discussed more fully in Chapter 4)* last anywhere from three to more than seven years.

In addition, smaller companies generally react more quickly to changes in the economy than larger ones, according to Susan Belden, senior editor of the newsletter *No-Load Fund Analyst*. Because of their extra sensitivity, small stocks will outperform large ones at the beginning of an economic recovery and underperform when recession is looming.

Different-size companies also respond differently to inflation. When the rate is rising, nimble businesses that have near monopolies in fast-growing niches generate better earnings than more unwieldy corporations operating in broader, highly competitive markets. And better earnings translate into higher stock prices. In his book, *Market Timing for the Nineties*, Stephen Leeb notes that during periods of high inflation, small stocks have returned 21 percent a year, far more than the 16 percent return of gold, the traditional inflation hedge.

Because their performance cycle complements that of large stocks, individually volatile small caps actually reduce the overall volatility of a portfolio to which they are added. Satya Pradhuman, senior quantitative analyst at Merrill Lynch, says that by devoting 10 percent of your equity funds to small stocks, you can

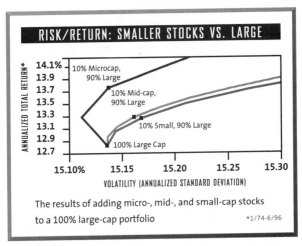

RISK/RETURN: SMALLER STOCKS VS. LARGE

ANNUALIZED TOTAL RETURN*

14.1% — 10% Microcap, 90% Large
13.9
13.7 — 10% Mid-cap, 90% Large
13.5
13.3 — 10% Small, 90% Large
13.1
12.9
12.7 — 100% Large Cap

15.10%   15.15   15.20   15.25   15.30

VOLATILITY (ANNUALIZED STANDARD DEVIATION)

The results of adding micro-, mid-, and small-cap stocks
to a 100% large-cap portfolio   *1/74-6/96

boost returns by 40 to 100 *basis points* (hundredths of
a percent) without increasing risk *(see the chart, above)*.

♦ Pradhuman warns that if you boost your small-cap
allocation above 20 percent, the extra returns come with
considerable extra risk. So if you're considering a larger
investment in small companies, ask yourself if you can
stomach the tailspins along with the vertical climbs.

♦ PBHG fund-family manager Gary Pilgrim advises
investors to "be very conservative about money you think
you might need over the next few years," using small-fry
funds to help put some punch into the rest of your portfolio.
Another way to reduce risk is to mix stocks that are insen-
sitive to the economy—among large caps, Campbell Soup
Co. is an example—with some that are very sensitive, such
as a steel company.

DIVERSIFICATION NEEDN'T STOP at the small-cap level.
Small stocks are themselves a disparate lot, and your
portfolio should probably contain both growth and
value companies and possibly also microcaps and
regionals.

GROWTH VERSUS VALUE

"Nobody would claim to be a nonvalue investor. It is certainly not the opposite of growth."
— CHARLES ROYCE, *president of Quest Advisory Corp., which manages the Royce family of funds, in an October 1992 interview with* Institutional Investor *magazine*

THE TERMS "GROWTH" AND "value" may apply less to companies and stocks than to two different ways of looking at and evaluating them—that is, to different investment styles. A stock cannot be both small and large (though two investors may place the cutoff at different points); it might, however, be categorized as both growth and value. That's because size is measured along one dimension—market capitalization—whereas growth and value involve two different axes: earnings growth and asset value. A stock's categorization, therefore, depends in part on the perspective from which it is being studied and on the emphasis given different factors. This section defines the growth and value perspectives in general terms. You'll get a more detailed look at the analyses they translate into in Chapter 3.

The growth approach to investing was popularized in 1939 by T. Rowe Price, founder of the eponymous fund company. Price believed that companies, like organisms, pass through three major phases: growth, characterized by increasing earnings; maturity, when earnings stabilize; and decline, when they fall off. The first phase, he felt, offers investors the greatest opportunity for gain with the least risk. Price's followers look for companies with expanding profit margins, quarter-to-quarter sales increases, and a history of accelerating earnings growth, year over year and quarter over quarter. If these criteria are met, growth investors are willing to accept a high share price relative to earnings, a measure known as the *price-earnings ratio,* or *p/e.*

Their reasoning is that when earnings have been growing at an ever-faster pace, they should continue to grow strongly enough in the future to narrow the gap with the share price in a short time.

Value investors, in contrast, generally shy away from overblown p/e's. That doesn't mean they discount the importance of earnings, but they are wary of relying on possible future achievements to justify high market valuations in the here and now. Instead, value advocates look at the present (and, to some extent, the past) situation for elements that support a price higher than the current one—for instance, low p/e and low *price-to-book* (the company's market cap divided by its total assets net of liabilities).

"We determine the enterprise's value, [which] may mean looking back a couple of years to when circumstances were better or considering the result of the sale of certain assets or the elimination of losses in certain divisions," Charles Royce explains in the October 1992 *Institutional Investor* interview. "And we try to invest at a discount to that value."

The market should eventually push the stock price up to, or even above, the company's true, intrinsic worth. When this happens, the value investor is gone.

"We like to come in early, when these things are undiscovered or unloved," says Bill Nasgovitz, manager of the small-cap Heartland Value fund. "And when they attract attention or move up in price, we'll gladly part with our stock."

Nasgovitz, Royce, and their fellow value investors are apostles of the almost-legendary Benjamin Graham, whose methods form the basis of the fundamental stock analysis employed today. Since the 1940s, when Graham's ideas started gaining acceptance, and largely because of his teachings, the market has become considerably more efficient, making it nearly impossible to find large stocks that meet his strict criteria. Today's value candidates are found primarily in the small-cap market, which is generally less well followed on Wall Street and is therefore less efficient.

Distressed companies constitute another major group of value candidates, mined mainly by contrarians. Michael Price, a value investor who manages the Mutual Series funds, described the scavenger style in a May 1996 interview with Bloomberg News's Tim Quinson: "Lawsuits, environmental spills, wrong part of the business cycle, companies with disappointing earnings—those are the ponds we fish in."

ONE STOCK, TWO PERSPECTIVES

IN THE COURSE OF AN ANALYSTS round table, I asked growth advocate Jim Oberweis Jr., of the Oberweis funds, and value investor Bill Nasgovitz, of Heartland Advisors, to discuss Just for Feet. The footwear superstore operator appears in both their portfolios, but in opposite positions: Oberweis is *long* the stock, meaning he actually holds it in his portfolio; Nasgovitz has *shorted* it—that is, he sold shares borrowed from a broker, planning to replace them with others bought later at a lower price. Why the different approaches?

Jim Oberweis: When we bought Just for Feet, it really was at an attractive valuation.... We look for 30 percent growth in revenues.... That's actually the bare minimum; in fact, in our portfolio, the average companies grow at a rate of 70 percent. The second thing we look for is 30 percent growth in earnings. Again, an average of about 70 percent in the portfolio.

Chris Graja: So they can't get their earnings by simply laying people off or cutting costs.

JO: Right. These are the most successful, best-managed companies in the business. However, like Bill, we don't want to pay a ridiculous price for the company. I would call us not so much growth investors as growth-value investors. We're looking to buy companies for a p/e not higher than half the rate of growth. So if a company is growing at 50 percent annually, we don't want to pay a p/e higher than about 25.

The rationale is that investors tend to overreact to bad news. David Dreman, a value contrarian and one of the past decade's best fund managers, has stated that while in-favor stocks are notoriously overpriced, out-of-favor ones are just as notoriously underpriced. The trick is to find fallen companies with both low debt and balance sheets strong enough to keep them solvent while good management teams figure out what went wrong and fix it.

Royce, illustrating that the distinction between

When we bought Just for Feet, I think we paid no higher than $33 ever and an average of about $27. The company is growing at 100 percent annually, in terms of both revenues and earnings. We had outstanding growth in both. And I think that continues. I think it's pretty much a fully valued company at this point. We wouldn't buy it at these levels. But we continue to hold on to it.

CG: Bill, what's the other side of that coin?

Bill Nasgovitz: Well, the flip side would be, we think the stock is fully valued. It is a great company. Great concept. They are a retailer of tennis shoes. No rocket science behind that concept. But at $45 a share, the stock is selling at approximately 60 times this year's estimated earnings. You know, 60 times earnings . . . if you bought the whole company at that price, you'd be getting 1.6 percent on your money. That just doesn't make sense to us.

CG: That's the earnings yield, one over the p/e of 60.

BN: That's the earnings yield. . . . When two-year Treasuries are yielding a lot more: 6.4 percent. So, the stock has had a big move. We think it's a concept that has worked, but margins will be squeezed as the company continues to grow and competitors step into the market. Now, we haven't made any money on the short side yet. It just went into the 50s and we shorted some more. But at this price, we think it's fully priced.

growth and value is one of style rather than substance, finds some of his value prospects among "fast-growth companies ... that have stopped growing as quickly as Wall Street wanted them to. The company may get its act together and be a 20 or 25 percent grower again.... But in the process of that shift, there are a lot of growth investors that become highly agitated." As an example, he cites women's apparel retailer Charming Shoppes, a onetime highflier that he picked up cheap when its earnings flattened. The chain rejoined the fast track after a short breather, and his fund got a nice boost.

BOTH THE GROWTH AND VALUE approaches have advantages. Each also has limitations, which the other side is quick to point out.

Value investors claim their style generates the best long-term results, pointing to evidence like that illustrated in the graphs *(right)*. According to these, a $1 investment in 1975 would have become $52 by 1997 if put in small-cap value stocks, compared with only $29 in small-cap growth, $12.72 in large-cap growth, and $22.79 in large-cap value stocks.

Going further, researchers at Tweedy Browne and investment firm Sanford Bernstein have stated that so-called small-cap outperformance during the past two to three decades is attributable less to size than to deep undervaluation. They point out that, except for three years in which small clearly outshone large, returns for both groups have been almost the same. But when the universe is divided between growth and value stocks, the latter have a significant and consistent advantage.

Moreover, if you adjust returns for risk, small-cap growth comes in dead last among the possible size and style combinations. This is hardly surprising, say value investors, since the growth strategy of buying expensive companies can easily fall flat if future earn-

VALUE VS. GROWTH PERFORMANCE

SMALL-CAP STOCKS

CUMULATIVE RETURNS OF $1.00 INVESTED IN 1976
- Value
- Growth

MID-CAP STOCKS

CUMULATIVE RETURNS OF $1.00 INVESTED IN 1976
- Value
- Growth

LARGE-CAP STOCKS

CUMULATIVE RETURNS OF $1.00 INVESTED IN 1976
- Value
- Growth

ings don't increase as fast as expected.

"The way some of these companies are priced, they better become the next Microsoft," Nasgovitz says, "because at 100 or 150 times earnings, one disappointment is going to be extremely painful."

Of course, not every small-cap growth company *is* a potential Microsoft. The chance that a $50 million company will become a $50 billion one is slim. First, the founders need to turn a brilliant idea into a product the whole country knows and uses. Then, when the company really takes off, they need to mutate from hands-on garage inventors to macromanagers. The biggest turning point, though, occurs when the up-and-comer is large enough to attract the attention of the big guys—well-managed competitors with rock-solid balance sheets that can afford to devote some of their resources to putting an upstart out of business.

Growth advocates, for their part, might counter that the statistics showing value's superiority are biased. The studies cited assume a "black-box" style of investing, in which someone blindly buys all the stocks ranked in particular quintiles by their p/e's. This is artificial. Even the most rabid growth investor will avoid the highest ratios. In fact, Claudia Mott, director of small-cap research at Prudential Securities, points out that small-cap growth funds on average outperform small-cap value funds; even Tweedy Browne concedes this in its September 1996 semiannual report.

The growth people also note that though one of their winners could well grow a thousandfold, percent increases for the top value picks are more commonly in the hundreds. Many value stocks, moreover, turn out to be "permacheap," their prices doomed to languish in the low figures. The fact is, most cheap stocks are cheap not because they have been overlooked but because something is gravely wrong with them. And even truly undiscovered stocks may stay underpriced for a long, long time. As Merrill Lynch's Pradhuman puts it, many value investors see value long before anyone else does and, as a result, end up hanging on to stocks through a long unprofitable period.

"When you talk about errors on the value side," says Nasgovitz, "we're generally there a little bit earlier than the rest."

WHERE DOES ALL THIS LEAVE YOU? On the fence, if you're smart. Neither the growth nor the value style of stock picking is infallible, but both are capable of producing winners. And though it's possible for one stock to attract both types of investors, the two groups generally have different takes and make very different choices. So if you combine both growth and value styles in your portfolio, you'll increase both its diversity and your chances of making successful investments.

Because of their different characteristics, growth and value stocks can perform different roles. The former produce spectacular price rises and just as spectacular falls; the latter, less spectacular but more consistent gains. So growth stocks can provide your portfolio with momentum, while value picks furnish downside protection.

Growth and value also thrive in different market situations. Though value, as I said above, seems to do best over the long term, in certain economic environments growth is dominant. Value, for example, is generally soundly beaten by growth when the economy is slowing, when interest rates are rising, and when the U.S. Treasury yield curve is flat *(see Chapter 4 for details)*. So my advice here is the same as it was for debt versus equity and large versus small stocks: If you want consistent and reliable returns, make sure both groups are represented in your portfolio. The proportions will depend on your goals and risk tolerance. The chart on the following page shows the risks and returns of different combinations of growth and value

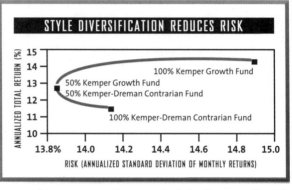

STYLE DIVERSIFICATION REDUCES RISK

100% Kemper Growth Fund
50% Kemper Growth Fund
50% Kemper-Dreman Contrarian Fund
100% Kemper-Dreman Contrarian Fund

ANNUALIZED TOTAL RETURN (%)

RISK (ANNUALIZED STANDARD DEVIATION OF MONTHLY RETURNS)

stocks, represented respectively by Kemper Growth and Kemper-Dreman Contrarian funds.

If you're in a high-income tax bracket, small-cap growth stocks have a definite edge.

An article in the September 1996 issue of *SmartMoney* points out that if you assume federal and state tax rates of 31 and 6 percent, respectively, small-cap stocks have outperformed large-cap ones during the past 15 years, and growth has beaten out value. Specifically, the average tax-adjusted annual return of the Russell 2000 index of small-cap stocks was 15.1 percent for the period, versus 14.5 for the large-cap S&P 500. During the same period, value stocks in the mostly large- and mid-cap Russell 1000 returned 14.7 percent, versus 14.9 for growth stocks in the same index. The reason for the relative success of the small and growth sectors is that returns of large-cap and value companies derive in great part from the reinvestment of taxable dividends; in contrast, small-cap and growth companies rely more on capital appreciation, which is taxed at a lower rate than income.

BOTH VALUE AND GROWTH INVESTORS hope their small-cap stocks will get bigger fast, either by maturing or by recapturing past glories. Investors in small regional and niche companies generally have more modest aspirations. They're content with solid, steady earnings in relatively noncompetitive environments. Regionals are usually not glamorous, but they may be the friendliest for you, the small investor. They're the ones most likely to be sitting in your hometown, or where your Uncle Bill works. In either case, you're in a position to get some perfectly legal inside information that could give you an edge over the big guys. All you have to do is read the local newspapers, drive by the plant, talk to employees and neighbors, customers, and suppliers.

SMALL AND SMALLER

"During the 43 years of our study, $10,000 invested in all the stocks in the Compustat database with a market capitalization below $25 million would have grown to over $29 million! Unfortunately, no professional money manager can realistically buy these stocks."

— JIM O'SHAUGHNESSY, *in* What Works on Wall Street

REGIONAL, GROWTH, AND VALUE stocks differ in the reasons they're small: because they're parochial, young, or misunderstood. Small stocks can also differ in their degree of smallness. The tiniest of the tiny are the microcaps.

I've defined microcaps as companies having market capitalizations under $250 million. Some in the business put the bar even lower. The Fremont U.S. Micro-Cap fund, for instance, has a median market capitalization of $149.10 million. As I've said before, boundary disputes are common. What isn't disputed, though, is that when you're talking returns, smaller is better. Over the past 20 years, Merrill Lynch's Pradhuman states in a 1995 *Business Week* article, companies with market caps of $60 million or less have produced average annual returns of 21 percent, compared with 17 percent for small-cap stocks and 13 percent for large-caps.

"Historically, this is the group that has given you the biggest bang for the buck," says Prudential's Mott.

Microcaps are even less well followed on Wall Street than the larger small caps. There are a lot of them, for one thing: Estimates range from 3,000 to more than 4,000. And they cost at least as much to research as larger companies in which institutions can take bigger stakes and make bigger profits. So about 45 percent of the tiniest stocks have no analyst coverage at all, according to Daniel P. Coker, quantitative analyst of NatWest Securities' Micro-Cap Research Group. Those companies that are covered aren't exactly smothered: Coker figures they average around 1.4 analysts each; the average is less than 1 for caps below $100 million.

That leaves the field pretty much open for you. Uncovering what's going on with an underfollowed company takes a fair amount of time and effort. But think of it as fun, and remember that this is one area where an amateur with a little horse sense and patience can sometimes outsmart an MBA with five investing theories.

"The world has adopted small-cap as a real genre," Quest Advisory's Royce, who specializes in small- and microcap stocks, told *The Washington Post*. "What's remaining [at the lowest levels of capitalization] is below the radar screen, and it's a large area for opportunity."

It's also an area where research really pays off. That's because a small company's performance is determined largely by its own actions and condition, rather than by the economy at large. "As you go down along the scale of size of companies, the success of the company and the investment are much more dependent upon individual company developments," says Robert Kern, portfolio manager of Fremont U.S.

Micro-Cap. "I like that the things you are analyzing are closely tied to the company, as opposed to some macroeconomic variable."

Mammoths like AT&T, which spread themselves over many businesses, can't grow much more quickly than the economy itself. Tiny companies, limited to a small slice of one niche, grow principally on the strength of their own products. Of course, if they rely on a few giant customers and these suffer a slow-down, the small suppliers will suffer, too. But really innovative products will always be in demand. Because microcap companies are relatively independent from macroeconomics, good research provides a real edge in this sector: You need a crystal ball to predict where the economy is headed, but a little hard work can uncover customer base and product innovation.

Still, this is a very risky area. The failure rate is much higher for microcap companies than for their larger cousins. Bigger businesses generally have a few past successes to build on, as well as decent managers, capital, and a few long-term contracts to stabilize their earnings. Call it the "survivor effect"—the same inertia that holds giants back in a rising market keeps them afloat in a sinking one. Tiny companies are more agile, but also more vulnerable.

In addition, microcaps are almost invisible and their market consequently illiquid. Want to sell Coca-Cola? Done. Want to sell Lifetime Hoan? Who's the buyer? For microcaps, the average daily trading volume is just 18,000 shares, compared with 54,000 shares for small caps and 505,000 for large stocks, says Pradhuman. Because demand is so low, a seller with an oversupply of micro shares will have to drop his or her price. By the same token, a would-be buyer may have to bid the price way up. This widens *bid-ask spreads*—the difference between where market makers will buy *(the bid)* and sell *(the ask)*. It also amplifies price swings. According to Ibbotson chief economist Paul Kaplan, microcaps are twice as volatile as large-cap stocks and a third jumpier than small ones.

PUTTING IT TOGETHER

NOW YOU KNOW YOUR PORTFOLIO should be divided into stocks, bonds, and money markets, and the equity portion between large and small stocks. You might also want to divide your small-cap investments between micro and somewhat larger companies, and among value, growth, and niche stocks. Fine. But how do you go about choosing what exactly to buy in the small-cap categories? The following chapters will provide specific tips. For now, though, here are some general rules and strategies.

Allocate a portion of your small-cap portfolio to mutual funds. Consider making that 100 percent if you don't have enough time to research your picks thoroughly or enough money to spread your risk around. Jim Oberweis Jr. feels that anyone who can't afford to buy 20 individual small-cap stocks should stick with funds. I'd modify that a bit: If you have only $10,000, say, to allocate to this sector, you could invest about $3,000 in one or two well-researched individual stocks and turn over the rest to the professional managers. Investors looking at small caps only for the diversification they provide might do best with an index fund, such as one of those discussed in Chapter 2.

Whatever you do with the rest of your small-cap investment money, mutual funds should probably be the vehicle for your microcap investing. A fund gives you diversification, which keeps any one failure from ruining your returns. If you choose well, you also get a skilled manager who has access to the companies' management and the research clout to keep you out of trouble.

Fund management is especially important in the microcap sector, with its relative independence from macroeconomic movements. Since managers can't just ride the trends, their fundamental analysis and business research can make a real difference. As a result, the gap between the best and worst performers in the microcap sector tends to be much greater than in other specializations. In 1995, for instance, Perkins Opportunity, which invests in upstart companies largely from the same upper-Midwest region where the fund is based, returned a stellar 70 percent; at the other extreme, Frontier Equity lost 1.26 percent.

Research, research, research. This advice applies no matter how you decide to invest your small-cap money. As will be explained more fully in the following chapter, you have to do a fair amount of homework to find funds with good track records and, once you've invested, to make sure they hold to their stated objectives. Research is truly crucial, though, when you're looking at individual stocks. As I've said before, the investor with more knowledge always has an edge over the one with less; small caps are one sector where you can glean information not known by the whole world. You also reduce your risks by researching your prospects' finances and weeding out ones that could be toppled by a bad quarter. All this is covered in Chapters 3 and 4.

Stay small. You don't have the time to analyze all 5,000-plus small companies. For your individual stock investing, you need to reduce your universe to segments where you have an edge and that you can research thoroughly. Many brokerage firms succeed by following companies in one industry or geographic region very closely. Alexander Paris, the president of Barrington Research, for example, focuses on companies based in the Midwest. The small-cap mutual funds you buy should probably also be small, limiting the assets they will accept to manage. Remember, this is an area where big guys often have trouble maneuvering.

Keep your costs low. One sure way to lower costs is to minimize your transactions. Trading stock costs you money in commissions and the bid-ask spread.

Small-cap transactions are particularly expensive, since spreads tend to be wide. Most small- and micro-cap stocks are traded over the counter, on the National Association of Securities Dealers Automated Quotations system, or Nasdaq. When you buy or sell shares of these companies, you're dealing not with other investors (as you do on an exchange) but with market makers. These market makers—brokerages, for instance—enter the prices at which they will buy or sell a stock onto an electronic system. The highest buy price and lowest sell price become the bid and offer you see when you get a quote. The difference between the two prices represents the brokerage's compensation for making a market in the stock. The smaller the volume of shares changing hands, the larger the spread.

Despite recent reforms, Nasdaq spreads are often as large as half a point; that means you're buying shares for 50 cents more than you could turn around and sell them for. So if you are to make any money on the trade, the stock's ask must rise more than a half point. On a $10 stock, that represents a 5 percent increase—huge in a market where the average annual return is just 12 percent.

Have a plan for when to buy and when to sell. This is important for funds, but critical for stocks.

Buying is easier. Your goal is to acquire stocks that Wall Street will latch on to a short time later, thus creating demand that will push up their prices. Not every company that produces a fine product and has sound finances fits the bill. Dozens of research studies have shown that stocks go in and out of favor. If you follow your collection of companies carefully and apply a few of the strategies described in later chapters, you should be in a position to scoop up bargains.

Selling is a tougher call; you'll find specific advice in Chapter 3. For now, just remember that you can lessen the pain of your sell decisions by setting both a goal and a cut-loss point for every stock when you buy it. If the share price reaches either level, you should reevaluate the company's prospects and its fit with your portfolio to see if there are any new reasons to hold it.

THAT'S JUST A QUICK TASTE. The following chapters will give you more detailed information and recommendations to really sink your teeth into. For advice on building a small-cap mutual-fund portfolio, turn the page. If you're eager to start on individual-stock investing, skip to Chapter 3 or, to get straight to the more sophisticated strategies, Chapter 4.

Mutual
FUNDS

N O MATTER how you handle the rest of your investments—carefully researching and selecting every bond and blue-chip yourself or handing the whole thing over to a financial manager—when it comes to your small-cap allocation, you should seek professional help. That means mutual funds. As I said in the previous chapter, most individual investors should have a portion of their small-stock portfolio in funds. The minimum is probably 50 percent. You might even decide to go for 100.

Mutual funds represent the easiest and cheapest way to buy diversification and good asset management. That's true for most investments, and it goes double for small stocks. Make that quadruple for microcaps.

This chapter won't tell you everything you need to know about investing in funds. For that, I'd suggest you look at *A Commonsense Guide to Mutual Funds,* by Mary Rowland. What I hope to do here is to convince you of the benefits of incorporating funds into your small-cap strategy and give you some pointers on how to accomplish that.

DIVERSIFICATION

"There are a small number of people, like [Warren] Buffett or Sam Walton, who become incredibly rich from one or just a few holdings. But you never hear stories about the people who go broke. Think of it this way: There are no guarantees when you invest in stocks. If you had $100 to play the lottery, would you put all the money on one number? Or would you want 100 different numbers? I think you're better off with more lottery tickets."
— CHRIS BROWNE, *a partner at investment advisor Tweedy, Browne Co.*

THE WAY I'VE BEEN THUMPING this theme, it could be a tax-cut plan in an election year. But believe me, diversification is a lot easier to execute, and the cost/benefit trade-off is a lot clearer.

There's a cost? Well, yeah. If you spread your investments among a bunch of different sectors and stocks, you're going to get less of a bang when one stock takes off than if you had made a concentrated bet on it. That's investor Warren Buffett's view. And that's why his strategy is to put all his eggs in one basket and watch that basket really carefully.

The trouble is, a concentrated bet that goes wrong can crack your whole nest egg. Buffett's strategy works only if you pick stocks as well as he does; most of us don't. We also can't take the huge stakes in companies that Buffett does and so don't have the same leverage with management to challenge decisions not in shareholders' interest.

Splitting your bets diffuses your risk, keeping any one failure from ruining you. That's an important consideration when you're dealing with small companies, which often don't have fat reserves to carry them through lean times. (Buffett, of course, buys huge companies that not only have ample financial padding but are themselves diversified across a number of businesses operating in a number of countries.)

"It's somewhat like trying to know when lightning will hit which trees," Quest Advisory Corp. president Charles Royce told *Institutional Investor* magazine in an October 1992 interview. "If you have enough trees, you'll still have firewood at the end of the season." Diversification also stabilizes your returns, since different sectors and styles tend to prosper at different times and in response to different economic factors.

But spreading your wealth among individual stocks is tough unless you have a lot to invest. A thousand dollars isn't going to buy you much of a stake in 15 to 20 companies—the minimum number you should hold, according to Jim Oberweis Jr., portfolio manager of the Oberweis funds. A thousand dollars is all you need, though, to buy a share of the average small-

cap mutual fund and a stake in its portfolio of
upwards of 75 stocks.

PROFESSIONAL MANAGEMENT

*"Individuals should own stocks. Then they'd see
how hard it is and let professionals do some of the
work for them."*
—BILL BERGER, *retired manager of the Berger Funds*

IN EVERY BUSINESS, THERE ARE artists and hackers. The
man who painted my house is an artist. He could
spackle and prime the dining-room ceiling while you
were eating Thanksgiving dinner, and you'd never
know he was there. Last summer I painted some
Adirondack chairs and wound up ruining a pair of
shoes, wrecking my new shorts, and splattering paint
in my hair. A lot of small-cap mutual fund managers
are artists; most of the rest of us are paint-spillers.

Wait a minute, you say, aren't we the little guys that
are supposed to have an edge in this sector? Sure, but
many of the best small-cap funds are little guys, too,
relative to the industry: Just compare the $184 million
in assets that Oberweis Emerging Growth was managing in November 1996 to Fidelity Disciplined Equity's
$2.134 billion under management.

With less investor money that must be kept working, funds like Oberweis can keep their portfolios relatively small. This helps them avoid one of the most
serious problems large investors face in the small-cap
sector. To juice returns enough to offset research
costs, a big institution with a huge portfolio has to
buy a sizable block of a successful stock. That's tough
when you're dealing with a company that has a small
market cap. A "sizable block" of its shares may represent a larger percentage of the total outstanding than
a fund's mandate—or a manager's prudence—
allows it to hold. A much more modest stake does the
job in a small portfolio, whose manager can thus

afford to spend the time and money necessary to find the best small companies.

So small-fund managers are little guys. But they're artistic little guys, with more research money and experience, not to mention better connections and backup, than us hackers. Analyst Daniel Coker, of the Micro-Cap Research Group at NatWest Securities, notes that huge information gaps exist between institutional money managers and even the best stockbrokers, and between brokers and most individuals. A manager like Michael Gerding, of international small-cap fund Founders Passport, will visit 300 companies a year. Others, like Oberweis, avoid direct contact with company management but have their own ways of digging up the reams of data they need. Just as important, from having studied thousands of these companies, the pros know what to look for in the piles of numbers and facts they gather and usually have both a talented staff and sophisticated models to analyze the data.

You might still be able to unearth some small gems that escape the pros' notice—the well-run factory down the street, say, or the company that makes the snowboards all of your kids' friends are bugging their parents to buy. The searching, though, takes time, effort, and more than a little luck. To figure out if the potential profits are worth the trouble, ask yourself whether your edge is greater than the average investor's—do you have special sources of information, and if so, how reliable are they? If you aren't too sure, spend extra time with your kids and let a fund manage your money. If you think you do have a bit of an advantage, you should still spend as much time as you can with your kids—the *only* risk-free investment—but maybe give up some sleep or devote one lunch hour a week to doing the research for the non-fund part of your small-cap portfolio.

CONVENIENCE AND COST

"Transaction costs are very high for small stocks, especially if you are wrong. When the stock is doing poorly and everyone wants to sell, that is where you really get hurt."
— ROBERT KERN, *portfolio manager of Fremont U.S. Micro-Cap*

YOU SHOULDN'T DO A LOT of trading, in either mutual funds or individual stocks. But even buying to hold involves buying, and you can't hold forever. So bear in mind that shares of a mutual fund are much easier and cheaper to purchase and redeem than shares of a small-cap stock. Consider, also, that every fund share represents multiple stocks—if you had to buy or sell all of them individually, your transaction costs would be multiplied, too.

When you trade stocks, both your principal in a purchase and your profit from a sale are eroded by commissions, fees, and spreads. The bite is particularly big in the small- and microcap markets: The limited numbers of available shares and of investors willing to buy or sell them make for very wide bid-ask spreads. The same factors can lead to delays in execution, particularly in sales of lesser-known microcaps.

In contrast, you always have a ready buyer for your mutual-fund shares: the fund itself. And if you deal directly with the fund or trade through a supermarket broker such as Charles Schwab, Jack White, or Fidelity, you may pay no transaction fee, or load. *(For more on fund fees, see "Masters of Their Domain," below.)*

That doesn't mean you get off scot-free. Funds have to pay commissions and deal with spreads when they trade for their portfolios, and those transaction costs (along with manager salaries and administrative and marketing expenses) reduce your returns. On the other hand, because they buy in bulk, managers usually get breaks from their brokers that you and I will never see.

NOW THAT YOU'RE SOLD, I hope, on putting at least some of your small-cap money into mutual funds, the next step is to choose one, or maybe a few. Ten years ago, that would have been easy. You were limited to 45 or so funds specializing in small companies. Times have changed, though. In 1995, according to *The Washington Post,* 318 funds had $43 billion invested in small-company stocks. To find the ones that are right for you, you have to do some research. This may not be as rigorous as when you're picking a stock, but you can't just stick a pin in your newspaper's fund listings. Look into who manages each fund's portfolio and how, what its record is, and the fees and other costs you'll have to pay.

THE NO-BRAINER APPROACH

Here's a good rule of thumb
Too clever, is dumb.
—OGDEN NASH

IF YOU WANT TO MINIMIZE your research time, stick to the type of fund that minimizes management. In other words, put your money in an *index fund,* one whose holdings—and, consequently, returns— mimic the composition of a market index such as the Russell 2000. The only thing these funds' managers have to do is keep up with changes in the companies making up the index. So trading and administrative costs, not to mention management fees, should be minimal: The Vanguard Index 500 Trust, for example, charges two-tenths of a percent in management expenses, compared with 1.33 percent for the average stock fund. The lower a fund's total expenses, the more of your money gets invested and generates returns. This is especially important in the small-cap market, where "round-trip" costs on stock trades can be 4 to 6 percent, according to Satya Pradhuman, senior quantitative analyst at Merrill Lynch.

Because indexing managers have so little leeway in managing, you don't have to worry as much about their investment philosophies and records as you would with an actively managed fund. Specifically, you don't have to worry that they'll stray from your objective, which in this case is to stay small. The organization that creates an index will remove stocks that no longer fit its defining criteria—such as market-cap size—and the funds that match the index must follow suit. As I'll discuss later, active managers often aren't as disciplined about cleaning house, tending in particular to let their average market cap drift upward.

An index fund also supplies automatic diversification. Since the market includes both growth and value stocks, for instance, the fund will, too. Different styles cycle in and out of favor. Combining them in one portfolio, as an index fund does, should provide more consistent returns over the long run.

 **Call Vanguard. Its Extended Market Portfolio invests in the Wilshire 4500, which contains all exchange-traded stocks not included in the S&P 500.**
The Portfolio, often tacked on to the firm's famed Index 500 fund to mimic the returns of the entire market, can be used alone as a low-cost way to gain exposure to small stocks. Vanguard also offers the Index Small-Cap Stock fund, which matches the Russell 2000. Other fund families have similar index funds. You might also check into Dimensional Fund Advisors' 9-10, 6-10, and small-cap value funds (though they require a $50,000 minimum investment, far higher than Vanguard's).

As long as we're talking indexing, why not go the whole hog and match the performance of the entire U.S.

equity market?

If you have $10,000 to invest, put $7,000 of it in the Vanguard Index 500 fund and $3,000 in the Extended Market Portfolio. According to Burton Malkiel's classic, *A Random Walk Down Wall Street*, a similar portfolio has outperformed the S&P 500 since 1973, with lower volatility. How's that for a free lunch? This one step will give you better returns than most of the Hermès-tie-wearing money managers get. Depending on your investment goals and the amount of risk you can tolerate, you may want to raise or lower the small-cap exposure very slightly. You'll also need to decide, when the outperformance of one sector changes the original allocation, whether to trade around and restore it—a process called "rebalancing"—or just let the investment ride. I'll return to this question below, in "To Balance or Not To Balance."

MASTERS OF THEIR DOMAIN

"Some individuals can invest successfully, but most don't have the patience or discipline to really be successful. That's what they are paying us for."
— CHARLES ROYCE *of Quest Advisory Corp.*

INDEXING HAS DEFINITE ADVANTAGES. But if you want high performance, not merely low maintenance, it may not be for you. Although actively managed small-cap funds have higher expenses and take more monitoring than index funds, their returns can be greater as well.

This was not obvious in 1995, when only 16 percent of managed funds bested the S&P 500 index, according to Steven T. Goldberg in the March 1996 issue of *Kiplinger's* magazine. But as Goldberg points out, 1995 was a special case. Blue-chip U.S. stocks led the world's markets, creating a situation "tailor-made for the S&P 500," he says. "Not only is the index composed almost entirely of large U.S. companies, but it also overweights the giants. The 59 biggest stocks accounted for more than half the index's rise.... In fact, while the S&P rose 37.5 percent..., the average stock in the S&P returned only 32.4 percent, just 1.4 percent more than the average stock fund."

The point is, in most years, a well-managed diversified fund that mixes in some small stocks (and possibly also foreign stocks and cash) will beat the S&P 500. Good management should add even more in the small-cap market, which is less efficient. Managers who can exploit this inefficiency to pick up undervalued treasures should outperform the Russell 2000, the Nasdaq Composite, or any other small-stock index. The catch is that you have to do a little homework to find these whizzes.

What do you look for, and where? Mary Rowland's book has most of the answers. For now, though, here are a few pointers.

Figure out what investment roles you want small-cap funds to play. You may use them to fill specific slots—growth, value, aggressive, contrarian, micro—in your otherwise individual-stock portfolio. Or they may be your only small-cap holdings; in that case, try to cover a range of styles and subgroups, either through a few diversified funds or through several more-specialized ones. Whichever strategy you follow, be sure that the funds you buy will do the jobs you chose them for.

Don't rely on a fund's name to tell you how it will function in your portfolio. Names are marketing tools, and there's no truth-in-labeling law here. For example, 39 percent of Fidelity Blue Chip Growth's assets in the first part of 1995 were in small and medium-sized technology companies, not typical blue-chip fare. Even worse, many funds that include "small cap" in their titles include some pretty large caps in their portfolios.

So look past a fund's title and read up on it in *Morningstar Mutual Funds,* a collection of reports on 1,600 funds published by the well-respected Chicago rating company *(see "Resources")*. A fund's report indicates such information as its median market cap, how its portfolio is allocated among various investment categories, and, in a short review section, how its manager has been implementing its stated goal. For more details, including what companies the fund holds, the size of its stakes, and comments about the fund's performance, get its semiannual report from the fund company.

Look for good performance over a long period. You want to gauge how a fund performs—both in absolute terms and relative to other funds in the same field—in bad markets as well as good. You'll find this info in Morningstar's newsletters and in the quarterly reports that the fund mails to shareholders. Some funds will be slow and steady; others will vary between stellar and dismal showings. Ask yourself how much volatility you can stomach. If a fund's average 5- and 10-year returns are good despite periodic dips and you won't need the money you put in too soon, you may decide to buy it and just lay in a supply of Maalox. Or you might opt for another fund that's consistently middle of the road and hold the antacid.

Make sure you understand the fund manager's general investment philosophy and are comfortable with it. Professional investors fall into two camps. Some, like Jim Oberweis, are big fans of spreading around the risk and the wealth; in summer 1996 his microcap fund owned about 90 stocks, none of which accounted for more than 3 percent of the portfolio's total assets. Other investors prefer to concentrate their resources; in the same period, the Robertson Stephens Contrarian fund had 22.3 percent of its assets invested in one stock. Big bets often win big, as witness the funds that posted huge gains in early 1995 because they loaded up on technology stocks. But they can also lose big, as witness the funds that were still in techs later that year.

More and more managers are taking the big-bet route, figuring it's the way to become rich and famous (not necessarily in that order). Decide whether you're comfortable with this style. Do you worry more about losing the farm or missing the boat? In either case, you shouldn't own more than one or two funds whose managers can take outsize stakes: 10 percent in one company is extreme even for sector funds, which focus on one industry group, as is more than 30 percent in a single industry. And those managers should have superb track records in picking winners. If you own more than one such fund, make sure they aren't both putting your money on the same horse, like tech stocks.

Check the investment policies in a fund's prospectus to see how much latitude the manager is given to concentrate investments, to short stocks, and to use derivatives. Then check fund holdings—detailed in the semiannual reports—to see if he or she actually does any of this. Remember, though, that funds only disclose these facts twice a year; what they do in between is anybody's guess.

Get copies of funds' newsletters. In these publications, managers will often discuss economic issues and the techniques they use in tending to their portfolios. Check whether any of the stock strategies described in the following chapters are utilized and how they are implemented.

Diversify, but don't dilute. You're paying a manager, whom you've supposedly screened carefully, for his expertise, so let it shine through. If you spread your investments among too many funds investing in too many styles and sectors, the effect of any one manager will be diluted. In that case, you might as well save on fees and put the whole shebang in an index fund.

Check expenses. Just because you decide to pay for active management doesn't mean you should get soaked. The higher a fund's expenses, the better it has to perform relative to its benchmark index to make investing in it worthwhile. Look for combined operating costs (administrative, management, and marketing) that are lower than 75 basis points. And go no-load. The load is the sales commission you pay when you buy or sell through a broker and sometimes even when you deal directly with the fund family: Front-end loads are deducted from the amount you invest; back-end loads (also known as *deferred sales charges* or *redemption fees*) are skimmed off the money you take out. Some firms even charge for reinvesting dividends or for transferring money from one fund to another. Any fund with such fees had better have a manager who is the Vermeer of small caps.

One Vermeer who has earned his fees is Robert Rodriguez.
His First Pacific Advisors Capital fund, which closed in mid-March 1997, carries a hefty 6.5 percent front load and charges 75 basis points annually in management fees. But both Morningstar and Bloomberg have ranked it No. 1 in five-year performance among small-cap funds. So investors who got in before the closing have gotten what they paid for.

Look for a low turnover rate. This refers to the percentage of the portfolio that is traded each year; for instance, a 50 percent turnover indicates that half the fund's holdings change annually. The higher the rate, the higher the transaction costs and capital gains taxes, which reduce your returns. This is a particularly important consideration in the small-cap market, where trades tend to be more expensive. (Rodriguez, for instance, keeps his Capital fund's turnover low, at 21 percent as of June 1996.)

Keep it small, especially when choosing a micro-cap fund. Any fund can become unwieldy when it becomes too large—even Warren Buffett's Berkshire Hathaway. In spring 1996 Buffett told investors in his enormously successful investment pool that neither he nor his vice chairman would buy Berkshire shares at their current price. Buffet said he felt his fund had grown to the point where performance might begin to suffer.

That point is much lower for small-stock funds. "As a small-cap stock fund gets bigger, it has two choices," says Acorn's Ralph Wanger. "It can own more stocks and risk becoming nothing more than an index fund, or else own larger stocks and become a mid-cap fund."

It's a matter of simple math. Many funds are prohibited by their mandates from owning more than 10 percent of a company, and prudence usually dictates much more modest stakes, particularly in small businesses. A small-cap manager might well keep his or her average investment to 2 percent. Given that the average small stock has a market cap of around $500 million, that comes to $10 million. So a fund like Acorn, with $2 billion to put to work, would have to spread its assets among 200 small stocks.

The question is, could the manager find that many exceptional stocks and would he or she have the resources to stay on top of them all? Laura Lallos, senior analyst at Morningstar, notes in the January 30, 1996, issue of *Financial World* that the difficulty of researching small companies limits the number that a fund manager can reasonably follow and invest in. In the same article, Bill Nasgovitz admits that he and his eight analysts were finding it difficult to do the research needed to put to work all the money flowing into his Heartland Value fund before he closed it to new investors in July 1995.

Managers who don't close their funds have two alternatives to expanding the number of companies they invest in. One is to increase the size of their average stake. But that can be risky in the relatively illiquid small-cap market, where it's tough to amass or divest a large block of shares without affecting their price. The other option is to abandon the fund's small-cap focus and look for larger companies.

As an investor, you don't want your small-cap money invested in large stocks, which should already be represented elsewhere in your portfolio. You also don't want to pay an active manager to put together an index fund, nor do you want the fund holding stakes too large to be traded quickly.

Check out the asset size of any fund you're considering. Anything above $3 billion to $4 billion would probably make it difficult for the fund to stay invested in small caps without becoming a crypto-index or a mid-cap fund. The absolute figure, however, is less important than its relation to the size of the fund's analyst and support staff. Despite a huge asset pool of $4 billion, T. Rowe Price's small-cap New Horizon fund has produced a five-year return of 22.2 percent because manager John Laporte has 20 to 25 analysts and researchers to rely on.

Next, make sure the fund's management is committed to closing its doors before assets get too large for the staffing to support. I recently bought the Oberweis Micro-Cap fund because it swore to stay lean and nimble enough to stick to its specialty: buying supersmall stocks. Its cutoff was $60 million—that's with an "m," not a "b"—which would make it a thousandth the size of Fidelity Magellan. (Magellan, by the way, closed its doors for 16 years, from 1965 to 1981, when its assets were only $424,488, because management felt it had become too big.)

"The issue is staying true to the label," says Nasgovitz. His Heartland Value microcap fund has a median market cap of $59 million. The much-larger Fidelity Low-Priced Stock, which also targets small companies, holds megacaps such as IBM and RJR Nabisco.

Finally, you want any shutdowns to apply not only to new customers but also to new money from old ones. Additional contributions made by existing investors after a closing can be substantial enough to cause problems. That's especially true if, as often happens, new investors rush to get in before the deadline. When Heartland Value closed after reaching $800 million in assets, it allowed existing investors to increase their stakes; by mid-1996 its assets had grown to $1.5 billion, according to Morningstar. Nasgovitz's fund is still a top performer, but others might founder under such a flood of money.

Players who don't move fast may find all the microcap doors shut: To invest successfully in Lilliputian companies, funds have to stay as lean as supermodels. On the other hand, new microcap funds keep being created. Heartland, for instance, introduced Small Cap Contrarian in 1995 as an alternative to its Value fund; Contrarian's record, though short, is encouraging, according to Morningstar. As more companies vie for the money returning to U.S. stocks from overseas, they will undoubtedly try to exploit interest in the hot micro sector. Just hope they don't market so many that managers can't still pluck up plenty of bargains with tweezers.

 Don't buy into a fund just before it closes.

In *A Commonsense Guide to Mutual Funds*, Rowland cites a 1995 *New York Times* article by Timothy Middleton showing that closings are generally followed by downturns in performance. The reason: By the time most managers decide to cut off new investment, they already have more money than they can profitably put to work.

Do buy when it reopens.

Middleton also points out that managers who close their
funds are putting shareholders' interests ahead of their
own, since their salaries are based on the size of assets
under management. So when managers decide to reopen,
you can feel fairly confident they see opportunities to keep
more money at work and more investors happy.

**Try not to buy any fund immediately before it makes
its annual capital-gains distribution to shareholders.**

The distribution diminishes the net asset value you just paid
for, returning money you wanted invested and making you
pay capital-gains taxes on it. It's as though you lent a dollar
one day and got it back minus a tax deduction the next. So
before you buy in to a fund, check its *record date*. That's the
day, usually falling between the end of October and year
end, by which you must own shares in order to get a payout.
If you find that the record date is near, wait until it passes
to make your purchase.

GROWTH AND VALUE

> *"I think investors, as they're looking at funds, are
> better off to balance between some of the more
> growth-oriented funds and some of the more
> value-oriented funds, and not really try and say,
> Is this right time to get in or the wrong time to
> get in?"*
> —CLAUDIA MOTT, *director of small-cap research at Pru-
> dential Securities*

PROS LIKE BILL NASGOVITZ and Jim Oberweis can make
good livings specializing in either value or growth.
You probably can't. If you want your small-cap portfolio to work for you in various economic climates,
make sure both styles are represented.

Growth and value thrive at different points in the
business cycle and under different interest-rate conditions. The *business cycle* is the period during which

the growth rate of the gross domestic product climbs to a peak, falls to a bottom, and then moves back up to the base line. At the beginning of this cycle, when company earnings and expectations about them are rising, small-value stocks tend to do best; after the peak, as the economy slows, small emerging-growth companies take the lead. Similarly, a significant drop in interest rates usually presages good times for value investors, while rising rates mean a small-cap growth spurt lies ahead. *(For a more detailed discussion of the business cycle and interest rates, see Chapter 4.)*

Growth and value stocks also complement one another in the way they perform. Growth companies tend to be shooting stars: They can rise spectacularly or plummet sickeningly. Value plays aren't as volatile, since out-of-favor companies generally trade closer to the worth of their assets. The downside of low volatility is that these stocks can be stuck at less-than-inspiring price levels for a long time. By combining the two styles in your portfolio, you get growth's momentum tempered with value's stability and downside protection.

"You don't intend to push out too far on the valuation spectrum," says Claudia Mott. "You hope that by having a little bit of earnings momentum built in, you're not just looking at very low valuation names that may not necessarily have much to drive them forward."

How you incorporate growth and value in your small-cap portfolio is up to you. If you like choosing your own individual stocks, you may feel more comfortable ferreting out the next Intel than researching turnaround candidates. In that case, leave the value-picking to pros like Charles Royce, whose Micro-Cap fund follows a strict value style and, according to Morningstar, generally produces good returns with low risk. On the other hand, you may be happier selecting companies on the rebound than new up-and-comers. So for your growth investing, you'd enlist a manager like Gary Pilgrim: His PBHG Growth fund is tending to the mid- rather than small-cap size, but its returns, says Morningstar, are still sizable, as are its risks. Or you might want to add both types of managers to your roster, particularly if you do all your small-cap investing through funds. *(A list of small-cap growth and value funds appears on page 78.)*

BORDER CROSSINGS

"A portfolio isn't efficient without an international component."
— BURTON MALKIEL, *the Chemical Bank Chairman's Professor of Economics at Princeton University*

FOR TRUE DIVERSIFICATION, leave home. Internationalizing your portfolio will stabilize returns while adding some zest. One nation's economy is always peaking when another's is falling off the edge. If you spread your money around the world, at least part of it is going to be working hard all the time.

Nineteen ninety-six was a good year for the dozen small-cap international funds tracked by Lipper Analytical Services. As of August 31, they had earned 10.7 percent, propelled in part by economic recovery and low interest rates in Europe. One drawback to these funds is that few have been around even three years. Top performer American Century International Discovery, for example, which returned 22.11 percent in 1996, opened in April 1994. Second-ranked Acorn International, with 1996 returns of 15.19 percent, is relatively mature, having been founded in September 1992. According to Morningstar, Acorn also seems less volatile than the front-runner, though the brevity of both funds' track records makes it difficult to tell.

Some of Discovery's volatility may be due to the 20 percent of its portfolio invested in the emerging markets of the lesser-developed world. That 20 percent is probably also largely responsible for the fund's high returns. Developing countries are expected to outpace the industrialized nations in economic growth over the next decade. That makes the prospects of small companies in the Third World very tempting. Malkiel, author of *A Random Walk Down Wall Street,* practically gushes about the benefits of adding an emerging-markets component to your portfolio. The caveat is that you need a long time-horizon to reap those benefits; the short-term volatility can be excruciating, as all too many investors discovered when Mexico devalued the peso at the end of 1994.

 Go international, not global.

They sound the same, but they're not. International funds invest exclusively outside the United States. Global ones can put their assets anywhere in the world—including the U.S., if they see opportunity there. As a result, a global fund could easily duplicate holdings in your domestic funds. That won't give you diversity.

 You can index internationally.

The Vanguard International Equity Index Emerging Markets portfolio provides exposure to the economies of the developing world by matching a custom benchmark created for the fund by Morgan Stanley. Excluded are countries whose markets are illiquid or that make foreign investment difficult or unprofitable. The Vanguard portfolio started up only in 1994, but Morningstar says it has outpaced its peers since then, attributing this performance to conservative country allocation: heavily Southeast Asian, with no African, Eastern European, or Middle Eastern exposure.

For a broader international exposure—to developed as well as developing economies—check out Vanguard's STAR Total International Portfolio. The fund allocates 44 percent of its assets to developed markets in Europe, 44 percent to developed markets in the Asia-Pacific region, and 12 percent to emerging markets.

BACKING THE HOME TEAM

"Why would you send your money anywhere you wouldn't go on vacation?"

— CHRIS BROWNE, *partner in investment advisors Tweedy, Browne Co.*

AN INTERNATIONAL PERSPECTIVE adds diversity to your portfolio. But staying close to home has benefits, too. With small companies, the guy who's there on the ground, ears and eyes open to catch developments as they occur, has a big advantage over the pro slaving at a hot computer hundreds of miles away. Regional funds invest in companies within a few hours' drive of their offices. So the managers and analysts can visit prospects, chat up their neighbors, employees, suppliers, and customers, and read about them in the local papers. With all that info, regionals should be able to dig up overlooked nuggets of intelligence and react to good and bad news before it reaches the Street.

Homestate Pennsylvania Growth fund, for example, has earned top-notch returns with below-average risk by investing primarily in companies located in Pennsylvania, according to Morningstar. This fund finds plenty of investment opportunities in a state with 540-plus public companies and an economy that, at $244 billion, is larger than those of many foreign countries. But one of its greatest strengths, says Morningstar, is manager Kenneth Mertz's ability to search out obscure but solid local companies that he can buy cheaply.

You can find out if a small-stock fund is a regional specialist the same way you'd determine if it follows a growth or value style: read its *Morningstar Mutual Funds* review, check its aims in the prospectus, and study its holdings in the semiannual report.

FUND MAINTENANCE

"You should make certain that each fund is doing what it is supposed to do."
— MARY ROWLAND, *in* A Commonsense Guide to Mutual Funds

ONCE YOU'VE PUT TOGETHER a portfolio of small-cap funds whose objectives match yours and whose managers have good records of keeping them on track, your hardest work is over. One of the advantages of investing this way rather than through individual stocks is that it's fairly low-maintenance. But don't just stick the funds' prospectuses and reports in a file and forget them. Nothing is forever—that includes fund managers, management styles, and performance, as well as your goals and portfolio allocations. It's your job to stay on top of changes and take whatever actions they may require. Again, look at Rowland's guide for details. Meanwhile, here are a few tips.

 When a manager jumps ship, follow.
Just a suggestion—but give it serious consideration, especially with small-cap managers. Many of these are inseparable from their funds: Wanger at Acorn, Nasgovitz at Heartland, Oberweis at Oberweis. Even where the identification is less strong, the man or woman at the helm is usually responsible for a fund's track record; you can't be sure the performance will be the same when someone else starts steering. A friend of mine just took over the management of a fund. He says he can't figure out for the life of him why the previous manager was holding certain stocks, and it will take him months to get his own team together.

The other side of the coin is that by following a manager you really like, you might get in on the ground floor of a good thing.
When Garrett Van Wagoner, the star stock picker of Govett

Smaller Companies, left that fund to set up his own at the beginning of 1996, many investors moved with him. During the first half of that year, the defectors had reason to rejoice: Van Wagoner's young Emerging Growth fund returned more than 49 percent, making it the best-performing small-company growth fund, according to *Barron's*. Govett, meanwhile, fell into the lowest percentile of all funds.

Van Wagoner suffered a setback in the second half of '96, dropping 18 percent from the end of May to the end of the year as the market turned against his aggressive style of investing. Nevertheless, analysts still believe that he is a top manager for investors who can take the falls with the rises. So, all in all, it pays to keep on top of who's coming and going, when and where. You can do that by subscribing to a newsletter like *Morningstar Investor* or *The No-Load Fund Investor (see "Resources")*.

❖ Look in a fund's annual report for its performance stats, both for the current year and for the past 10 years.

Compare this year's figure with the returns of a benchmark like the Russell 2000, which should be included in the report. Make a similar comparison with the fund's peer group; Lipper Analytical Services, *The Wall Street Journal,* and *Barron's* all publish performance statistics for style and segment groups. Then turn to the historical performance. You'd like to see steady or improving numbers.

❖ But check for patterns, too.

As I've said before, different types of stocks do better in different environments. Make sure your fund's performance is consistent with its style, and that at least some of your other holdings show complementary patterns.

Read your newspaper's stock pages. If you own a fund that invests heavily in one sector, check how those stocks are doing, then compare your fund's performance. If, over a few months, the individual stocks are booming and the fund is stagnant, something's wrong. The unfortunate souls who owned Steadman Technology Growth in 1995, for instance, must have wondered if they'd warped into a parallel market. Although tech stocks, which make up a large part of Steadman's portfolio, soared in the first part of the year, the fund's returns were negative. Definitely time for investors to head for the door—if they weren't halfway through already.

See what your fund managers have to say for themselves. They all have a chance to explain their performance in the annual and semiannual reports.
Look for a candid appraisal, including an indication of what to expect from the market and their probable response. In addition, some funds, such as those in the Heartland, Robertson Stephens, and Founders families, equip their 800 numbers with recorded monthly messages in which the managers discuss their takes on the economy and what they're doing to adapt to any changes they foresee. See if the explanations make sense to you and if you agree with the general investment philosophy expressed. This is also a good way to check for changes in viewpoint that could indicate "style slippage," coming up next.

Don't assume that a fund is going to stay in the slot you bought it to fill.
Small-cap funds with too much investment money flowing in often start loading up on mid- or even large-cap stocks. Managers may drift to whatever style or sector is currently hottest. "Style slippage" would be fine if you were doing all your stock investing through one fund and just wanted to get the best returns currently available. But it is a headache if you buy specific funds to play specific roles in your portfolio—whether to provide general small-cap exposure or to specialize in a segment such as value or growth.

Check a fund's holdings in its annual report.
If you bought it for the manager's domestic small-company focus, and it has IBM, Microsoft, and Teléfonos de México in its portfolio, pull out. Stocks like those may boost the fund's

returns, but they don't do anything for your diversification. And they could duplicate other of your holdings if you also own large-cap domestic and international funds.

 Read the proxy statements.
When funds want to change investment policies—raise market cap, leverage, add derivatives, increase fees—they have to spell out the proposal in one of these statements, so that shareholders can vote on it. If you don't like a proposed change and it passes, you can vote again, with your feet, by moving your money to another fund.

TO BALANCE
OR NOT TO BALANCE

"Every crowd has a silver lining."
—P.T. BARNUM

IN SETTING UP A DIVERSIFIED PORTFOLIO, you allocate a certain percentage of your funds to each of the styles and segments you want represented; for instance, as I noted on pages 57–58, you might want to duplicate the performance of the entire market by putting 70 percent of your money in Vanguard's Index 500 fund and 30 percent in its Extended Market Portfolio. But one reason you diversify is that you expect different types of investments to perform differently: small growth stocks will wipe the floor with small value one year, and the next they'll both be flattened by large consumer companies. Such outperformance by one sector in your portfolio is going to upset the balance of styles you started with. Going back to those index funds, if small stocks do much better than large ones, your 70/30 allocation could easily become 50/50.

What should you do about the unbalancing? You have a choice: let your profits run or restore your original allocation. Intuition says run with it. After all, you risk throwing good money after bad if you move assets from a strong manager or market sector to a weak one. Not to mention the taxes you must pay when you take your capital gains. But there are advantages to rebalancing. It keeps your portfolio diversified, and it exploits market cyclicity—the out-of-favor style or sector that lagged one year often takes off the next. If you rebalance rigorously, you'll be buying low and selling high, just like a good contrarian.

◈ If you're a rebalancer, sit down at least once a year with your fund statement or statements; figure out what percentage of your portfolio each sector or style represents. Then compare those figures with your ideal distribution. If they're different, sell some shares in the funds that have grown beyond their allocations and buy more in the ones that have shrunk below theirs. In the indexing example above, you could restore the 70/30 distribution by selling part of your Extended Market Portfolio investment and using the proceeds to buy more of the Index 500 fund.

But my advice to a pure indexer is, don't lose sleep over this. Indexing isn't supposed to exercise your gray cells. If you don't need to draw on your investments for several years, leave your portfolio alone. As the goals you're saving for near, start moving money from small stocks into larger stocks and bonds. This isn't science, but by reducing your small-cap exposure—and stock exposure in general—you increase the odds that the cash to pay for fast-approaching expenses will be there when you need it.

STRESS TESTS

"As far as the laws of mathematics refer to reality, they are not certain, and as far as they are certain, they do not refer to reality."
—ALBERT EINSTEIN

INSTITUTIONAL INVESTORS LOVE to quantify things—for instance, how much money they'd lose if the market looped back to 1987 or Klingons invaded Earth. That's why they love stress testing. It allows them to make official-sounding statements like "I can be 73.2 percent certain that the maximum one-week loss my portfolio will sustain is 23.8 percent." Cool.

I don't know about you, but I don't really need to know my profit and loss in 75 different scenarios. I'd rather spend the time on stock research or—better still—with my family. However, there is a quick and dirty version of the stress test that I do find useful: You just estimate what would happen under a worst-case scenario if all your fund managers decided to max-out their allowable sector bets.

The first thing to look at is how exposed your entire stock allocation could leave you. Take out your latest statement and a calculator. Write down the dollar value of all your stock funds and add them together to get the total you have invested in equities. Now, what's the worst that could happen? We probably can't beat the 50 percent drop in the market between 1973 and 1974. To see how much you'd lose in a similar meltdown, multiply your total stock figure by 0.5. Could you absorb a loss of that size while you wait for stocks to recover? Your answer will depend on your other investments and how close the bills you're saving for, like college tuition, are to coming due. If you couldn't tough out the waiting period, consider allocating more of your savings to principal-conserving investments such as bonds.

Next, take a look at your managers' sector bets. This requires a little more work. For each fund in your portfolio, determine from the prospectus the maximum percentage of assets the manager can allocate to any one sector, then multiply the dollar amount of your position in the fund by that percentage. For instance, if the manager of a fund in which you've invested $100,000 is allowed 20 percent concentrations, your maximum sector exposure for that fund would be $20,000. Add together the figures you get, and the result is your dollar exposure if all your funds' managers decide to take their maximum allowable stakes in the same sector.

Again, what's the worst that could happen to you in, say, four months? Well, that's how long it took computer stocks to drop 30 percent in 1995. So to compute the dollar loss you'd suffer in a worst-case scenario, multiply your sector dollar exposure by 0.3. In my example, that one fund investment would lose $6,000.

If right about now your palms are sweaty and you're short of breath, calm down. Just because your fund managers can take maximum sector stakes doesn't mean they will, or that they'll all max-out the same sectors at the same time. Second, big sector bets pose more of a danger in funds with large asset pools and portfolios, which usually can't move in and out of stocks as quickly as nimble smaller funds can. Third, at certain times in the business cycle, you might actually want a fund to be concentrated in very defensive industries, such as food and drugs.

Still, as I've said earlier, you shouldn't own more than one or two funds whose managers are allowed to take outsize stakes in one sector. The bottom line is that you don't want to get badly hurt. And though trading and sector bets can score big in the short run, which determines most portfolio managers' salaries, they don't pay off over the long term—*your* horizon.

For most of your small-cap investments, you should be looking at a 20-year time frame. Over periods like that, three things seem to generate the best returns, and none of them is trading. The first is the earnings performance of individual companies; with a horizon of 20 years, I'd put my money on a fundamentals guy over a trader. The second element is diversification—not excessive, just owning a broad-enough cross-section of the market to reduce risk and to benefit from whichever area of the economy is prospering. The third and last is minimizing expenses: the fewer unnecessary trades a fund manager makes, the better your returns will be.

SOME SUGGESTIONS

THE SMALL- AND MICROCAP SECTORS are hot right now, and funds are popping up all over to take advantage of investor enthusiasm. In the boxes on this and the following pages, I've listed a few funds that have reasonable track records or whose managers have proved themselves with similar styles elsewhere. To help you choose which ones to fill which slots in your portfolio, I've broken them down by style and segment. But don't take my word for any of them. Do your own research: Look in *Morningstar Mutual Funds,* read the fund prospectuses, scan some of the newsletters and

SMALL-CAP VALUE FUNDS

FUND NAME	5-YR RETURN AS OF 1/31/97*	PHONE
Barr Rosenberg U.S. Small Cap	21.37	(800) 447-3332
Heartland Value	19.99	(800) 432-7856
MAS Small Cap	19.15	(800) 354-8185
Franklin Balance Sheet Invest.	19.1	(800) 342-5236
Fidelity Low-Priced Stock	19.1	(800) 544-8888

* AFTER EXPENSES; NOT INCLUDING LOADS

SMALL-CAP GROWTH FUNDS

FUND NAME	5-YR RETURN AS OF 1/31/97*	PHONE
AIM Aggressive Growth	23.32	(800) 347-4246
Retir. Syst. Emerging Growth	23.07	(800) 772-3615
RSI Retir. Emerging Growth	20.96	(800) 772-3615
Parkstone Small Cap	20.4	(800) 451-8377
Consulting Group SC Growth	20.18	(212) 816-8725

* AFTER EXPENSES; NOT INCLUDING LOADS

Web sites listed in the "Resources" section. Then, once you've committed your money, be sure to monitor your choices' performance in the newspaper, online, and in the funds' own reports.

THIS CHAPTER HAS PRESENTED the ground rules for investing in funds in general and in small-cap funds in particular. You might decide that this is the way to go with your entire small-company portfolio. Or you might want to do some of your own stock picking. Either way, you will find information to help you in the following chapters. For individual stock investors, there's advice on putting together a list of candidates, deciding which to buy when, and biting the bullet when it comes time to prune your portfolio. But

SMALL-CAP BLEND FUNDS

FUND NAME	5-YR RETURN AS OF 1/31/97*	PHONE
Rockwood Growth	18.57	(888) 762-5966
Seligman Frontier A	18.13	(800) 221-2783
Acorn	17.22	(800) 922-6769
Managers Special Equity	17.04	(800) 835-3879
Lord Abbett Developing Grth A	16.37	(800) 874-3733

* AFTER EXPENSES; NOT INCLUDING LOADS

INTERNATIONAL SMALL-CAP FUNDS

FUND NAME	12/31/95– 8/31/96	PHONE
Amer. Century Int'l Discovery	22.11	(800) 345-2021
Acorn International	15.19	(800) 922-6769
Founders Passport	12.93	(800) 525-2440
Morgan Stanley Int'l Small Cap	12.61	(800) 548-7786
Montgomery Int'l Small Cap	12.39	(800) 572-3863

* AFTER EXPENSES; NOT INCLUDING LOADS

SMALL-CAP INDEX FUNDS

FUND NAME (NOT RANKED)	PHONE
Vanguard Index Ext. Market (Wilshire 4500)	(800) 662-7447
Vanguard Index Small Cap (Russell 2000)	(800) 662-7447
Rydex OTC (NASDAQ Composite)	(800) 820-0888
DFA 6-10 (small and microcap)	(310) 395-8005
DFA 9-10 (microcap)	(310) 395-8005
Schwab Small Cap Index Fund	(800) 435-4000
Federated Mini-Cap (Russell 2000)	(800) 341-7400

SOURCE: BLOOMBERG L.P.

those choosing to stick with funds can benefit, too,
using the tips on assembling and tending to an individual small-stock portfolio to understand how fund
managers operate—especially the ones handling
your money.

CHAPTER

BUYING
Individual
Stocks

ALL RIGHT. YOU now know that to boost your portfolio's long-term performance and stabilize returns you should mix in small-cap companies. The previous chapter discussed using mutual funds for that purpose. Here, the focus shifts to individual stocks—which to buy when, and how long to hold them. These are crucial considerations for people ready to assemble their own small-cap stock portfolios. But the information is important even for fund-only investors. Don't forget—when you buy a fund, you are authorizing someone else to buy and sell individual stocks for you. Knowing how that's done makes you a smarter consumer.

This chapter outlines a general plan for creating a portfolio of small-cap stocks and maintaining it through rebalancing and disciplined selling. Chapter 4 takes the process one step further, describing strategies for ensuring that you buy at fair prices and at the right times.

INVEST, DON'T SPECULATE

"I like to tell a story about a man who wants to walk his dog across the park. He should have the sense to stay on the walkway, but the dog is going to wander off to one side of the path to chase a butterfly or to the other to get a sniff of something. The path is the shortest route from point A to point B, but if he assumes that the dog knows a better way, he'll wear himself out. ... The path, of course, is earnings, and the dog is all of the things you hear in the press that make you want to be a trader."
— BILL BERGER, *retired manager of the Berger Funds*

SMALL STOCKS BRING OUT the speculator in people. Mention them at a cocktail party, and someone's sure to start talking up a miracle company: It's working on a process to turn swamp water into clean, edible fuel and is about to go public. It has no product or earnings yet, but it could dominate the $1 trillion energy market.

Yeah, and you could hit the lottery. Still, I wouldn't call filling out the "Pick 6" every week a savings plan. This book isn't about taking a one-in-a-million chance to hit it big. It's about maximizing investment returns while minimizing risks. That means putting together a small portfolio of stocks in small, stable companies whose prospects you like and that you feel comfortable living with for a while. For that you need strategy, not speculation.

THE STRATEGY: BUY TO HOLD

"It's our experience over the years that really the best strategy is to remain fully invested and ride the cycle up and ride the cycle down. Hopefully, over a long period of time, you wind up with average returns higher than the Dow indexes. And that's really what we're looking to do, not to try and pick exactly when it's going to go up and go down."

—JIM OBERWEIS JR., *portfolio manager of the Oberweis funds*

WHY INVEST FOR THE LONG HAUL? Wouldn't you be better off jumping in and out, buying at the lows, selling off at the peaks?

Nope.

First, most of us would probably jump when we shouldn't. Market timing is a tough trick even for pros like Jim Oberweis Jr. "Although sometimes we may guess what the markets are going to do, it is only that," he says. "And we wouldn't act on that, and we wouldn't invest on that. We think market timing over any substantial period of time is virtually impossible. I know of no one who has done it over any long period of time successfully. And we would urge investors against doing that."

Second, high turnover is highly expensive. *Turnover*

refers to the percentage of your portfolio that changes over a particular period; for instance, if you swap around half of your holdings in a year, your annual turnover is 50 percent. The problem with this is that large chunks of any profits made from those swaps are eaten up by capital-gains taxes, commissions, and spreads. This is especially true when you're dealing with small- and microcap stocks. Those markets are relatively illiquid, and the volume of trading is small. As a result, spreads are wide and swapping quickly in and out of a company almost impossible. Sellers of lesser-known microcaps can wait days to find buyers, and then they may have to dole out their shares over long stretches of time to keep from wrecking the price.

"One of the problems of a small-stock portfolio is that trading costs are very high—not only commissions but your effect on the price when you try to buy or sell 5 percent of a company," Ralph Wanger, manager of Acorn Fund, says in a February 1995 interview with *Kiplinger's* magazine.

The problems of accumulating or unloading large stakes in small stocks generally don't concern individual investors. But they are important considerations for funds, even relatively small ones. Consider the case of Pulaski Furniture Corp., described by Preston Athey, manager of the T. Rowe Price Small Cap Value Fund, in a February 1995 *U.S. News & World Report* article. At the beginning of 1995, Athey's position in Pulaski, a Virginia furniture maker, was worth about $2 million. That represented a 17 percent gain since 1991, when the manager started buying the shares. If Athey had decided to realize his profit, could he have just dumped the company and counted his cash? Hardly. The fund's 100,000 shares represented more than three weeks of the stock's average trading volume. He would have had to parcel them out over a month or more. Because of such problems, and to control costs, Athey keeps his fund's turnover to a low annual rate of about 20 percent.

You'll probably never have to worry about moving the market with your purchases and sales. Still, the low liquidity of small caps can cramp your trading style, widening spreads and perhaps preventing you from buying or selling when you wish at the price you want.

The buy-and-hold approach avoids the pitfalls of trading costs, illiquid stocks, and mistimed leaps. "The whole point of investing is to buy good stocks, lock them up for 10 years, and wind up with more money than you started with," says Bill Berger.

But that entails living with your picks for a long time. Along the way, you're sure to encounter some rocky periods. Stocks are volatile, and investors in the smallest companies suffer through the most extreme price moves. To weather the ups and downs, you must have faith in your selections.

"Acorn has a 20 to 25 percent turnover rate, which means that we hold stocks four to five years," Wanger says in the *Kiplinger's* interview. "If you are going to hold a stock that long, you need a reason to think that the stock will do better than average over a very long period of time."

Your reason had better be a lot more solid than assurances from your drinking buddies that a company is going to be the next Microsoft. Finding true distance runners involves research, which takes time and patience. You might wind up passing on a long shot that goes on to win big, but you'll also avoid the ones that throw their riders on the turn or fade in the stretch.

"Invest in haste, repent at leisure," says Robert Rodriguez, manager of First Pacific Advisors' Capital and New Income funds, adding, "There's always another streetcar coming along."

Rodriguez is a good man to listen to: FPA Capital has been the No. 2 small-cap fund over the past 10 years, and, according to mutual fund rating company Morningstar, New Income has some of the best returns of any bond fund, along with very low risk.

WHAT TO DO

"I like [Warren] Buffett's theory: When you're born, you get a card with 20 investment decisions, and each time you make one, you get a punch, so you'd better make them count."
—ROBERT RODRIGUEZ

HERE'S THE BASIC PLAN (details come later): First, decide what portion of your small-cap holdings you want to be individual stocks, as opposed to mutual funds. Remember what I said at the end of Chapter 1: If you can't afford to buy shares in at least 20 small companies, do the lion's share—say, 70 percent—of your investing in this sector through funds. Once you've decided how many stocks you're going to look for, create a list of companies that have solid fundamentals and for which you have an edge. By *edge,* I mean that you understand their businesses and their prospects better than the average investor does. Then, using information from sources such as financial statements (which you can download from the Internet), winnow this collection down to 20-plus names you really like. If that seems too few, remember that the best analysts in the world focus on a small number of companies, usually in a single industry. Chances are you can't efficiently follow more—or more diverse—stocks than they can. Rodriguez, for one, prefers to hold between 25 and 30 companies and adds only one to five new ones a year to his portfolio. "I don't see how anybody can follow 50 to 100 companies," he says.

"What's more conservative?" asks Robert Sanborn, manager of Oakmark, the No. 1 aggressive-growth fund since 1992. "Owning 20 stocks in businesses you understand that are priced right and have good management? Or owning 500 stocks in many businesses that you don't understand, many of which are run by rotten people and many of which are priced insanely?"

A few very successful stocks are all you need, anyway. In a 1993 letter to shareholders, Acorn Fund's Ralph Wanger observed that just three great picks had made the difference for him between mediocrity and outstanding results: Houston Oil & Minerals, an obscure exploration company, added to Acorn's portfolio in 1973, that rose by a factor of 24 and saw Wanger through the ruinous 1973–74 bear market; Cray Research, in which he purchased a $1.5 million stake in 1978 that he ultimately sold for $20 million; and International Game Technology, a block of whose shares, picked up in 1988 for $5 million, was worth $80 million by mid-1995. Concluded Wanger: "It's a little bit like baseball. Babe Ruth hit a lot of home runs, even though he struck out a lot. The big winners can really carry the team to victory."

Once you've got your own 20-plus potential sluggers, your next step is to find out as much as possible about them. That means calling the companies, visiting, getting on mailing lists, and trolling the Internet. The information you gather during this research will help you determine which of your prospects are fully valued or overpriced and which are cheap.

Cheap is what you're looking for. Remember, not every good company is a good stock. The business can be sound and the management solid, but if the market has already factored in all those pluses, the share price has nowhere to go. Your job is to hunt for good companies that haven't yet been fully recognized as such. The efficient-market gang would say they don't exist, or at least are very rare. But even those guys would admit that you have a better chance of finding unmined lodes among companies like surgical-device maker Cabot Medical, followed by just one analyst, than among the market's Intels, which are scrutinized by more than 40 analysts each.

Finally, for every stock you decide to put money into, you should create a dossier, including a statement explaining why you bought it and what would make you sell. You'll review these notes periodically to see whether you need to rebalance your portfolio.

That's the general project. Now for some specific tips on how to implement it.

LOOKING FOR IDEAS

"I take an eclectic approach to finding new ideas. I go to lots of trade shows and read scads of trade journals. For instance, I spent three days last week at InterOp, the [computer] networking show in Las Vegas. Elvis and I were walking the floor. I also cull lots of IPO prospectuses and sometimes go to several road shows a day."

— *From an April 1995 interview in* Barron's *with* G A R R E T T V A N   W A G O N E R, *who at the time managed the Govett Smaller Companies fund and now runs his own group of funds*

INVESTMENT IDEAS ARE ALL AROUND you: in the industrial park across town, at the trade show you visit for business, in your local newspaper and the industry newsletters and journals your company subscribes to, even at the hardware store where you shop. Once you start looking, you can't miss them. If those sources don't inspire you, here are some other ways to work up a list of possible purchases:

◆ **Study the semiannual reports of some small-cap mutual funds with good performance records to find out what they hold.** Top value and growth funds like Rodriguez's FPA Capital and Garrett Van Wagoner's Micro Cap are good places to search. *(For others, see Chapter 2, page 78.)*

◆ **Call regional brokerages for leads.** Many of these firms specialize in small companies operating in their parts of the country that often escape Wall Street's radar screens. The brokers will be happy to earn a commission on any purchase they help you identify. A list of regional brokers and their phone numbers appears in "Resources."

◆ **Quiz people working at firms in fields in which you have an interest.** That's what Garrett Van Wagoner does, according to Peter Kris, managing director of the Van Wagoner funds. "[Garrett] wants to know what the new ideas are," says Kris, "who is starting up new firms, if they are capable managers, and who their competitors are likely to be."

◆ **Subscribe to _The Red Chip Review_ and scan the _Value Line Investment Survey_ at your library.** The _Review_ is a weekly newsletter that covers the small- and microcap markets and profiles individual companies. The _Survey_ is a compendium of one-page company reports published by Value Line, an investment advisory service that ranks stocks according to safety and their projected performance over the next 6 to 12 months _(see "Resources")_.

SORTING AND SIFTING: THE S&P PLAN

"You want to own tennis balls, not eggs, because tennis balls bounce."
—BILL BERGER

TO TURN YOUR INVESTMENT ideas into that list of 20-plus solid small-cap prospects you need to find out about the companies behind the ideas. It takes work, but you've got to do it: Stint the research at this point, and you risk disaster.

What if you don't have the time, skill, or patience for financial analysis? Get pros to do some of the legwork for you. That doesn't mean laying out $100 an hour. By limiting your field to stocks covered by Standard & Poor's Corp., you're essentially hiring a stable of well-trained researchers and analysts at far less than minimum wage. Since the S&P companies are all closely followed, you'll miss out on the truly buried treasure, but if your analytical skills aren't well honed, those stocks aren't for you, anyway.

To enlist S&P's help, just shell out $24.95 for the annual *Standard & Poor's SmallCap 600 Guide.* The S&P 600 is an index of 600 small companies—those in the 50th to 83rd percentile in terms of market value. The stocks must be listed on one of the exchanges or Nasdaq; be priced above $1; and meet various ownership, seasoning, spread, volume, and financial criteria—the companies can't be in bankruptcy, for example.

Many small stocks are eliminated from the index by the screening process. Microcaps in the lowest 17 percent in terms of market cap ($0 to around $150 million, in 1996) are omitted as well. For stocks that aren't included, you might be able to find information at the *Bloomberg Personal* Web site (www. bloomberg.com). For all the companies that *are* in the index, however, the guide contains two-page research reports that provide overviews of their strengths and weaknesses, including up to 10 years of financial data. The info may be slightly out-of-date by the time the guide is published. If you need more current data, you can either have the S&P fax an updated report to you by calling its Reports-On-Demand service at (800) 292-0808 or (800) 546-0300, or you can download one from its Internet site (www.stockinfo.standardpoor.com).

The reports are in the book in alphabetical order, so looking up a prospect by name is a cinch. It's a little harder to troll for small companies in a particular region or business, as you might want to do if you're using the guide as a source of ideas. To help you out, we've presented two lists of the 600 in the Appendix, one broken down by state and the other alphabetical, showing industries and providing Internet addresses for companies with sites as of February 1997.

BESIDES PRICE, RATIO, AND financial-statement data and analysis, the S&P guide provides summaries of a company's business, operation, and past stock performance, as well as quantitative evaluations of the stock's prospects and attractiveness as an investment. The book's introduction explains what the various numbers, letters, and symbols in the reports mean and gives useful definitions of financial terms and ratios.

The S&P pros have read and analyzed the raw financial documents for you and packaged the essentials into easy-to-digest bites. This doesn't absolve you from doing your own research, though. If you're interested in a very small company or one screened out of the S&P index, you'll have to do your own analysis. Even if all your prospects are included, you should go to primary sources, such as the financial reports and proxy statements described below, for more recent data, to cross-check conclusions, and to fill in the reports' outlines. That said, the information in the guide will give you a good start, enabling you to pick out the companies you want to spend your research time on.

What do you look for in a guide report? If you want to do a thorough balance-sheet analysis, including evaluating the data and ratios relative to the norms for the company's industry, I'd suggest a little book called *The Guide to Understanding Financial Statements*, by Geza Szurovy and S. B. Costales, or the famous *Security Analysis*, by Benjamin Graham and David Dodd. Any library should have several reference books. Even an old accounting text from a yard sale would probably give you the basics. In the meantime, here are some quick pointers, including what professionals such as Bill Berger, the Heartland funds' Bill Nasgovitz, and Jim Oberweis want to see. Remember, though, the criteria aren't foolproof. If they were, I'd have better things to do than write this book.

READING THE REPORTS

"Spend at least as much time researching a stock as you would choosing a refrigerator."
— PETER LYNCH, *former manager of Fidelity Magellan fund*

HOW YOU READ A PARTICULAR company's report in the guide depends in part on what type of business you believe it is. You should be looking for two types: good businesses you can buy at great prices and great businesses you can pick up at good prices—in other words, fairly priced, quality growth and value stocks.

Some criteria are equally valid for both growth and value companies, though possibly more pertinent to one group than the other. For instance, professional investors and managers seem to agree that any buy prospect—small or large, growth or value—should show a history of earnings. "I simply refuse to buy a small stock unless it has earnings," says Doug Marx, a broker for investment advisory firm Piper Jaffray in Sioux City, Iowa.

Most pros also look for a record of recurring increases. "We look for earnings acceleration—this quarter compared to the same quarter of the last year, and this quarter compared to the previous quarter. We like to see both of those," says Oberweis. "I also look at the revenues and then compare all of this to the price you're paying for the stock to make sure what you're doing is reasonable."

The pattern may not be as clear-cut, however, for value stocks. Many of these are fallen growth stocks and could show a recent or current decline in

income. You'll be hoping that the dip is just temporary and looking for signs of an earnings rebound.

Some more research tips that apply across the
whole small-cap sector:

**Check out the Quantitative Evaluations section,
particularly the Outlook ranking, which represents a recommendation to buy, hold, or sell.**
You've gone to the S&P guide for the experts' help,
and here is where they really deliver. Based on S&P's
quantitative models and market data, the items in this
section indicate the opinions about the stock held by
the service's analysts, as well as by investors in general
and by company insiders in particular. They're good
guideposts, but always make up your own mind—it's
your money that will go down the drain if the experts
are wrong.

Take advantage of S&P's ratio analysis. These figures, found in the Per Share and Balance Sheet sections, are proportions that you can (and should) calculate yourself later from the financial data in a
company's statements. Having pros do the work for
you at this stage, though, is a convenient shortcut. All
of the ratios are important, but none is essential.
Remember, small and microcap companies almost
have to have something wrong with them, particularly
if they're value stocks. So a poor showing in one area
shouldn't be a knockout blow but rather a warning,
indicating a weakness to watch carefully.

◆ **ROE.** Bill Berger stresses the importance of strong
return on equity (calculated by dividing average common equity into income net of preferred dividends). This indicates that management is getting a
real bang out of the bucks stockholders like you
give it. Berger's emphasis is shared by Bob Barker,
the head of investment firm Barker Lee & Co.

"A stock sells essentially on its earnings," Barker

said in a February 1996 episode of "Adam Smith's Money World." "If you can find a company with a high rate of return—therefore, earnings on the capital it has—and a strong growth trend, you know that the stock is going to perform with the growth of the business."

Berger, a self-proclaimed chicken who doesn't "want to be up all night," likes to see an ROE of at least 20 percent. This is more than many small companies can deliver; you may want to set your sights a little lower—to, say, 15 percent.

◆ **ROA**. But you don't want attractive returns on equity that are generated by leveraging earnings. To guard against this, look at the company's *return on assets* (assets divided into net income). A low ROA (10 percent or so) might indicate that management has produced a high ROE by deriving a lion's share of earnings from assets funded with loans and bond issues rather than stock sales. That's not good news for investors. As Berger puts it, "Who needs a company that borrows a lot of money?" That's especially true of small companies, which must borrow at far higher rates of interest than big ones like Disney, which in 1993 issued 100-year bonds at an interest rate just slightly higher than that for Treasuries.

◆ **Current ratio.** Will the company be able to pay its bills in the short term? The answer depends on its liquidity, which is measured by the *current ratio*. This figure is calculated by dividing *current liabilities* (the debts coming due within one year) into *current assets* (those expected to be cashed in or used up producing revenue during the year). You'd like to see a ratio of around 1 or 1.5, indicating more than enough assets to cover obligations. This is particularly important for a value play, which might be in the process of clawing its way back to profitability.

On the other hand, too high a current ratio is not

great, either. The company should be using its funds to grow, not just socking them away against expenses. One of Kirk Kerkorian's major beefs against Chrysler in his early-1996 stockholder campaign was the size of its cash holdings, which had risen from $1.5 billion in 1990 to $5.5 billion by 1995.

◆ **Payout ratio.** A company's *payout ratio* is the percentage of its earnings that it distributes as dividends. Sixty to 80 percent should be the max. Anything above this would be too hard for a value company to sustain, and a real growth company should be able to make you a bigger profit pouring its revenues back into its business than you could make yourself by investing its dividends.

Under Balance Sheet Data, check *cash* and *cash flow*. The first is money in the bank—hard cash and government and other marketable securities. The second is net income plus depreciation, depletion, and amortization. Both figures should be trending up.

Value investor Bill Nasgovitz has a tougher requirement: He wants the cash figure to be larger than the company's market cap (also shown in the report, under Key Stock Statistics). Stocks that measure up are available, he claims, although "not as much in a bull market, such as we've had, as, let's say, in 1973 or '74, a big bear market." One example that Nasgovitz discovered was Crown Books Corp., which he bought in spring of 1996 at less than cash per share.

Also in the Balance Sheet section of the report, review the past six years of liability and equity figures. Benjamin Graham, the father of value investing, required that a company's current liabilities added to its long-term debt be less than its *book value*—its total assets net of liabilities and intangible assets, such as goodwill. (Multiply the figure under Per Share Data by shares outstanding to make the comparison). That's still a good guideline. The point is, any company you invest in should be able to honor its obligations in hard times. And small caps have enough problems in slow economies without a high level of debt.

"Small companies can stub their toes," Nasgovitz explained on the February 1996 "Adam Smith's Money World." "One customer might account for 25 percent of their business. So if they get a downturn in orders, do they have the financial ... capacity to withstand a downturn?"

William O'Neil, author of *How to Make Money in Stocks* and founder of the *Investor's Business Daily (IBD)* newspaper, adds that firms with a lot of debt can get clobbered during periods of high interest rates. He feels that the lower a company's ratio of debt to equity, the better and safer it is, and he likes to see reductions in debt over a few years. Another measure is debt as a percent of capital (found in the Ratio section). For companies in Nasgovitz's Heartland funds, the average is 19 percent; for Charles Royce's Premier fund, 16.6 percent.

Look for a good story. The numbers and ratios tell you with certainty only where a company has been and is now, not where it will be in a year. For that, you want to see something in its Profile and Business Summary—a new product, new management, new market—that promises to fuel its growth or, in the case of a value stock, turn the business around. A catalyst is particularly important in the microcap sector. "Many companies that are very small deserve to be," says Daniel P. Coker, quantitative analyst with NatWest Securities' Micro-Cap Research Group. "They're often family-run and have only one good product." That's nice for the family, but investors need growth.

"For us, the payoff comes from finding small companies with earnings and then trying to identify a change that the company is making or responding to that will propel earnings further," says Piper Jaffray's Marx. "Using this philosophy, we find a lot of good companies with great products."

One company that's been catalyzed is Vans, Inc. The footwear maker rode high in the early '80s, as fans of *Fast Times at Ridgemont High* rushed out to buy the same Vans sneakers they'd seen Sean Penn slap himself in the head with in the film. But the company overexpanded. It declared Chapter 11 bankruptcy in 1984 and languished for a decade in the shadow of competitors such as Nike and Reebok. Then in 1995, former chief exec Walter Schoenfeld came out of retirement and oversaw a restructuring. The result: 55 percent growth in sales of Vans sneakers and snowboard boots. Just what the broker ordered.

Be on the lookout for market dominance or leading products in a growing market. Robert Rodriguez requires that any company he invests in be No. 1, 2, or 3 in its industry in terms of market share. Van Wagoner doesn't insist on top-three ranking, according to an April 1995 *Barron's* article, just a growing business. He'll go for an "up-and-comer that the big guys have just started to take seriously, [with a product or service] that's changing or influencing [the] industry."

Oberweis also stresses product. He looks for companies that have "a better hamburger, if they're producing hamburgers, or frozen yogurt, if it's frozen yogurt," he said on "Money World." "If [consumers are] buying 50 or 80 or 100 percent more each year [of] whatever [a company is] producing, that tells me it is doing something unique, something different, and something right that ought to catch our attention."

The business profile and summary in the report should tell you about market share. You might also check your newspaper for stories about the business or call the company itself or one of its competitors. Other sources are industry trade journals, which you can find at the library, and *Hoover's Handbook of American Business.*

A niche is nice. It's easier to dominate a market if the market is small. That's why Acorn's Ralph Wanger searches for companies in niche businesses, such as Harley-Davidson. Harley is "the only motorcycle maker in the United States," Wanger says in the February 1995 *Kiplinger's* interview, "and the ones outside the U.S. aren't that exciting. What you've got in Harley is maybe the best brand name in the U.S. Coca-Cola is a good brand name, but people don't tattoo it on their bodies."

Another niche player, Guest Supply, illustrates the potential for growth in such positioning. You know those miniature shampoos, hair conditioners, lotions, and sewing kits you find in hotel bathrooms? Well, Guest Supply makes most of them. The company supplies 14 of the 15 largest chains in the United States, including the Motel 6, Marriott, Hyatt, and Hilton Hotels chains. But it has plenty of room to expand, according to Coker. He estimates that Guest now reaches only about one-third of all hotel properties. And a large number of the company's existing customers purchase just a small percentage of the items it can provide: paper products, cleansing chemicals, and textiles, in addition to soaps, oils, and creams.

Try to determine just how safe your pet pick's franchise is. Does it have major competitors? Is its market wide open or protected by barriers, such as high start-up costs or government regulation? The quality of a company's competition can have a significant impact on what you'd be willing to pay for its stock. For example, the upside of turnaround star Vans may be limited by the fact that it's sharing market space with Nike. If a company's report doesn't list its main market rivals, call it up and ask for names of competitors; see if it will recommend a trade paper that will fill you in on major industry issues. The ideal scenario is no competition in a growing industry that is difficult to get into, such as prescription drugs; the worst is a toehold in a slow-growing industry, such as printing, that is dominated by firms that could squash your prospect like a bug.

Reap the downstream benefits of technology. One of Acorn's key investment techniques is finding companies that will be secondary beneficiaries of new inventions. Wanger points to the TV stations and cable companies that were spawned by television and, more recently, to International Game Technology, which puts microprocessors into the video games and slot machines it manufacturers.

"IGT benefited marvelously from technology," he says in the *Kiplinger's* article. "It reinvented the humble mechanical slot machine, which inside looks like an old cash register, full of springs and cams and levers, ... by replacing the works with a microprocessor.... It's a new device that offers more interesting games, eliminates maintenance, allows you to get progressive jackpots or add lottery components. All of a sudden, casinos are taking out craps tables to put in more slot machines. An IGT slot machine sells for $5,000. If the company tried to sell the same microprocessor for your kid to put inside a personal computer, it couldn't get $500 for it."

Apply the "quit test." This is Wanger's favorite criterion. As he explains in *Kiplinger's*, "You find a company that excites you so much that you say, 'This is so exciting and so much better than what I'm doing running a mutual fund that I'd like to quit this job, buy 100 percent of the company, and run it.' That's not practical, but sometimes people actually do it. One of the stocks we own is Systems & Computer Technology. It was followed by a nice young brokerage analyst we talked to frequently. One day he said, 'I'm not going to be talking to you again as an analyst.' I said, 'What happened? Did you get indicted again?' And he said, 'No, I'm going to work for Systems & Technology in its marketing department.' I sure as heck bought more of that stock."

Don't ignore what other investors think about the company. You can figure this out by looking at *relative strength:* the rate, relative to other stocks in a specified index or industry, at which a particular stock rises or falls in a rising or falling market. A high relative-strength ranking means that the company's shares have tended to climb higher and drop less precipitously than those of its peers—music to a buyer's ears. The Qualitative Evaluations section of the report contains a Relative Strength Rank figure, indicating how the stock has performed compared with all the others in the S&P universe on a rolling 13-week basis. The rankings range from a low of 1 to a high of 99. Oberweis requires a rank of at least 75 and prefers 90 or 95.

"I'm a believer that there are some other pretty smart people who invest in the market," he says. "If [my other requirements] are all [met] and the relative strength isn't, I better do some more homework and figure out why the stock isn't performing."

THE CRITERIA DISCUSSED SO FAR are valid for both growth and value stocks. The S&P reports also contain information that you may weigh and interpret differently for one group than for the other. Say you find a growth company with a good story and solid earnings that doesn't have an enormous amount of debt. You might next look at its price-to-earnings ratio. You'll find this under Per Share Data in the guide report, though you might also want to check the current value in the Wednesday *Investor's Business Daily* or on the *Bloomberg Personal* Web site. The number will probably be much higher than the maximum 15 or so you'd want to see in a value stock. That's because you're expecting earnings to grow quickly, narrowing the gap. The question is, is your expectation realistic?

For an answer, begin by reviewing past earnings growth. If there is an upward trend that seems to be steepening, you're on the right track.

Oberweis wants to see year-over-year increases of at least 30 percent in both earnings and revenues. "We never buy the biotechs or Netscapes of the world," whose revenue gains often don't translate into earnings growth, he says. He also requires a p/e no higher than ½ the growth rate—a ratio of 25, for instance, calls for 50 percent growth—and evidence that the company can sustain its earnings pace. The fastest-growing buggy-whip maker, he points out, wasn't much of a buy when the automobile was being introduced.

Oberweis, though, is unusually strict among growth investors. Van Wagoner will settle for year-over-year earnings growth equal to 20 percent and no lower than the p/e. Alexander Paris, president of Barrington Research, requires five-year profit growth greater than 10 percent and a p/e not more than twice this figure.

◆ **Check the company's profit margins, represented in the S&P report by the % Net Income of Revenues, under Balance Sheet Data.**

You'd like to see the margins increasing, a sign that the company is either cutting costs or selling its product at higher prices, or both. At the same time, be on the lookout for quick nonoperational fixes—such as layoffs—which produce boosts in profits the company might not be able to repeat. Be wary of spikes in earnings that are not paralleled in revenues.

WITH A VALUE STOCK, YOUR FOCUS is different. Primarily, you want to see low p/e and price-to-book ratios. (Price to book isn't given in the report, but you can calculate it easily by dividing the listed book value into the share price.) It's as though you were buying the whole company: The higher its earnings and asset value in relation to its purchase price, the sooner you get back your outlay and start making a profit. "We look at the balance sheet as much as we look at the earnings statement," says Bill Nasgovitz. "What's the book value? What's going to hold this stock up if the plane crashes and things turn out to be fairly negative?"

Investment advisor Tweedy, Browne Co., in the booklet it sends to new and prospective clients, cites several studies showing that stocks with low p/e's have consistently delivered higher annual and cumulative returns than those with higher ratios and that among low-p/e stocks, small-caps outperform large ones. Other research has found that small stocks with low p/e's not only post higher returns than the market but do so with less risk. (Remember, though, that these statistics assume a "black-box" style of investing, blindly buying all the stocks in a particular p/e range without any other screening mechanism.)

FPA's Robert Rodriguez requires that a stock's p/e be less than 15.
This is a good guide, but you may want to be less absolute. Look for ratios that are 25 percent lower than the industry norm. You can calculate your own industry averages from the p/e's for similar companies listed in the newspaper, or ask your broker to look them up on the firm's Bloomberg terminal.

◆ **Look for companies whose earnings yields are comparable to the yield on triple-A-rated corporate bonds.**
Earnings yield—the reciprocal of p/e—is what the return on your investment would be if the company paid out all its earnings as dividends. Benjamin Graham required an earnings yield twice the bond yield, but parity is more a realistic goal today. So, if corporate yields are 8 percent, you'd look for a p/e no higher than around 12.

◆ **Remember: A low-p/e company whose earnings are expected to grow is better than one having the same p/e but no growth prospects.**
As Warren Buffett has said, growth and value are "joined at the hip."

PRICE TO BOOK TAKES precedence over p/e for Charles Royce, president of Quest Advisory. "We do not buy stocks from a p/e standpoint," he says in an October 1992 interview with *Institutional Investor*. "As value investors, we're often buying companies that have taken the past year off, [so] their last-four-quarter p/e might be 48." You have to look beyond current earnings, he feels, to past performance and to other factors indicating a low valuation. One of the most important of these for Royce is the price-to-book ratio: "Our average there is about 1.5, compared with a range of about 3.5 to 4 in a growth portfolio."

Stressing price to book works for Royce—his Micro-Cap fund, for example, is praised by Morningstar for its "distinctive style and limited downside volatility." The statistical evidence is less clear. Academics Kenneth R. French and Eugene L. Fama have determined that for price-to-book ratio, as for p/e, lower is indeed better, and the lowest ratio combined with the smallest cap is best. Other studies, however, have been inconclusive. At Prudential Securities, for instance, director of small-cap research Claudia Mott, analyst Daniel Coker (now at NatWest), and Kevin Condon (now at B.T. Securities) found the benefits of low price to book significantly "less robust" than other valuation measures.

One problem with using this criterion is that "low" is relative when talking about price to book. Manufacturing and capital-intensive businesses have more tangible assets and therefore higher book values than creative, knowledge-based ones. As a result, the price-to-book ratios of utilities in general are lower (at about 1.5) than those of software companies (about 9.5). But that doesn't make utilities necessarily better values. Another problem stems from accounting conventions. Assets such as real estate are carried at "historical cost," the price paid to acquire them. This could be quite different from their current market value. Accordingly, price to book can paint an overly optimistic or pessimistic picture of a company's financial health.

For a company to be truly cheap on a price-to-book basis, its ratio should be lower than its industry's norm. To check this out, look at the reports for other companies in the same business and compare ratios. Also the S&P and Bloomberg Internet pages *(listed in "Resources")* sometimes show industry averages. Or ask your broker to use the Relative Value (RV) function on his or her Bloomberg terminal.

Stocks with the lowest price to book may be the best selections when you're worried about the market, since they seem to weather downturns better than highfliers do. But take into account other fundamentals, too.

P/E AND PRICE-TO-BOOK RATIOS are the primary value indicators. But they aren't the only ones. Two other signals to look for in the reports:

A pattern of buying by a company's officers and directors. This could indicate that its stock is underpriced. The Tweedy Browne booklet points out that insiders often have "insight information" about operational changes or hidden assets, such as excess real estate, that could boost earnings. It cites several studies showing that stocks bought shortly after significant insider purchases became public outperformed the market index by large margins. For the inside track, check the Insider Activity section under Quantitative Evaluations. You can get additional information from newsletters such as the *Vickers Weekly Insider Report* and *Insiders' Chronicle* or at the associated Web sites: www.quote.com/info/vickers.html and www.cda.com *(see "Resources")*.

A company whose market cap equals 66 percent or less of its *net current asset value*. NCAV is not listed, but you can compute it by subtracting current liabilities and long-term debt from current assets. According to the Tweedy Browne booklet, Ben Graham earned 20 percent a year from the 1930s to 1956 by buying shares in companies that met this criterion. The booklet also cites modern studies showing that such stocks, if held at least two years, outperform even the ones in the lowest price/book category. One reason these companies are attractive is that they are often takeover targets. But the holding period is important—you may have to wait awhile before the stocks actually move.

You won't find a lot of companies today that meet Graham's 66 percent mark. As a compromise, many value investors will buy stocks at slightly above their net current asset values. Two companies trading below or close to their NCAVs in the fall of '96 were Deb Shops (with a market value and NCAV of $58.6 million and $54.4 million, respectively) and Crown Books ($52.23 million and $53.2 million). Nasgovitz has been an enthusiastic buyer of Crown: As of June 1996, Heartland Advisors owned nearly 680,000, or

12.83 percent, of the shares outstanding.

But bear in mind that cheap stocks are usually cheap for a reason. A high NCAV relative to market cap, for example, may mean the company has a large backlog of products (included in its current assets) that nobody wants and that it will have to discount to unload. Or its current assets may be swelled by accounts receivable that it will never collect, or perhaps the owners are liquidating the business. Read the company's profile to see what sent your value prospect down the tubes and if there's any reason to foresee a turnaround. Then check Balance Sheet Data to make sure that the company is solid enough to stay afloat while you're waiting.

TWEEDY BROWNE ANALYSTS LOOK at a value prospect as though they were underwriting an insurance policy on it. "We want married couples with a clean driving record who drive Volvos and walk to work," Tweedy partner John Spears told me one day at lunch.

You may have to put off this kind of examination until you've sorted out your prospects using the S&P guide and are collecting and analyzing your own research materials (*see "Find Out About Fundamentals"*). At that point, for example, you can determine the balance-sheet health of a low-NCAV prospect by checking what percent of its current assets are in inventory and in accounts receivable: If the proportions are out of line with industry norms, you might want to steer clear. On the other hand, a large percentage of cash (including marketable securities) is generally a good sign. Crown Books had $158.1 million in current assets in late 1996, of which inventory accounted for $111.3 million (not bad for a book retailer) and cash for $30 million, or $5.56 a share— a nice amount, considering that the stock was trading in the $11 range.

Even before the data-collecting stage, though, you

can search for survival signs in the S&P reports. Low debt is important. So is a high current ratio. Also examine the price chart on the first page of the report, as well as more recent prices, in the newspapers or on Nasdaq's Internet page, at www.nasdaq. com—if the stock is still dropping, consider putting your buy on hold until it stabilizes.

INFORMATION, PLEASE

"The first and foremost rule is to really get to know your company. And this entails getting all the financial information on the company that you possibly can and getting on the phone and talking to the people who run the company, talking to the people who are buying products from the

GOOD GROWTH, FINE VALUE

IF YOU'D LIKE TO TAKE A CUE FROM Philip A. Fisher and Benjamin Graham, venerable growth and value investors, respectively, here are a few of their key criteria. Some you'll be able to check on in the S&P guide; for others, you'll have to read the companies' reports and proxy statements, scan news and industry articles, and talk to management or other company representatives.

Philip Fisher—whose book *Common Stocks and Uncommon Profits and Other Writings* reportedly influenced Warren Buffet as much as Graham's *The Intelligent Investor* did—suggests that the following indicate a good growth stock:

◆ products whose sales have the potential to increase significantly for several years
◆ a management determined to develop new products when the potential of currently successful ones has been fully exploited
◆ effective research and development in relation to sales
◆ a successful sales organization

company, talking to anyone you can think of that would have some sort of insight into this company's prospects."
— GORDON ANDERSON, *managing editor of* Individual Investor *magazine, on "Adam Smith's Money World"*

AFTER USING THE S&P GUIDE to pan your list of prospects, you'll be left with 15 to 20 that could turn out to be golden. But before taking a stake in any of them, you need to do more research, to find out as much as possible about their operations and finances, as well as about any developments, reorganizations, or projects that could propel them to a higher plane.

- ◆ strong profit margins
- ◆ efforts to improve profit margins
- ◆ no outstanding labor or personnel problems
- ◆ a backup team of managers capable of running the show if something should happen to the CEO
- ◆ good cost analysis and profit controls
- ◆ a long-range profit strategy, including plans to cut costs, raise prices, develop new products
- ◆ a management that keeps shareholders apprised of the company's affairs in good times and bad.

For a value stock, look for these criteria, from Janet Lowe's *Value Investing Made Easy:*
- ◆ price amply supported by underlying value—that is, lower than its breakup value, or what its individual parts would be worth if they operated independently and had their own stock prices
- ◆ if possible, share price below net current assets
- ◆ quality. "Investors do not make mistakes, or bad mistakes, in buying good stocks at fair prices," said Graham.

Try the product.

This is a Peter Lynch classic. If you like what a company produces, others probably will, too. That means increasing sales, which should translate into good earnings and so higher share prices. It's simple advice, but even the pros follow it when they can. Steve Shapiro of Founders Asset Management in Denver told me that he and a couple of the fund's managers happened to drive past a Rainforest Cafe around the time the chain was planning its initial public offering. Shapiro's passengers yelled at him to stop, and the whole group piled out of the car, credit cards drawn, to sample as many menu items as possible and quiz other patrons. Caution: Customer satisfaction can't be your only criterion. In late 1996 Rainforest, with about $460 million in market capitalization, had only a few operating outlets—not exactly a dream purchase, no matter how good the service.

LOOK LOCAL

"All our companies are just a car ride away."
— JOSEPH BESECKLER, *founder, Homestate Pennsylvania Growth fund, in the May 1996 issue of* Individual Investor

WHEN YOU INVEST NEAR HOME, you have access to legal inside information. (I won't go into what constitutes the illegal kind, but as long as you aren't buying or selling a company's shares based on what you know as a director or heard from one, you're probably safe.) You can find out more about a hometown firm in your local newspaper than any out-of-town investor will read in the national press. And it's easy to see for yourself what's going on. All you have to do is drive by: Is the plant dark most of the time? Or is it running extra shifts, a sure sign that business is good? Is the company hiring or laying off staff?

For more information, talk to people who work there: Have employees received competitive raises? And visit on days the community is invited inside. Is the working environment clean and safe, showing concern for employees? Can workers communicate easily with managers, or are the two separated by several floors and forbidding receptionists?

I like to walk into a company and see nice but not opulent digs filled with busy people. I don't want to be able to tell the difference between management and the workers. When managers are mixing with the staff, sporting the same frayed sleeves and dirty hands, it's a sign that, like my boss, Mike Bloomberg, they know "every damn thing that's going on."

Joseph Beseckler is a local man. His Homestate Pennsylvania Growth fund invests at least 65 percent of its assets in companies that are headquartered in Pennsylvania or have substantial operations there. That gives it an edge, Beseckler says in *Individual Investor* magazine. The fund's analysts can easily visit all of the companies they cover, which, moreover, are generally underfollowed by Wall Street.

You can also leverage local connections for leads on businesses outside the area. Piper Jaffray broker Doug Marx, for example, takes advantage of having personal-computer maker Gateway 2000 as a neighbor. "I get a lot of good information about computers and tech stocks just being here and talking to people in town," he says.

Tweedy Browne's John Spears enlisted family help while researching Fleming Cos. The company wholesales groceries, produce, and dairy products to supermarkets, so Spears talked to his family grocer, who generously answered questions about Fleming and its competitors. These insights helped Spears make a more informed investment decision.

Spears, who also quizzed his pharmacist about two drug distributors he was deciding between, cautions that a company's customers, suppliers, and rivals aren't always willing to dish the dirt. Even the big guys have trouble getting this information. But that means if you succeed, you've got a real scoop.

Frequent travelers can cultivate personal connections in several localities. One money manager I know who specializes in the retail industry has the knack of getting out of companies before bad news hits. Her secret, she says, is visiting malls whenever she's on the road and checking up on her companies' outlets. She schmoozes with the managers over coffee and snacks, getting good gossip in return.

FIND OUT ABOUT FUNDAMENTALS

"The best way to get to know a company is to get the annual report and read it cover to cover."
—BILL BERGER

OF COURSE, UNLESS YOU LIVE in a very unusual town, not all your small-cap prospects are going to be local. You can't get the same insider's insight into companies that don't field a float in your local Memorial Day parade. But you can still find out more about how they work.

The companies themselves are great sources of information. The Securities and Exchange Commission requires them to publish financial and business data in their quarterly and annual reports and proxy statements. These contain updated versions of the raw material—the fundamentals—that the S&P experts massage and condense in the fundamental analyses in the guide.

Although Berger recommends a more thorough study, you can probably concentrate on the areas mentioned in the tips below: the president's letter, balance sheet, statement of cash flows, and income statement (in the reports), and the executive compensation section of the proxy statement. For companies not in the S&P guide, that's where you'll find the data you need for your own analyses. For companies that are covered, these primary sources provide a sort of reality check on the reports' figures and opinions.

 The company's balance sheet should be "strong."

Many of the figures and ratios that contribute to this strength were discussed above, in connection with the S&P reports—low debt relative to equity and book value, increasing cash, a current ratio greater than one, for example. Again, if you want to do a thorough balance-sheet analysis, refer to *The Guide to Understanding Financial Statements* or an accounting text.

 But regard corporate figures with suspicion.

That's another of Benjamin Graham's rules. Management puts its own spin on the facts, and even experienced analysts can have a tough time determining if the company's accountants are playing hocus-pocus with the numbers. A 1990s corollary: Regard anything you see on the Internet with even greater suspicion.

 On the income statement, study the sales figure.

Ideally, it should be equal to or greater than the company's market cap. "We look for a low price-to-sales ratio," says Oberweis. "Typically, someone who goes out to buy an entire company says, 'Okay, what am I paying for a company with revenues of such and such?' We'll also look at that, because we're buying pieces of the company."

Some investors substitute *price/sales* (calculated by dividing sales into market cap) for price/earnings in their financial analyses. There are two reasons for this: One, unlike sales, earnings can be heavily influenced by accounting decisions concerning inventory, depreciation of assets, and extraordinary charges. Two, p/s is a better indicator than p/e for companies whose earnings are temporarily low or negative. A word of caution: A Prudential Securities study by Claudia Mott and Daniel Coker found that although p/s differentiated winners from losers, it didn't do so better than p/e, nor did it produce consistent results. Probably the best bet is to use both measures to cross-check each other.

◆ **Robert Rodriguez likes to see something left over when he subtracts capital expenditures from cash from operations (both found on the cash-flow statement).**
The remainder is called *free cash flow,* and it is essentially a measure of the company's ability to generate enough money to fund its own growth and still have a cushion for unforeseen costs or opportunities.

◆ **If the company distributes earnings, look for an above-average dividend yield, calculated by dividing the share price into the dividend per share.**
A high yield (around 3 percent) is attractive, as long as it's not paired with a high payout ratio *(see above).* Tweedy Browne cites studies showing that the companies with the highest dividend yields have also produced the highest investment yields. Bear in mind, though, that this measure is more significant for small-cap value than for small growth stocks, which seldom pay much of a dividend, and may be meaningless for microcaps.

◆ **Buy the formula.**
Here are three equations, courtesy of Peter Lynch, Benjamin Graham, and Michael Berry, intended to help investors decide if they're putting their money in the right place.

◆ **Earnings growth + dividend yield / p/e > 1.5.** In English, the sum of the company's expected annual earnings growth rate and its dividend yield should be more than half again as great as its price-earnings ratio; Lynch adds that twice as great is excellent. This is essentially the inverse of Oberweis's requirement that a company's p/e be no more than half its rate of earnings growth, but Lynch has made it less stringent by including dividends in the calculation. You'll find expected earnings growth rates—composites of analyst predictions based primarily on estimates provided by the companies' investor relations groups—in the S&P reports on the Internet or at the

Web site for Zacks Investment Research. Or call the companies themselves for these numbers.

◆ **The intrinsic value of a stock = eps x [(2 x earnings growth) + 0.085] x 4.4/AAA-bond yield.** According to Ben Graham's formula, a stock should be selling for the company's annual earnings per share times twice the expected earnings growth rate plus the appropriate p/e for stocks with static growth (8.5), times 4.4 divided by the yield on triple-A corporate bonds. To see how this works, imagine that crockery maker Feet of Clay, which has 10 million shares outstanding, has earned $20 million this year, or $2 per share, and has an expected growth rate of 5 percent. Assuming that triple-A corporates are selling at 7.33 percent, the intrinsic value of the stock is $2(2 x 0.05 + 0.085) x 4.4/0.0733 = $2(0.185) x 60 = $22.20. If Feet of Clay is selling for less than $22.20, it's cheap; above this figure, it's overpriced.

◆ **The rule of 2-2-2.** Mike Berry, a former manager of the Dreman small-cap value fund who now handles the mid-cap portfolio at Heartland, looks for stocks characterized by three "2s": First, they should be trading at **half** the market multiple—that is, half the average p/e for the appropriate index. Second, the companies should be growing their earnings at **twice** the market rate. Third, their price to book must be less than **two.** Berry's rule is basically a summary of value criteria, spiced with growth. (You'll find market multiples and growth rates in *Barron's* and on the Bloomberg Web page; *IBD* also carries multiples.)

 But don't sweat the math.

These are rules of thumb distilling the insights of market experts, not precise recipes to be followed mechanically in arriving at your investment decisions. Stating them as formulae is misleading—it makes them appear more scientific and less biased than they are.

One place bias can enter is in the expected growth rate. Growth is notoriously difficult to forecast, and estimates are often influenced by considerations not strictly financial. In the past, companies and the analysts following them may have overemphasized good news to stir investor enthusiasm. Lately, though, they seem to be taking the opposite tack. Management has learned that bad things happen when announcements of actual earnings fail to live up to earlier predictions: At worst, angry shareholders sue; at best, the stock takes a nosedive. When the expectations prove too conservative, on the other hand, share price usually soars. So managements "tend to work with analysts to keep estimates low," says Jim Oberweis in his September 1996 *Oberweis Report,* a newsletter for shareholders.

Ask companies' investor relations offices for their reports or search the Internet.

Reports filed electronically with the SEC are available through Edgar—short for Electronic Data Gathering, Analysis, and Retrieval—which you can access at www.sec.gov/edgarhp.htm. Company addresses and phone numbers are included at the bottom of the S&P reports and are listed in the Appendix. This information is also available in *Nelson's Directory of Investment Research,* an annual publication found in most libraries and bookstores *(see "Resources").* Or call (800) 555-1212 for directory assistance—almost every company has a toll-free number these days.

Look into obtaining press releases.

Ask the investor relations office about getting on a mailing list or go back to the Internet. Some companies have sites that receive their releases; others send them to free services on the Net. One caution: There can be too much of a good thing. Bill Nasgovitz says he once received eight positive press releases from one company on the same day. He got nervous and sold. Sure enough, bad news lurked behind the spin—the stock dropped like a split-finger fastball soon after.

Avoid companies whose financial statements aren't audited by one of the Big Six firms: Arthur Andersen & Co.,

Coopers and Lybrand, Deloitte & Touche, Ernst & Young, KPMG Peat Marwick, and Price Waterhouse & Co.
"We've had a number of frauds over the last 10 years," says Bill Nasgovitz. "And in each case, they were non-Big Six auditing firms." A reputable accountant's approval doesn't mean that the company is a good investment. It does mean that the report preparers have followed generally accepted accounting principles. That should make it easier for you to see what's going on and to compare the company's figures with those of others in the same industry. Oberweis also looks for "hidden footnotes" and anything else indicating that "the company is doing something a little bit unusual."

VIEW FROM THE TOP

"The smaller the firm, the better the management needs to be."
— ALEXANDER PARIS *of Barrington Research*

NO MATTER HOW GOOD a company's balance sheet looks or how strong its brand name is, a group of bad managers can ruin it in a heartbeat. In a small company, the people at the top are particularly important. Often the business is their baby, and it lives or dies on their business smarts. Unfortunately, say some analysts, many entrepreneurs are not just crazy about their companies—they're just plain crazy. So before investing, get to know the people in charge.

Rodriguez prefers it if managers have been in place for at least two years, giving him material on which to judge them. He wants to see that they have developed a definable image for their company. Here are three ways to develop your own image of the management and its goals:

Read the letter to shareholders in the annual report. This will give you a sense of how the company officers think they're doing and where they want to go from here. Value companies, which are often fallen angels trying to fly again, should discuss their problems openly and be specific about solutions.

Look for how a company intends to increase earnings. Peter Lynch lists five ways—cutting costs, raising prices, expanding into new markets, selling more in old markets, and disposing of losing operations. "I ... want to see a management that can articulate how they're going to grow the company, what they're doing to develop products and expand distribution," Garrett Van Wagoner says in an April 1995 *Barron's* interview. "I've also got to make the judgment that management is good enough to complete their plan."

Read the compensation and insider holdings sections in the proxy statement sent out before the shareholders meeting. These will tell you how management compensates itself and lower-level employees and how much of a stake managers have in the company.

For Van Wagoner, the more stock insiders own, the better. "I want to see that management has enough financial incentive to be rewarded if [its] plan works," he says in the *Barron's* interview. "Professional managers are well and good, but that's not who I want running my company."

Nasgovitz agrees, adding that when "insiders—officers and directors—have a large percentage of stock ownership, ... their interests are aligned with the public shareholders'." What percentage is "large"? Genesee Corp. is considered closely held with 12 percent insider ownership. But Marc Robins, editor-in-chief of *The Red Chip Review* newsletter, demands even greater commitment. "Stock ownership of 20 percent [is] a good base level. To me, if insiders own this size position, they must have the kind of commitment that, over time, will pay me the kind of return I desire," Robins writes in the May/June 1997 issue of *Bloomberg Personal* magazine.

You might also take a look at the bios of the board of directors, if these are included. Outside members often ensure that insiders keep shareholders' interests in mind.

Try to meet managers face-to-face or talk to them on the phone. Nasgovitz, whose team visits more than 500 companies a year, says that value investors "love to go out and kick the tires, check if the bricks are in place and if management's there working full time, part time, what their incentives are, how eager they are to show up at work every day. In the value camp, we're generally buying distressed merchandise or wallflowers—things that, perhaps, are not in favor. And management is a critical element in terms of our analysis."

This isn't everyone's point of view. Oberweis, for one, avoids direct contact. "Over a long period of time," he says, "it really doesn't add that much value to our investing process." Worse, getting to know the people who run a company makes it harder to be objective about its prospects and to sell the stock when these prospects seem dim.

Royce, too, doubts that "meeting eyeball-to-eyeball with the CEO is necessarily going to get you anywhere." He believes that contact with outsiders connected in various ways with a company is just as important, and possibly more enlightening.

"You want to talk with suppliers and other people who have known management for a long time," he says in the October 1992 interview with *Institutional Investor* magazine. "There are subtle things you want to find out, such as the culture of managements, their integrity, whether they change their minds too frequently. You want to know other ingredients besides just the facts."

Most analysts probably belong to the Nasgovitz camp. Lisa Gray, a stockbroker in Memphis, for instance, feels that by visiting the managements of small companies in its neighborhood, a firm's research team can give its clients access to the best information possible.

David Schafer of the Strong Schafer Value fund also favors close-up looks at companies and their managers. He tells of visiting Jaguar in the early 1980s, when neither the car nor the stock had many fans. Schafer was the only analyst who bothered to visit the beleaguered British automaker, and he got an exclusive on its new manager and how he was handling problems with the company's quality-control program. The biggest obstacle was posed by frequent defective shipments from outside suppliers. So the manager ordered any broken part to be dumped on his desk. He then personally delivered it to the CEO of the offending supplier. Impressed, Schafer bought a block of Jaguar stock for his fund, which he sold for a huge profit when Ford Motor Co. bought the company in 1989.

If you also prefer the Nasgovitz approach, there are several ways you can get a more personal feel for management. It's easiest, of course, when the company is local. You may be able to go to an open house there or get invited to a local chamber of commerce meeting. You might even attend the annual meeting, if you can get a ticket as a nonshareholder. Nasgovitz has been known to drive by a company's parking lot at 6 A.M., looking for managers' cars, and then again at 7 P.M., to make sure they're still there. Long hours, he feels, are a clue that management regards this as more than just a job; when that's no longer true, he says, the company's best days are over. If he sees a luxury car in the lot, he'll often ask whose it is. He'd rather hear that it belongs to an intern's parents than to a fat-cat executive.

If you're really lucky, one of the officers of a company will be teaching a class at a local night school or community college. Enroll—you'll learn something about business and should hear good stories about life in the trenches.

For companies not in your neighborhood, you can always fall back on the telephone. Don't worry that managers will refuse a call from a small investor. As *Individual Investor*'s Gordon Anderson explained on "Money World," "Most of these small companies are entrepreneurial. And an entrepreneur—I know this from the way we do business—it's your pride and joy. It's your baby. You want to talk about it because someone's interested."

If management is rude or evasive, stop right there. Any company that doesn't treat its shareholders, or prospective shareholders, with respect is not a good investment.

When you get an officer of the company on the phone, take a few interrogatory tips from Ron Ognar, manager of the Strong Growth fund. According to the May 1996 issue of *Mutual Funds* magazine, Ognar asks "about company goals, earnings projections, operating margins, growth rates. How long will it take you to reach your targets? Can you go higher? Get there faster? Do you have enough cash and borrowing to make an acquisition? Who's the competition? Do you confine your service to the United States? How do you put a five-year plan together?"

Ognar also quizzes executives about how much stock they own and how far down the corporate ladder stock options are distributed. He wants to know about a CEO's personality and management style, how top managers are recruited, and if they have frivolous plans, like buying jets for executive travel. One last question: How would the company hold together if the CEO "went to the Fiji islands for six months?"

Find out when the company plans to make its next earnings announcement. Then ask whether the figures are expected to meet, exceed, or fall below Wall Street predictions, and the reason for any difference. This is very important. Analysts deduce future quarterly and annual earnings from statements by the company, combined with their own readings of industry and larger economic trends. Based on their deductions, they issue buy, sell, or hold recommendations that may affect the stock's price. When analysts' expectations collide with reality, the market reaction can be violent. That's good news if they've guessed too low, bad news if they were overly optimistic. So be on the lookout for surprises—and for no surprise, as well: Because of the new estimate conservatism noted above, an announcement that merely meets expectations now often depresses share price. As Oberweis points out in his September '96 newsletter, "We investors aren't stupid. After a while, we figure out that a $0.15 estimate from an analyst really means that they are expecting $0.17 or $0.18 per share for the quarter." So actual earnings of 15 cents are disappointing.

Try to discover how the company treats its employees and the community.

"Look for companies that educate their employees and treat their customers and shareholders well and are good corporate citizens," says Bill Berger. "It isn't about capital anymore. It is about brainpower. It's a people world. Service is the key."

Berger cites the example of check printer Deluxe Corp. "A company that really educates its employees can dominate a market. Deluxe became a leader because its employees didn't make mistakes, so every bank gave them business."

NOW, WHAT ABOUT THOSE PENNY STOCKS?

"Penny-wise is pound-foolish."
—BENJAMIN FRANKLIN

AFTER READING ALL THIS about how crucial careful research is, you're sure to hear about a couple of guys who played a hunch and turned a penny stock into a 10-bagger. (For the non-Lynchites in the audience, that's a stock selling for 10 times what you bought it for.) Two friends of mine recently did just that with a company called Advanced Viral Research Corp.: They paid about a dime per share, and in a few weeks, the stock was selling for more than a buck.

I know what you're saying: A few stocks like that, and you can retire 20 years before you'd planned to. The trouble is that for every 10-bagger, there are scores that will take your money and just bag it. And telling the first type from the second is difficult, because penny-stock companies usually don't list on a major exchange and so don't have to report to the SEC. It's even harder to tell if this week's winner will become next week's impossible-to-unload turkey. Investors in Comparator Systems, a maker of fingerprint-ID software, learned that firsthand: During three days in May 1996, they saw their share price balloon 30-fold, to 1⅞ from ¹⁄₁₆, then watched it deflate just as dramatically, to six cents in September.

One thing I can tell: Advanced Viral Research Corp. wouldn't have passed my battery of tests, starting with the Crayon Criterion. Peter Lynch has often said that if you can't draw a company's product with a crayon, you don't understand its business. That means you don't have an edge and should stay away. AVRC produces and markets an antiviral peptide-nucleic acid complex under the name Reticulose. I'm out of the game right away. I studied biology and chemistry in college, but now I couldn't tell the difference between a peptide and a riptide.

How about fundamentals? A look at the company's income statement shows that it's had minimal sales in 1992, '93, '94, or '95 and that its expenses are mostly administrative. It's been losing an average of more than $500,000 a year, and it isn't clear where additional money will come from. No analysts cover AVRC, so you can't check with them.

The company does have shareholder equity. Must be a lot of insiders buying, right? Wrong. In the past two years, officers of the company have bought exactly zilch, while selling off more than 2 million shares.

So what made this stock move? The company claims its product can counteract a number of viruses that stimulate interferon production, such as those that cause influenza and hepatitis—maybe even AIDS. AIDS is a hot topic right now, and hot topics sell stock. In the 1960s, during the outer-space craze, the joke on Wall Street was that National Cowbell had just changed its name to International Bovi-sonics and the stock was going wild. The same goes for AVRC: We don't understand the business, but, hey, the cure for AIDS, that could be huge.

Another thing that put this company on the map was a report in the June 1995 issue of *Hot Stock Whispers,* by George Chilekis, saying the company was about to announce that an eminent medical doctor from a highly respected U.S. hospital had signed on as a scientific consultant. Chilekis also suggested the possibility of a joint venture with a well-known pharmaceutical firm and predicted that the shares should soar upward (can you soar downward?) on the release of this oft-whispered rumor.

Let's count that up: whispers, rumors, and unconfirmed reports. Why would most people rather buy a stock on evidence like this than on a rock-solid set of financial statements? It's just human nature, I guess.

What can we conclude? First, two people a lot less cynical than I am have made a boatload of money. Second, the public loves to build castles in the air. Third, and most important, betting on penny stocks isn't investing—it's speculating or gambling. You can make a lot of money investing in companies that promise to cure AIDS or match fingerprints, but you can lose a lot, too. Those stocks are manipulated easily and often. Many of the people investing in them are probably unsophisticated. So they're easy marks for shady dealers like the ones rounded up in 1996 by the FBI for bribing brokers to tout penny stocks to their clients.

My advice: Over the long run, you will get killed if you put money in penny stocks. One in a thousand may make you a bundle. But the whole thesis of this book is reaping rewards while reducing risk. If a company has no assets, no earnings, and no product, you're running lots of risk. And you don't need to rush in—you can still make a fortune on a company after it develops its product.

If you can't resist the lure of the "pink sheets," which list penny-stock bid and ask prices, buy *Walker's Manual of Unlisted Stocks (see "Resources")*.

The manual contains four years of financial info on 500 of these companies. But that's only a beginning. Be prepared to dig a lot harder than you would for a listed stock, even a microcap. As Jack Norberg, a pink-sheet specialist and president of Standard Investment in Tursint, California, told *Business Week*, "You have to take a hobby approach to investing in this area. This is not for the passive person."

ANTI-ANXIETY INVESTING

"The key to this whole game is winning by not losing."

—CHARLES ROYCE, *in the 1992* Institutional Investor *interview*

AFTER YOU'VE FINISHED YOUR digging and gathering, your sifting and sorting, you should be left with about 20 solid prospects. Some of these you'll buy; others you'll keep an eye on for the future. The next chapter will describe strategies you can use to decide which investments to make, when. But before choosing your purchases or even a strategy, you should decide on an overall investment philosophy—particularly, how much risk you're willing to take for the possibility of higher returns.

I know, I've been pushing prudence. But even prudence allows for different degrees of risk tolerance. Your job is to figure out where you fit on that scale—whether, say, you'd get worse palpitations watching your stocks' prices bounce up and down or seeing them rise more slowly than the small-cap leaders.

"When I first meet a client, we write out an investment philosophy for their portfolio," says Piper Jaffray's Doug Marx. "I try to find out what my customer's risk tolerance is. Piper has a series of questions we ask, and then I add my own, like what would bother you more, to be in cash with the stock market going up or to be invested with the market going down?"

So do some soul-searching. The results will help you determine what risk controls to build into your portfolio and where to set your sell signals. It will also give you a measure for evaluating your holdings' performance, which you should do every quarter to see if you need to rebalance or otherwise restructure your portfolio.

THE DEAN OF INVESTING FOR high risk-adjusted returns is Quest Advisory's Charles Royce. His Royce Premier fund has the lowest risk in the small-cap field, according to Morningstar. Royce himself was named in a 1995 poll of professional money managers, published in *USA Today,* as one of three colleagues to whom they'd entrust their own money. So he's a good man to turn to for tips on how to build an ulcer-free portfolio.

Royce points out that every portfolio is subject to four types of risk—valuation, financial, portfolio, and market—each of which requires a different management technique. Essentially, the portfolio-building tips given so far have addressed the first three risks: Investing in companies with low p/e and price-to-book ratios reduces *valuation risk,* the tendency of a stock price not adequately supported by business fundamentals to collapse when the market mood turns pessimistic. Strong balance sheets and adequate cash flows provide companies with a margin of safety against *financial risk,* which arises from unforeseen external changes. Diversification prevents concentrations in particular industries or sectors that might boost returns but could just as quickly drag them down: *portfolio risk.*

To manage the last type—*market risk*—you need to look at a measure called *beta.* Market risk refers to the "rising tide lifts all ships" phenomenon: The prices of all securities in a particular class tend to move up and down more or less together. Beta measures the degree to which the price movement of an individual stock conforms to that of the equity market as a whole (usually represented by the S&P 500). A beta of 1 indicates perfect lockstep; 1.5 means that the stock's price will rise or fall half again as much as the index; 0.5, that it will move only half as far. Certain rare securities, such as gold stocks, have negative betas, indicating that they swim against the current, rising as the market falls and vice versa.

Royce keeps his Premier fund's market risk low by investing in nonmainstream companies—those with minimal institutional ownership—whose betas mostly fall between 0 and 0.65. His reasoning: "If you don't want to get hit by a bus, stay out of the middle of Sixth Avenue." By staying out of the high-traffic zones of the market, Royce achieves stability: Premier will not soar with the hottest small-cap funds in a bull market, but it will drop less drastically when the bears take over.

Royce's style is not for everyone. Some Premier investors were unhappy with returns in the booming 1995–96 market that lagged those of more aggressive growth-oriented funds, such as Gary Pilgrim's PBHG Growth. However, if you lack the resources to recover gracefully from the rough landings that such highfliers make from time to time, you should probably aim for Royce's steady rather than for Pilgrim's spectacular results. Learn from 1995. According to the *Chicago Tribune*, the average stock fund returned 31 percent during the first nine months of that year, but only 3 percent in its fourth quarter. Funds with risk-control procedures did considerably better in the last quarter, posting double-digit returns by getting out of tech stocks and into new groups of companies that were rotating into favor.

When pros like Nasgovitz and Oberweis talk to brokers, they make clear what kind of stocks they're interested in and how they approach investing and risk.
That way, any stock suggestions they receive have a better chance of meeting their criteria. Try it. You'll save yourself and your broker a lot of time.

You can check out your stocks' betas in the Key Stock Statistics section of the S&P reports; for companies not in the index, check with a broker.

CARE AND FEEDING
OF A PORTFOLIO

"Reviewing a company when earnings come out and when new balance sheets come out is not a time-consuming process, especially if things are tracking.... Unlike other businesses, though, prices in this business change all the time, so you have to keep yourself in a ready position to take action. You must be organized in some disciplined way to buy and sell your securities on shifts in prices, which can happen very suddenly, or you will miss opportunities. We plan what we'll do with a stock at different price levels—add or subtract to our positions, or sell."
—CHARLES ROYCE, *in the 1992* Institutional Investor *interview*

ONCE YOU'VE SETTLED ON YOUR investment philosophy
and risk tolerance and made your stock purchases
with these factors in mind, you'll have some cleaning
up and organizing to do. In the course of your
research, you will probably have accumulated a huge
pile of paper, which the 20 mailing lists you're now on
are going to make even huger. To be able to access all
the information contained in that pile, you have to
put it in some order. You could flow it into a spreadsheet on your computer or stuff it in a file cabinet you
pick up at a yard sale. At the very least, you should fill
out an index card for each company, listing key telephone numbers and reference sources, as well as what
it does and what your edge is. (A sample of the work-
sheet Nasgovitz fills out for each of his purchases is
shown on the following two pages.)

Make up a card even for the companies you've
decided to pass on for now. Their time may come,
when the economic climate changes or you have
more money to invest. The vetting you've already
done will reduce the amount of research you'll need
to do in the future. Then, as new prospects come to
your attention, create files and fill out cards containing the information you dig up on them and noting
why you like their prospects.

For each stock you do invest in, write down your
reason. Briefly state a goal toward which you can
objectively measure the company's progress. "If you
can't summarize your argument in three sentences,
you don't really understand it," says Acorn portfolio
manager Terry Hogan, who gives as an example "This
company will turn around in two or three years." In
addition, describe the catalyst that you expect to trans-
form the business, either turning it around or accelerating its growth.

Understanding why you bought a stock is crucial,
because this will help you decide later whether to sell
it. And knowing when to sell can be more important

WILLIAM NASGOVITZ'S 10 POINTS

Security: ABC Corporation   **Date:** 1/1/97
Location: Milwaukee, WI   **Analyst:** JK
Ticker: ABCD   **Desc:** Manufactures widgets
                                 Phone: (555) 555-5555

| 1 **Low P/E Ratio:** | Earnings: | '96 | $1.86 | A |
| | P/E: | | 12.9 x | |

| 2 **Low Price/Cash Flow Ratio:** | Cash Flow: | '96 | $3.21 | A |
| | P/CF Ratio: | | 7.5 x | |

| 3 **Book Value:** | | '96 | $11.91 | A |
| | Tangible: | '96 | $11.25 | A |

4 Financial Soundness:

Debt: 25.0%

5 Positive Earnings Dynamics:

Fiscal Year: Dec

	QI
'96	0.26 A
'97	0.55 E
'98	0.60 E

Earnings Notes:

6 Ownership: Insider: 25%

Buyback: Y
Authorized to repurchase

7 Management: Smith has over 20 years' experience in the business. New Vice President has 15 years'

8 Hidden Assets: ABC owns 30% of XYZ Forging Corp. (private company). Carried on books at cost. Fair

9 Catalyst: Recent acquisition will double revenue and

10 Chart: Off recent highs - consolidating gains.

Price:	$24.00	Contact:	Joe Smith
# Shares:	5.0 m	Broker:	HAI
Rating:	BUY	Industry:	Manufacturing

						Yes
'97	$2.55	E	'98	$2.90	E	
	9.4 x			8.3 x		

						Yes
'97	$3.65	E	'98	$4.20	E	
	6.6 x			5.7 x		

						No
'97	$14.45	E	'98	$17.35	E	
'97	$13.50	E	'98	$16.65	E	

Net Net Working	Price-to-sell	Dvd/Sh.:	
Capital: $2.5	Ratio: 50%	$0.20 Dvd Yld:	Yes

Q2	Q3	Q4	Yes
0.45 A	0.52 A	0.63 A	
0.60 E	0.70 E	0.70 E	
0.75 E	0.80 E	0.75 E	

		Yes
Institution: 30%	Insider Activity:	
	Smith (President) bought	
	2,000 shares @ $15 on 6/96.	
Poison Pill: Y	Pct: 20%	
500,000 shares.		

experience and a reputation as a shrewd manager.	Yes

market value significantly higher.	Yes

will be accretive to earnings.	Yes

	Yes

SCORE | 9/10

SOURCE: HEARTLAND ADVISORS, INC.

than knowing when to buy. As Bill Berger says, "You've got to weed the garden."

Strategies for when and why to unload your hard-won shares are discussed in the next section. Right now, you just need to know that there are basically two reasons to sell: success and failure.

It may be the company itself that succeeds or fails with a product. "One of the things we have in our database is the reason we own the stock," says Hogan. "It will say something like, 'I own this stock because these guys have a new drug for multiple sclerosis that's going to make the company grow very rapidly.' Now, one of two things can happen: Either some hamster in the lab gets diarrhea and the drug goes into the ash can—at that point you should sell the stock, because the reason you bought it doesn't exist anymore—or the drug succeeds. The stock goes from $10 to $50, and then its run is over. If a stock looks like it's getting really overpriced relative to our model, we have to take a look at it."

Alternatively, it may be the company's stock whose performance meets or falls short of your goals for it. To be able to judge this when the time comes, you should make two other notes on your index cards: a target price, at which you think the shares will be fully valued, and a stop-loss figure, indicating how far you will allow the price to fall before you bail out. When a stock reaches your target or stop-loss price, search for signs either that it will continue to grow or that its decline is just a temporary setback in an otherwise steady ascent. If you don't find any, you should probably sell.

The point of having all this information in one accessible place is to make it easier to reevaluate your portfolio and see what changes you need to make. You should go through this process roughly every three months, when the quarterly reports start rolling in: Check fundamentals for improvement or deterioration. And see if your reason for buying a company is still valid, becoming a reason to hold it. For instance, if your rationale for purchasing Microsoft Corp. in the 1980s was "It's the leader in building the software that runs personal computers," you're probably still a holder. On the other hand, if you bought Kmart Corp. because "It is and will remain the dominant retailer in the United States," you should have given up on it a while ago.

⬧ **To set a target price, first use the company's expected growth rate to come up with what analysts feel its earnings per share will be three or five years down the road. Then, based on the current average p/e for the sector and how dominant you think the company will be in its market, figure out what its future p/e will be. From this you can calculate the target price.**

Say you're considering Up 'N' Coming, which has a projected earnings growth rate of 30 percent and a current p/e of 10 in an industry whose average is 20. You believe that in five years, Up 'N' will be a major player in its market. So you figure its future p/e as 22. To reach that ratio, given earnings growth of 30 percent, the company's share price will have to increase 66 percent. Do the multiplication and you have your target.

⬧ **When a stock reaches your target, reexamine the company to see if something has happened since you set your price objective that would lead you to adjust it upward.**

Your mailing lists and local contacts may have told you about a new product or management scheme that the general investing public hasn't glommed onto yet. If you believe the share price will soar when this information becomes common knowledge, set another target and sit on your hands for the moment. If you can't find a compelling reason to raise your objective, though, and you see other investments that promise significantly more growth, you should probably make a trade. Marc Robins, of *The Red Chip Review*, calls this "swapping up in quality."

⬥ **Set your stop-loss on a small stock at 15 to 20 percent. But you may want to give a few special stocks more leeway.**

The more lenient stop-loss for superior companies was suggested by a study my colleague, Bloomberg markets editor Bill Hester, and I did on additions to the S&P 500. Our thesis was that these companies would outperform. What we actually found was that they did about the same as the index as a whole, maybe slightly better. As a sidelight, though, the study turned up an interesting pattern: Many of the stocks that later went on to produce big gains first took huge hits, dropping more than 15 percent before rallying. That's a *large* stock swinging widely over the course of one year; you can expect *small* caps to be much more volatile. The bottom line: For most stocks, consider cutting your losses at 15 or 20 percent. With superior businesses you're sure are solid, let your money ride a bit longer. But be disciplined. No stock should be on parole indefinitely.

⬥ **For a value stock, look to see if that catalyst—a new product, a reorganization—you'd hoped would turn the company around is on the horizon or is having the effect you'd hoped for.**

Heartland's Nasgovitz says he generally gives a company two years to prove it isn't "permacheap." He may decide to hang on longer, though, if he finds a reason to keep the faith: a high-powered management or balance sheet or a significant competitive edge in its industry. Nasgovitz cites a company the fund bought recently at less than cash per share. "Things are not going to change that dramatically in the short run," he says. "We think it's a great opportunity, based on its balance sheet, so we'll hold on and hang in there."

DUH BEARS—WHEN
THE MARKET FALLS

"The man that once did sell the lion's skin while the
beast lived, was kill'd with hunting him."
—WILLIAM SHAKESPEARE, Henry V

MANAGING YOUR PORTFOLIO in a down market can be scary, particularly if you've never suffered through one before. Chances are pretty good you haven't: According to Bill Nasgovitz, more than $4 out of every $5 invested in the stock market today has never seen a 10 percent correction, let alone a real bear attack.

Well, fasten your seat belts, it's going to be a bumpy ride. "Stocks, over the long term, might go down one out of three years," Nasgovitz says. "We haven't had that kind of market for a long, long time. We had the crash back in 1987, but it was very quick and over in a period of months. And then it was up, up, and away again. So I think the stock market probably is due for much rougher years ahead. The S&P 500, I think, should have a lot more down years than it's had over the past 15."

The good news: He also thinks that small caps, which have lagged a bit for the past 11 years, may be ready to outpace the pack. But Nasgovitz himself, tongue firmly in cheek, admits to "eternal hope." So make sure you're prepared for the worst.

Review your investment goals, taking into account your stage of life and long- and short-term financial needs. If you're going to need to cash in some securities to meet obligations in the near future, you're better off doing it now than after the market has corrected.

Consider a fund, such as Heartland's Small Cap Contrarian or Robertson Stephens Contrarian, whose objective is to make money in both rising and falling markets.

Think through your game plan thoroughly. Then stick to it.

Investors who panicked during the 1987 crash sold into a declining market. Those who held were buoyed as the market reached unprecedented heights. "Make fewer investments, and know what you own," advises Rodriguez. "That takes out a lot of the uncertainty and fear."

Don't try to time the market.

"If you start investing in equity funds, yet we have a down year, probably the worst thing [to] do is yank that money out, stick it somewhere else, hopefully catch when the market turns around again and get it back in," says Prudential's Mott. "You're better off to try and sit it out, even though you may get your quarterly statement and not be too happy with the numbers that are on there."

SELLING

> *"There's no black box for when to sell, like sell your winners when they are up 50 percent, and sell your losers when they are down 20 percent. It sounds seductive, because your upside is 2.5 times your downside, but it isn't that cut-and-dried."*
> —ROBERT RODRIGUEZ

WHEN DO YOU SELL A STOCK? The answer most people would like to give is never, but that isn't realistic. Most of us aren't good enough at stock picking to find companies that will continuously outperform the market. At some point, almost every purchase you make will have to be sold, either because you screwed up and it's an abject failure or because you were brilliant and it met your objectives and now has nowhere to go. You aren't divorcing your spouse or selling a friend down the river. Just Do It.

One of the biggest mistakes small-cap investors make is falling "in love with a company," *Individual Investor*'s Anderson said on "Adam Smith's Money

World." "They come up with a scenario by which this little company, this tree, grows to the sky. And they lose sight of the fact that not every tree grows to the sky. And they don't sell when all rational indicators say, Get out of this stock."

It is because so many of us tend to let emotions into our investing that stop-loss and target prices are important: They make us deal with hard facts. Say a stock you bought at $10 goes to $13 a share. Emotionally, you'd be tempted to let it ride. Realistically, though, you should ask yourself if the share price has anywhere to go after a 30 percent rise, which is huge. Setting a target price at a reasonable level will force you to ask that question.

Selling the losers is relatively easy. It's also vital to your survival as a stock picker. In his book, *IBD*'s Bill O'Neil quotes the famous investor Bernard Baruch: "Even being right three or four times out of 10 should yield a person a fortune if he has the sense to cut his losses quickly in ventures where he has been wrong."

One signal that you might have been wrong about a company is a drop in its share price below the stop-loss you set for it—for most small stocks, about 15 or 20 percent less than the level at which you bought it. Having said that, the decision to sell at this point is not mechanical. If what you've learned about the company and its business leads you to believe that this drop is a just a detour on an upward road, you might decide to hold.

"If you know why you bought a company and can ask what's wrong and if anything has changed, you can be a lot more rational when the stock price is down," says Rodriguez. "Sometimes when a stock is down 50 percent, you don't want to be selling; you want to be buying more."

Another thing to watch is earnings. They are what drive stock prices. So a negative surprise—when a company's actual earnings come in below analysts' expectations—should have you looking for the door.

"What tends to happen," Oberweis says, "is when a company has one bad quarter, things are actually happening behind the scenes that may not be obvious, but they tend to have a second or a third bad quarter down the line, as well."

It's the old cockroach theory: If you see one, you know plenty more are around. The same goes for bad quarters.

"One of the traps that people get into," says Prudential's Claudia Mott, "is not believing when a company has its first negative earnings surprise. For example, the company misses a quarter, [you tell yourself] it's only a one-time thing—next quarter is going to be fine. Lo and behold, come the next reporting season, you get hit with another negative surprise. ... All too often, especially in small caps, it's the beginning of the end."

Oberweis doesn't believe in second chances. "My father always uses the analogy that he's been married to his wife for 29 years now, and when she makes a mistake, it's all right, he can learn to live with it," he says. "However, it's not true with the companies we invest in. One bad quarter, and we're headed for divorce court. And we're going to make very little exception to that. ... This discipline's a major part to our investment philosophy."

That's the main reason Oberweis doesn't want to get to know the people who run the companies his funds own. After you spend time with management, he says, it changes "from company ABC to Bob's company. Whenever a report comes out and they show a negative quarter, Bob's immediately on the phone telling me, 'Look, Jim, it was a bad quarter. ...A few orders came in late, but they're going to get booked in the coming weeks. Next quarter we'll be fine.'"

Shelby Davis, manager of the New York Venture Fund, is more lenient. "A company is a collection of people," he says. "I don't throw my son out of the house when he has a bad report card, and I don't throw a company [out of a portfolio] because they miss one quarter's earnings."

NatWest's Dan Coker also weighs in on the side of leniency. His point is that with small companies, you need to regard both expected and announced earnings with a certain skepticism. Revenues and profits in this size segment are volatile, reducing the accuracy of predictions. Figures, moreover, are rounded: Actual earnings of 24.49 cents would be reported as $0.24, appearing to fall one full cent short of an estimate of 24.51, which is rounded to $.25.

Both Davis, whose son has taken up the family business, and Oberweis have been successful with their opposite approaches. Most of us, though, would do best to follow a middle course, basing decisions to sell on a combination of factors. One of these is valuation. A single negative surprise could well torpedo a company whose p/e is high, either absolutely or relative to those of similar companies, but it might leave unscathed a company with a very low ratio.

Check the stock's relative strength.

Relative strength, as discussed above, is a measure of how your stock's market performance stacks up against that of other companies in its industry or an appropriate index. This is crucial when you're considering breaching your stop-loss. If your stock has previously risen higher and has now fallen less sharply than its sector or the broader market, it may be a leader worth hanging on to. During the big plunge in tech stocks in 1995, for example, Intel Corp. dropped significantly, but by far less than its peers. The people who held on to the semiconductor maker are now happily counting their cash.

You can calculate relative strength by dividing the percent change in the index into the percent change in the share price. Your stock is outperforming if the result is greater than one in a rising market, or less than one in a falling market. For a more complete description, take a look at Tom Dorsey's book, *Point & Figure Charting (see "Resources")*. Dorsey is a master at explaining technical analysis in clear terms.

DUMP THE WINNERS?

> *"We do take a long view, and we tend to buy cheaply, so usually price is not the problem. Opportunity cost is the problem. You can own something for 10 years and make 20 percent. So you have to be vigilant about what you own, and you have to draw lines in the sand about the limits of your patience. But frankly, the wind blows over the lines all the time."*
>
> —CHARLES ROYCE, *in the 1992* Institutional Investor *interview*

THE STOCKS THAT HAVE MADE you money are tougher to let go. You know them, and when you sell you'll have to pay hefty capital-gains taxes. Paul Nadler, one of the most dedicated finance professors around and a former Rothschild Co. chief economist, teaches students a good rule of thumb: Before selling a decent stock that has given you a good run, find a replacement whose prospects are 50 percent better. That's how much extra return is needed to offset the commissions and taxes you'll have to pay on a trade.

A friend of mine says the small-cap mutual fund he manages will sell a stock that's been a winner in three situations:

◆ The stock meets the price objective set for it, and the fund's analysts can't find a reason to raise their target.

◆ A major brokerage issues a sell recommendation on it. Brokers don't say the 'S' word often. When they do, the company CEO generally calls to raise hell and promise never to do another lick of business with the firm. So if these guys do pull the emergency brake, something's really wrong. A second reason to heed their warnings is that other investors will. When mutual funds start unloading their huge stakes in a company, its share price will go down the tubes.

◆ Fundamentals shift significantly. This change can be anything that affects earnings power or assets, such as a major law suit, a failed product, the death of a dynamic manager, or the emergence of a serious competitor. Oberweis, who follows this rule as well, defines the fatal blow as anything that compromises the special advantage over competitors that first attracted him to the company.

 Oberweis will also look closely at a stock whose relative strength weakens or whose earnings growth slows. The first, because it indicates investor disenchantment, which he takes seriously; the second, because it may mean the company has lost its competitive edge.

 Keep an eye on the p/e.
As a strict value investor, Bill Nasgovitz buys out-of-favor stocks priced at, say, six or eight times earnings and sells them when they reach 20 or more and are becoming Wall Street sweethearts. That may be a little rigid for you, but you should start getting antsy when a stock's p/e approaches parity with the company's expected five-year earnings growth rate. As Oberweis says in his July 1996 *Oberweis Report,* when ratios get high, investors may be "discounting bright prospects so far into the future that the price of the stock no longer makes rational investment sense." (He begins to worry at around 70 times earnings.)

"Some of the research we've done has shown that you can probably go to almost 1.5 times growth before you start to see the stocks begin to underperform," says Claudia Mott. "But that is obviously still a very high valuation point, if you look just on an absolute basis. And unfortunately in times when the market's not just going up, those are the kinds of stocks that usually are going to get hurt more. So you do leave yourself open to a little bit more downside risk, if the market starts to correct."

SOME INVESTMENT PROFESSIONALS practice a defensive discipline of selling off portions of winning holdings. Piper Jaffray's Doug Marx will often sell a third of a position that has appreciated 30 percent, another third when it is up 50 percent, and the final third when the stock has risen 100 percent. "It won't get you any 10-baggers," he says. "But you protect your wealth and make sure you keep your profits."

Robert Rodriguez makes what he calls "keep myself honest" sales, unloading around 10 percent of his position in a stock whose price has risen significantly. But the FPA manager believes in adjusting his discipline to fit the company. As illustrations, he cites retailers Ross Stores and Claire's Stores. Rodriguez bought the two stocks at roughly the same time and watched them appreciate about the same amount. In August 1996, however, he decided to sell Claire's and keep Ross. The reason: He considered Claire's share price reflective of the company's current value; on the other hand, he had invested in Ross as a play on California's recovery, which he believed was still in progress.

Sell if the company's p/e seems out of line with its market and market dominance.

That's why Rodriguez decided to unload Nike, the oldest position in his fund. He bought the stock in 1984 for a split-adjusted price of less than $1 and sold it at $80. At that level, he explains, the sneaker maker had "the valuation of Coke and McDonald's. Although Phil Knight, Nike's chairman, thinks they deserve it, there is a key difference: Coke and McDonald's have been successful in selling to several generations of people, and until Nike proves they can do that, I don't think they deserve the same valuation."

ONCE AGAIN, YOU MIGHT NOT want to play strictly by the numbers. Any emerging-growth company will have periods when its valuation is horrendous—as much as several hundred times earnings. Smart, persuasive people will start saying how overvalued the stock is. Eventually it will fall from the sky, and for a time nobody will want to own it. But the guys who get the 100-baggers are those who hang on through thick and thin. I wish I could teach you how to tell a keeper from a flash in the pan. One piece of advice I can offer is that you're most likely to go the distance and possibly score big if you build your portfolio around a diversified group of relatively conservative picks while devoting a small portion to the flashy ones.

A football analogy: A big-play offense is successful only if you also have running backs who can pound out short yardage and a defense that can hold the other team after an interception.

I asked Bill Berger where you get the courage to hold a stock when it gets pricey or falls out of favor. His answer: "Common sense. Know everything about the company—that will give you the confidence."

AN S&P ALTERNATIVE: *IBD*

"We're looking for a company that is making a product that you and I are buying 50 or 100 percent more [of] every year, and are likely to continue doing so for some time."

—JIM OBERWEIS JR.

FOR A SMALL PORTION OF your portfolio, consider following a strategy similar to the one the folks at Oberweis use. You can either shell out the money for *The Oberweis Report* or try to do what Jim Jr. does, yourself.

First, go through the list of companies in *Investor's Business Daily, The New York Times,* or *The Wall Street Journal* and pick out the ones whose earnings and revenues are increasing at rates greater than 30 percent a year. Then, check this list against the stock tables in the most recent Wednesday *IBD,* and discard any stock whose p/e is higher than half its growth rate.

Next, test the stocks' relative strength—keep only those ranked 70 or better. (Oberweis performs this step later, but doing it here will save you research time.) Just for the heck of it, take a look at the companies' earnings-per-share rank, too; you'll vet their financials before you put any money down, but at this point the EPS ranks provide you with a good basis for comparison. You are probably looking for 70 or better here, as well.

By now your list should be considerably smaller. For those companies in the S&P 600, check the guide to make sure their earnings have been growing and to see what the analysts say about their business prospects; insider activity isn't an Oberweis criterion, but it wouldn't hurt to look at that, too. If a company isn't in the 600, you'll have to check the financials on your own, the quicker the better—a few weeks, and you've probably missed the boat. Ask your broker to fax you some data. But remember that many of these companies are not closely followed.

Now buy the stocks that pass all the tests. To monitor the companies, do what Oberweis does: Find out when they're going to announce their earnings, and ask their investor-relations people what they told Wall Street to expect and what the Street estimates are. If the figures are negative, sell right away: You don't want to see companies like this go from making 50 percent more each quarter to losing money.

Finally, wait for the earnings reports to come out. If a company continues to grow rapidly, you can probably count on another quarter of decent gains. If earnings are weak, you're outta there.

 As a shortcut, you can let your fingers do the walking: **The Friday *IBD* contains a list of all the stocks on the exchanges and Nasdaq that are priced above $7 and within 15 percent of their 12-month highs and whose earnings-per-share and relative-strength rankings are better than 85 percent.**

There's your candidate roster. Just research the businesses and place your bets. For each stock, the paper also shows the highest-performing mutual fund with a large stake in it. You can invest in the funds holding most of your favorites, or just use this information to see where the smart money is going.

COST CUTTERS

ON A BUSINESS'S INCOME STATEMENT, you don't want to see all the revenues being eaten up by expenses. In investing, too, you want to prevent costs from cutting too deeply into your profits. One way to accomplish this, as I hammered home in Chapter 1, is to keep your trading at a minimum by buying to hold.

You'll still have to buy and sell sometimes, though. When you do, try to keep it cheap. Among the expenses you can control are your broker fees. If you feel comfortable forgoing some of the advice and other services offered by full-service brokerages, you can reduce transaction costs by using their discount colleagues *(see "Picking a Small-Cap Broker" on the following page).*

Another cost-cutter is to place limit, rather than market, orders. A market order gives your broker permission to buy or sell shares at the best ask or bid available when the trade is executed. Since execution is rarely immediate, the price you actually get may be considerably different from the one in effect when you placed your trade. Moreover, since market makers' quotes are good only for specified numbers of shares—by law, at least 100, though dealers will often go higher—a large order or one involving an illiquid stock could be filled at two different prices.

A limit order, on the other hand, can only be filled at the price you specify or better. So when you place

PICKING A SMALL-CAP BROKER

YOU'LL DO MOST OF YOUR STOCK TRADES, and possibly your mutual-fund transactions, as well, through brokers. These come in three varieties, distinguished by the types of services they offer and the size of the commissions they charge to execute trades.

Full-service brokers, such as Merrill Lynch & Co. and Smith Barney, offer the largest palette of services: advice on money management, for instance, and recommendations on financial instruments based on their own staff research and analysis, as well as a certain amount of hand-holding. They also have the highest commissions: anywhere from $80 to $150 for a 100-share trade, though some firms offer special deals in which a client pays a relatively low flat fee to do a certain number of trades a year. If you're an experienced investor, you may not want to pay the full brokerage fees for your normal transactions. On the other hand, regional brokers, like Raymond James in St. Petersburg, Florida, can provide you with research on small local stocks that you might miss on your own *(see "Resources" for more names).* And full-service brokers that specialize in microcaps may be the best sources for the detailed information you must have to invest in this lucrative, but very volatile, segment. They not only can give you research on their favorite microcap stocks but are also the best sources for microcap initial and secondary public offerings. *(See Chapter 4 for more on IPOs.)*

Discount brokers, such as Charles Schwab, Fidelity Investments, and Jack White, are considerably cheaper. These charge from $30 to $40 for a 100-share trade, often less if it's done by computer. They won't give you advice, but they do provide other services, such as asset accounting and research reports from outside sources like S&P. If you feel comfortable finding your own candidates, and digging to get the real dirt on them, you might use a discount broker, possibly in addition to a full-service one for the more eso-teric IPO and secondary-offering markets. Each spring *SmartMoney* magazine publishes surveys of discount bro-kers, rating them on various criteria, such as service, costs, and customer satisfaction. Check out the most recent sur-vey before opening an account.

Deep-discount brokers, such as National Discount and Brown & Co., often have minimum commissions of $35 or less for big trades that involve money in one of their money market funds. Many also offer flat rates, say $15 or $20 for an unlimited number of shares of a Nasdaq stock. (Remem-ber, though—you still pay the spread.) This is a real advan-tage when you're investing in very low-priced microcap companies: Even a deeply discounted per-share commission on a trade involving a few thousand dollars worth of a $0.25 stock could come to hundreds of dollars.

If you're new to investing it might be a good idea to start with a full service or discount broker until you get more familiar with the market. Once you know what you're doing you can try out a deep discount broker.

A few tips:

◆ **Look small.** Doug Marx, a broker for regional invest-ment firm Piper Jaffray in Sioux City, Iowa, suggests that a broker from a smaller, local firm has a better handle on small companies because it will take the time to get to know their operations and to build relationships with management: "This is a relationship business, and you tend to do business with people most like you. As a small midwestern firm, we focus on small companies with a very good work ethic."

◆ **"Ask where [brokers] get their ideas and what their sell discipline is,"** says Marx.

◆ **Be prepared.** Lisa Gray, a Memphis stockbroker, sug-gests "you find a broker who has a plan for all market conditions."

one, you know what you'll get. Except that you may get nothing if you are trying for a better price than the market makers are currently offering. To get immediate execution, put your sell or buy order in at the current bid or ask price; even then, if the market moves against you, the order won't fill and you'll have to decide whether to lower your sights or wait for another move—this time, you hope, in your favor.

A limit order can be either *day* (in effect until the end of that day's trading) or *GTC* (Good Till you Cancel it). By tacking on an *AON* (All Or None), you can require that your entire order fill at one time or not at all. This avoids the multiple commissions you'd pay if a dealer filled your order in several installments over several days. The problem with this tactic is that the market makers might not take an AON order if it is "too large." AON orders they do take are put at the end of the queue and will therefore be filled last. So to be sure of execution, place one early in the day.

NOW YOU'VE GOT DOWN THE BASICS of small-cap investing and have learned two ways to build and maintain a portfolio of individual stocks. In the following chapter, you'll find more strategies for searching out and selecting investments and for deciding when to commit your hard-earned cash. But the first lesson is the most important: Do your research and find the best stocks available; then be ready to split when better ones come along.

CHAPTER

4

Trading
Strategies

ORE INVESTMENT ideas than money—institutions generally don't have this problem; many individuals do. The previous chapter set you on your way to a solution by showing you how to screen for the stocks with the highest ratio of reward to risk. But chances are you'll still be left with more candidates than you have money to buy or time to follow. So you need to make some hard decisions: Do you spring for the growing company that's capturing the market for satellite-dish beanies? Or do you opt for the fallen angel whose ex-CEO, now in the witness-protection program, has been replaced with Warren Buffett's godson?

This chapter contains suggestions and strategies for making those decisions. Sometimes it's a matter of understanding which broad economic trends may favor one group of companies over another. In other cases, more-localized signals will help you narrow your stock searches or provide a finer mesh for sifting companies to buy from those to watch. None of the strategies is fail-safe. But knowing how to apply them could improve your investing odds. John Spears, a partner at investment advisors Tweedy, Browne Co., contends that even small tilts in your favor make huge differences in the returns of a portfolio held for 20 or 30 years. This book is about giving yourself the edge that will tip the scales.

THE BIG PICTURE

"My point of view has tended to be that when small does well versus large, that has mostly to do with what's going on with the U.S. economy. If you go back and look over the course of postwar history, small caps tend to do best when we're coming out of a recession. It tends to be their periods of best return when we are coming out of a very weak economic cycle. I think the problem,

*though, is that not every recession has led to one
of these fabled multiyear small-cap cycles."*
— CLAUDIA MOTT, *director of small-cap research at
Prudential Securities*

NATIONAL AND GLOBAL economic trends and events
affect which groups and subgroups of investments do
better than others. By diversifying your portfolio
among the various groups, you achieve stable returns
without constantly having to adjust your holdings to
the current environment. Still, you shouldn't ignore
the larger economic effects discussed in this and the
following five sections: the business cycle, both domestic and international; fluctuations in interest rates and
in spreads between different credit ratings; foreign
exchange movements; and small-cap under- and overperformance. Keeping track of these trends and
understanding how they boost or batter which classes
of securities will help you make successful investment
decisions.

 Vote Democrat.

I don't mean to be partisan, but small-cap stocks do better
under Democratic than Republican presidents, according to
a Liberty Financial Cos. study reported on in the August 27,
1996, *Investor's Business Daily*. From the beginning of the
Hoover administration to the present, the report says, small
stocks have risen an average of 22.8 percent annually under
Democrats, compared with 1.9 percent under Republicans.

ONE OF THE BIGGEST NATIONAL economic trends is the
business cycle, discussed in Chapter 2, pages 66–67. It
plays a major role in equity performance: At different
points in the cycle, small or large stocks, growth or
value, will outperform.

The effect is illustrated in the chart at right, which
graphs the relative returns of small growth and value
funds against the business cycle, represented by one-

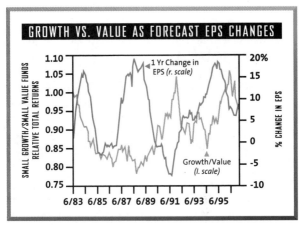

GROWTH VS. VALUE AS FORECAST EPS CHANGES

SMALL GROWTH/SMALL VALUE FUNDS RELATIVE TOTAL RETURNS (l. scale)

% CHANGE IN EPS (r. scale)

1 Yr Change in EPS (r. scale)

Growth/Value (l. scale)

6/83 6/85 6/87 6/89 6/91 6/93 6/95

year changes in expected earnings per share. When a cycle is just beginning, value stocks tend to do best, according to studies performed by Merrill Lynch senior quantitative analyst Satya Pradhuman. During this phase, earnings (and expectations about them) rise in general, but those of turnaround stocks tend to snap back spectacularly, producing double-digit growth that attracts investors' attention.

Small caps as a group often outperform at the top of the cycle. Large stocks have been played out, and investors must turn to smaller and smaller ones, which haven't been bid up as high, to prolong their roll. The strong bull market of 1995 was a classic case. Big companies had notched up their best showing since 1987, and investors began to look beyond the Microsofts, Intels, and IBMs, which had seen huge gains in the first half of the year, to tinier, less well-known—and cheaper—tech stocks.

People "are always chasing returns," James Floyd, of the Leuthold Group, told *Investor's Business Daily* in August 1995. "And things have turned away from the bigger companies to the smaller ones."

After the cycle's peak, as a slowing economy puts a brake on corporate profits, value stocks fall behind.

SOURCE: MERRILL LYNCH QUANTITATIVE ANALYSIS, I/B/E/S, MORNINGSTAR

At this point, says Pradhuman, emerging-growth companies, which still have some earnings momentum, attract investors. During the "soft-landing" period of July 1994 to March 1996, for example, Merrill Lynch's index of small-cap value mutual funds returned just 24.2 percent, compared with 50 percent for small-cap growth funds and 51 percent for the large-cap Standard & Poor's 500 index.

But when recession looms, investors flee small caps altogether for the relative safety and liquidity of large stocks. The best performers in this climate are consumer companies like Philip Morris Cos. and Johnson & Johnson, whose profits are very stable.

"[Small companies] can thrive in a soft-landing environment," John H. Laporte, who manages the $2.1 billion New Horizons Fund, says in a June 1995 *Washington Post* article. "They also can do fine in an environment where corporate earnings flatten out. If, on the other hand, we see a major recession, . . . they will not do well."

In a true bear market, small-cap stocks really suffer. Russell Creighton, senior vice president of Barnett Trust Co., points out in a 1994 *Pensions & Investments* article that when investors can't stand watching their principal erode any further, they start selling their holdings. And this drives down small stocks, which have fewer shares and fewer potential buyers, faster and farther than large ones.

"The liquidity problem is one of the key risks to small stocks," Pradhuman says. "All you need is the same amount of sellers for small as for large stocks, and small stocks go down more because of wider [bid-ask] spreads."

Creighton cautions that a recession now could hit small caps even harder than in the past, because of the growing institutional interest. "Billions of dollars have been put into the markets in the last several years, primarily through mutual funds," he says. "A lot were small cap in the last three years. Mutual fund managers will be forced to sell. We have never had a period with this many small-cap funds trying to liquidate."

On the plus side, the same factors—illiquidity and institutional participation—can drive small stocks to new highs in a generally rising market. Stephen Lieber, chairman of Lieber/Evergreen Asset Management, notes in the *Pensions & Investments* article that "in a strong market, limited liquidity is an aid. There's less stock around, so if you want it, you have to chase it."

 Don't try to time the market.

After reading about the correlations between the business cycle and stock performance, you might be tempted to try to rebuild your portfolio every time you think you see a new phase starting. Don't do it. First, even the pros can get the signals wrong. Second, the signals point to trends, which are a property of groups and which the individual stocks you hold (or plan to buy) may or may not follow. Third, as Claudia Mott's quote at the beginning of the section points out, even the groups don't always follow the script. And fourth, when they do, the market generally anticipates, rather than follows, economic developments.

"In equity, you're worried about what will happen, not what has happened," Mark Riepe, vice president of consulting firm Ibbotson Associates, told *Pensions & Investments*. "Stocks more often than not are predictors of business cycles." So by the time you see an economic trend forming, it's too late to act on it.

Your best course is to buy the best companies available, then review them when they hit your stop-loss or target price *(see Chapter 3)*. However, if you're on the fence about a purchase or a sale, the current stage of the business cycle could be a factor that tips you one way or the other.

"We pick stocks because, individually, they are attractive," Charles Royce, president of Quest Advisory, says in a 1992 interview with *Institutional Investor* magazine. "And we can't rely on macro factors to be part of the decision process. Often, too, you get high performance in periods of overvaluation."

My advice: Handle the business cycle with care. That goes for the other big-picture trends described below, as well. Your best course is to diversify. If she were constructing a portfolio, Claudia Mott says, she would "try to run both disciplines—valuation on the one side, earnings momentum on the other—and structure a portfolio that would look very much like the S&P 600 small-cap index."

A GLOBAL PERSPECTIVE

"More great companies, less coverage."
— Founders Passport Fund manager MICHAEL GERD-
ING's Miller Lite theory of international small-cap investing

THE UNITED STATES, OF COURSE, is not the only country with a business cycle. Nor is the U.S. cycle the only one that an investor should consider. Even in our increasingly global economy, nations are rarely in sync—one region's growth will be peaking when another's is just beginning or falling off the edge. The United States, for example, lagged European Community countries in the early '90s only to jump ahead in the middle of the decade.

That doesn't mean you should move your money around the world, chasing the latest hot economy. Rather, you should exploit varying regional cycles as you exploit complementary sector performance: by diversifying.

Small companies are the best medium for global diversification. Most large companies draw at least some of their income from operations abroad. Because of their foreign affairs, they can't be pure domestic plays. On the other hand, their earnings and stock prices are still tied mainly to their home economies, so they don't provide true foreign diversification, either. To get the purest exposure to each country's cycle, you have to go down the scale, to small companies that do all their business within their own borders.

Another reason to invest in small foreign companies is that they're where the greatest opportunities are. Two-thirds of the world's market capitalization now lies outside the United States, points out Michael Gerding, of the Founders Passport Fund. And, adds Ralph Wanger, the small-cap part of this is generally less efficient. "In many of the emerging markets abroad, it's like the 1960s were here," Leah Zell, the Acorn International fund manager, told *Kiplinger's* magazine in August 1995. "There are fewer analysts, and it's easier to find a good company that's not widely followed."

Put the emphasis on "good." "These aren't bamboo companies in Vietnam," says Gerding. "These are world-class companies, with some of the smartest managers in the world."

The easiest and safest way to internationalize your small-cap holdings is through mutual funds.

Foreign markets present challenges that even pros find daunting. Gathering information on the companies is difficult, as is interpreting what you manage to dig up. Paradoxically, investors often have fewer problems in emerging markets, many of which have adopted U.S. accounting standards; some companies in these countries even have Big Six accounting firms for their outside auditors. In contrast, Germany's and Switzerland's accounting rules—particularly those concerning cash reserves and earnings—are very different from their U.S. counterparts. This makes comparing Swiss and German companies' financial statements directly with those of U.S. companies very difficult, if not impossible.

Beyond these obstacles, most governments impose limits and taxes on foreign investors and their profits. You're better off letting a mutual fund manager worry about these headaches, as well as about whether and how to hedge against foreign-exchange risk. Recently, small-cap international funds have been particularly attractive, outperforming those with more general international holdings during the first half of 1996, according to the November 1996 issue of *Bloomberg Personal* magazine. For specific tips on investing in international small-cap funds, see Chapter 2, pages 68–69.

INTEREST RATES

"Not surprisingly, when 90-day Treasury-bill rates are overlaid with growth and value cycles, the cycles tend to follow with a reasonable degree of closeness, after a time lag, the longer-term direction of interest rates."

—KENNETH FISHER *and* JOSEPH TOMS, *president and senior vice president, respectively, of Fisher Investments, in* Small Cap Stocks

THE ECONOMIC CYCLE IS closely allied to the level of interest rates. Money, after all, is the lifeblood of business, and many companies rely on borrowing for their transfusions. When interest rates are low, as they generally are during and just after a slump, companies can fund their projects more cheaply. As a result, their earnings tend to pick up. When rates start to rise again, in response to an expanding economy and fears of inflation, margins erode.

Since earnings drive share price, the equity market mirrors interest-rate levels, rising as they fall, falling as they rise. Research by NatWest Securities analyst Daniel P. Coker confirms this pattern. One focus of his study was stock-market performance during the month following an initial Federal Reserve Board interest-rate change (one reversing the direction of the preceding moves). Coker found that since January 1948, initial rises in the *discount rate* (the rate the Fed charges member banks) were followed by market declines averaging 2.1 percent; initial Fed easings produced average one-month rises of 2.8 percent.

The effect is exaggerated among small-cap stocks. These "are very [influenced] by interest rates in terms of valuations," says Bill Keithler, of the Berger Small Company Growth Fund, in the 1995 *IBD* article. "When rates are going up, it's very tough sledding." According to the NatWest study, the average one-month declines for large, small, and microcap stocks in response to a Fed tightening were 1.9, 2.5, and 2.6 percent, respectively; the same groups rose 2.2, 4.9, and 6.1 percent after an easing.

The reason for the difference in interest-rate sensitivity is suggested in a 1995 paper by Merrill's Satya Pradhuman. Although large companies usually borrow in the bond market, he explains, many small companies, because of their lower credit ratings, must borrow from banks at prime. The prime rate is higher than interest rates for investment-grade debt; it also rises faster and falls more slowly. So small-cap earnings tend to respond more dramatically than large-cap earnings to changes in the Treasury rate (the benchmark for corporate bonds).

Kenneth Fisher and Joseph Toms, in the book *Small Cap Stocks,* report similar correlations for value versus growth stocks: "We found that when interest rates drop significantly, with a time lag, a value cycle ensues. Likewise, when rates rise significantly, again with a time lag, the result is a growth cycle."

Why? Because value companies generally carry much more debt, both short- and long-term, than growth companies, which can raise capital more cheaply by issuing stock. Fisher and Toms point out that high p/e ratios, a growth characteristic, translate into cheap capital: Selling stock at 30 times earnings is equivalent to borrowing at a yield of ⅟₃₀, or a 3.3 percent interest rate, which is well below the usual prime rate. In contrast, a p/e of 10, more characteristic of value stocks, translates into a capital cost of 10 percent, and that's seldom better than prime.

So rising interest rates will hit the profits and prices of value companies harder than those of more modestly leveraged growth firms. Conversely, value stocks should shoot up higher under the impetus of falling rates.

Merrill Lynch strategist Steve Kim has found that the slope of the current Treasury yield curve can also be used to forecast whether growth or value will be the better performer. The curve is a graph plotting Treasury yields against various maturities, from three months to 30 years *(see the chart below)*. Its normal shape is gently "positive," with yields rising gradually as maturities increase. This configuration reflects the fact that investors ordinarily require somewhat higher rewards for taking the greater risk of tying up their money for a longer period.

The yield curve may steepen if a Fed lowering of short-term rates, to stimulate economic growth, raises fears of inflation that keep long-term rates from falling proportionately. This signals a good environment for value stocks, which tend to outperform in a hot economy. Conversely, a flatter curve results from

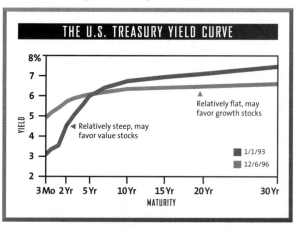

THE U.S. TREASURY YIELD CURVE

Relatively flat, may favor growth stocks

Relatively steep, may favor value stocks

■ 1/1/93
■ 12/6/96

YIELD

MATURITY: 3 Mo 2 Yr 5 Yr 10 Yr 15 Yr 20 Yr 30 Yr

SOURCE: BLOOMBERG L.P.

a tighter monetary policy, designed to cool the economy, and fewer long-term inflation fears. This configuration is better for growth stocks, which can post decent earnings even when growth is slow.

Don't fight the Fed. Rising interest rates mean tough going for stocks, especially small ones. You increase your odds of success tremendously if you take fewer risks and remain hard-nosed about your stock selection criteria when the Fed is tightening.

CREDIT SPREADS

"I'm a bottom-up stock picker. I can't forecast the market or the economy; my shareholders have empirical evidence of this."
—JAMES BARROW, *manager of the Vanguard Windsor II mutual fund*

THE ABSOLUTE LEVEL OF corporate bond rates is one indicator of what to expect in the small-cap sector. The gap between rates for companies having different credit ratings is another. Both Ibbotson Associates founder Roger Ibbotson and Merrill's Satya Pradhuman have shown that when the spread between the interest rates for lower and higher credit ratings tightens, small caps tend to outperform *(see the chart on the following page)*.

One explanation for this relationship is that spreads narrow when the economy is strong, making lenders optimistic about the prospects of risky ventures and willing to give them money at attractive rates. So small companies, which generally fall into the high-risk group, find it easier at these times to get the money they need to feed their rapid growth.

This was certainly true in March and April 1996. From May 1994 to March 1996, investors had required an average of 40 basis points to switch from the security of AAA-rated (bombproof) bonds to

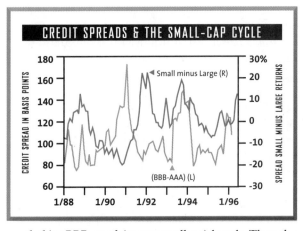

Again, don't use this information to try to time the market. However, if you are deciding between a large stock and an equally attractive small one, a tightening of spreads or a change in the shape of the curve could tip the balance one way or the other. For instance, if you see in *IBD* that the yield difference between AAA- and BBB-rated bonds has narrowed, you might opt for the small company over the large.

shakier BBB-rated (water-repellent) bonds. Then the economic rally began. This panicked traders, who started smelling inflation, and encouraged low-grade-bond investors, who believed it would help riskier businesses. As a result, 10-year bonds backed by the U.S. Treasury lost 9 percent of their value while debt of lesser credits rose a few percent. Meanwhile, funds like Oberweis Micro-Cap and Van Wagoner Emerging Growth jumped almost 50 percent.

♦ *Investor's Business Daily* **carries information about the Treasury curve and credit spreads. This is often provided by Bloomberg News (BN), so the Bloomberg Internet page (www.bloomberg.com) is another good place to look, as are the bond columns in** *The New York Times* **and** *The Wall Street Journal.*

SOURCE: MERRILL LYNCH QUANTITATIVE ANALYSIS

THE DOLLAR

"But then one is always excited by descriptions of money changing hands. It's much more fundamental than sex."

— N I G E L   D E N N I S , *English novelist and playwright*

HERE'S ANOTHER CONNECTION: The *dollar exchange rate* (how many dollars a unit of another currency will buy) is linked to companies' foreign earnings, which, in turn, are linked to their share prices. When the dollar weakens against foreign currencies, U.S. businesses with overseas sales benefit. Not only are their products now more competitive with foreign-made ones, but their yen or franc earnings translate into many more dollars. Eyeing these profits, investors pour money into the stocks of companies with foreign exposures, most of which are large. A strengthening dollar produces the opposite effect. The overseas profits of large companies are eroded, while home-bound small-cap earnings, unaffected by currency fluctuations, draw investor interest *(see the chart on the following page)*.

The first scenario was played out in 1995. From spring to year end, a weak dollar energized the earnings and share prices of large U.S. multinationals such as Coca-Cola Co., Gillette Co., and McDonald's Corp., which draw as much as 40 percent of their revenues from abroad. Meanwhile, small stocks were hit with a double whammy: higher interest rates, which made financing expensive, and a dearth of the overseas business that equity investors were seeking. By mid-1996, though, the second scenario was materializing. Rates had eased, the dollar was strengthening, and profits from multinational operations abroad were becoming slimmer. Analysts saw an opportunity for small, domestic companies to shine.

SMALL-CAP CYCLE & THE DOLLAR

Small stocks tend to outperform large stocks when the dollar appreciates against other currencies.

💎 **Finding exchange rates and other currency data is easy—just look in the newspaper. Using this information is more problematic.**

All it tells you is which sectors are likely to do better than others. But doing better is not the same as doing well. If you drop only 10 percent while the market drops 20, you've outperformed, but your family still starves. The dollar's relative strength should serve mainly as a warning signal. When it's very weak, as at the end of 1994 and the beginning of 1995, you'd better have rock-solid convictions about any small stock you choose over comparable large ones. A strengthening dollar, on the other hand, lowers the bar.

THE SMALL-CAP CYCLE

"People think small caps tend to outperform for seven years and then underperform for some period of time, [but] the relationship really isn't that perfect. ... I think it is very hard to time."
—CLAUDIA MOTT *of Prudential Securities*

SMALL-CAP "OVERPERFORMANCE" CYCLES				
PERIOD	DURATION (IN YEARS)	CUMULATIVE SMALL-CAP RETURN	ANNUALIZED SMALL-CAP RETURN	EXCESS RETURN VS. S&P 500
1932–37	4.8	946.0	62.5	16.0
1940–45	6.0	534.1	36.0	13.0
1963–68	6.0	267.7	24.2	10.8
1975–83	8.5	1072.6	33.6	14.5
1991–94	3.3	142.8	30.8	11.3
Average	5.7	592.6	37.4	13.3

IN ADDITION TO ALTERNATING periods of earnings growth and stagnation, falling and rising rates, wide and tight spreads, and dollar weakness and strength, many analysts detect cycles of small-cap under- and overperformance *(see the chart above)*. These cycles last from three to more than seven years, depending on who's counting.

The June 1995 *Washington Post* article cited earlier delineates two recent cycles based on the performance of the T. Rowe Price New Horizons Fund. New Horizons was founded in 1960 as the first small-cap fund and has been used ever since as a barometer for the sector. The *Post* article points out that from June 1983 to October 1990, the fund lost 1 percent while the S&P 500 was gaining 138 percent. That seven-year period was one of the all-time worst for small-cap stocks. The tide turned in October 1990. From that point until March 31, 1995—despite losses during parts of 1992, 1993, and 1994—New Horizons climbed 167 percent, compared with only 88 percent for the S&P 500.

Why do small stocks clobber or get clobbered by large stocks for years at a time? Probably for the same reason that last year's audience favorites will be next year's box-office poison: overexposure. When one group of stocks is in favor, their valuations become extreme. Investors looking for bargains suddenly rediscover last cycle's darlings, which have been snubbed and are now attractively cheap. Money flows into that sector, and the cycle starts all over again.

You can see this process at work by looking at two indicators: first, the relationship between the average p/e of the New Horizons Fund and that of the S&P 500; and, second, small-cap market share. The theory behind the first indicator is this: Because New Horizons invests in fast-growing small companies, you expect its average p/e to be higher than that of the index, which contains slow growers such as Bethlehem Steel *(see the chart below)*. When the two averages are about equal, therefore, small-cap stocks should be cheap. They may have fallen far out of favor, or the market may not yet have caught on to a recent spurt in income growth. Either way, small stocks are a good buy. This can't last, though—investors will soon rediscover the sector and bid up prices. When New Horizons' average p/e reaches twice the S&P's, small stocks are considered overheated.

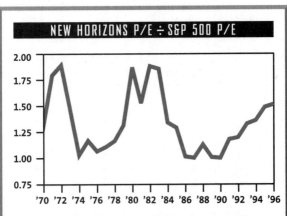

NEW HORIZONS P/E ÷ S&P 500 P/E

NOTE: THE AVERAGE (UNWEIGHTED) P/E RATIO OF COMPANIES IN NEW HORIZONS' PORTFOLIO DIVIDED BY THE P/E RATIO OF THE S & P 500 INDEX, 12 MONTHS FORWARD, AS OF 12/31/96. EARNINGS PER SHARE ARE ESTIMATED BY THE FUND'S INVESTMENT ADVISOR FROM EACH QUARTER END.

The second indicator, small-cap market share, is defined by Fisher and Toms as "the percent of the aggregate value of the total stock market represented by small caps." This number, the authors say, indicates "faddishness."

"When a style has a large share of the market compared to history," they write, "[it] has become more popular. When a style has a low share of the market compared to history, it ... has been losing popularity. Generally, styles that are too popular have already been bid up in price—all the buying has been done." They note that small caps went from a market share of only 14 percent in 1974 to a peak of 22 percent in 1983. In hindsight, they say, 1974 was "the best opportunity to own small-cap stocks since the end of the Great Depression."

♦ **When the S&P 500 index's average p/e and inflation are both running high, the whole market may be due for a downturn.**

According to Gail Dudack, chief market strategist at UBS Securities, when the Consumer Price Index added to the average p/e of the S&P 500 exceeds 20, trouble is brewing.

The chart below shows that the average p/e of the stock

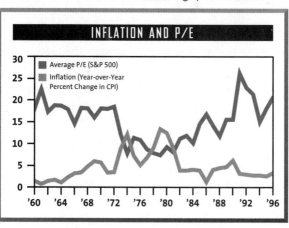

INFLATION AND P/E

- Average P/E (S&P 500)
- Inflation (Year-over-Year Percent Change in CPI)

SOURCE: BLOOMBERG L.P. AND T. ROWE PRICE ASSOCIATES, INC.

market moves opposite to the direction of the inflation rate. This means that one of the most dangerous times for stocks is when p/e's are high and inflation starts to rise. That was the situation in the early 1970s. During the post-World War II, pre-Vietnam war nirvana of the early 1960s, low inflation had supported high stock prices. Then inflation heated up, making life in the '70s and early '80s miserable for investors.

Watch out when the cash levels of small-cap mutual funds are low—a down cycle in small stocks is about to begin.

As Prudential's Claudia Mott points out, minimal cash reserves mean the funds are fully invested. So they won't be pouring a lot of new money into small-cap stocks, and growth will probably stall *(see the chart below)*.

AGGRESSIVE GROWTH MUTUAL FUNDS

Below-average cash levels tend to mean below-average returns.

CASH LEVEL	SUBSEQUENT RETURN (%)		
	3 MONTHS	6 MONTHS	12 MONTHS
<9.7%	2.6	4.6	8.0
Average of 9.7%	2.9	5.8	11.2
>9.7%	3.3	7.0	14.6

NOTE: DATA COVER THE PERIOD JANUARY 1971 THROUGH SEPTEMBER 1995.
RETURNS ARE FOR THE NASDAQ COMPOSITE AND DO NOT INCLUDE DIVIDENDS.

Once again, though, don't restructure your portfolio according to where we are in a small-cap cycle. Sure, you'd like to jump in at a bottom and out again at a top. But it isn't that easy.

THE JANUARY EFFECT

"Or is it the January defect?"
—S A T Y A   P R A D H U M A N, *senior quantitative analyst at Merrill Lynch*

THAT DOES IT FOR BIG PICTURE trends. Here's a more modest cycle—one you can pretty much count on year by year. For the past couple of decades, stocks have generated the lion's share of their annual returns in one month: January. The best explanation for this "January effect" is taxes. Simply put, at the end of the calendar year, investors sell shares that have fallen in price so they can book losses and reduce their tax bills. Then, after the 30-day waiting period required by law, they buy back the losers they still have faith in. The result is a market decline at year end and a rebound the following January.

This pattern, which has been confirmed by various researchers, is particularly marked among small caps. In fact, a large percentage of the returns that have made the smallest stocks the best long-term performers have come in January. According to NatWest Securities' Coker, since 1926 microcaps have returned 8.7 percent on average during January, compared with 1.4 percent for all months. Merrill Lynch's Pradhuman adds that small value stocks have been the biggest gainers. Connected to this is the fact, also cited by Pradhuman, that the effect has been most pronounced in Januarys following years of poor small-cap performance.

How can you exploit the January effect in your investment strategy?

An easy way would be to buy a no-load small-cap mutual fund in December, after it distributes its capital gains *(see Chapter 2, page 66)*, and then sell it again at the end of January. Or you could use fundamental analysis to define a subset of small caps that appear oversold and perform the same trades on them.

If you choose to follow either of these schemes, commit only a small portion of your investment funds, just enough to boost your annual returns. Your general plan should still be to buy excellent companies and hold them for a long time. In this context, the January effect might help you time your trades. For instance, if a small value stock is on your radar near the end of the year, you might wait until prices drop in December to pounce. Conversely, December is probably not a good time to sell shares, unless you want to take a tax loss.

If you like the tax strategy behind the January effect, implement it early.

That's the advice given by Bloomberg applications specialist Sanjiv Gupta in a November 15, 1995, Bloomberg News article. "Smart year-end tax sellers will do it [in November]," he says. "They will get a better price for their shares than they can a month [later]. And—if they are reluctant to part with their losers—they can buy them back at bargain prices in December, when others are dumping them. The wash rule says that when you take a tax loss, you cannot buy the stock [or fund] back for 30 days. Selling early means that you will be in a position to buy them back at the end of December."

TO MARKET, TO MARKET ... IPOs

"When you're working your way toward all-time high levels of IPO activity, it usually means the market's getting a little overvalued. People are obviously trying to take advantage of a very favorable window to get their financing done."
— CLAUDIA MOTT *of Prudential Securities*

ANOTHER PLACE TO LOOK for smaller-scale signals and trends is the IPO market. An *initial public offering*, or *IPO*, is the first sale of a corporation's stock to the wider community. It's done to raise money and also, sometimes principally, to let existing investors reap big profits on their shares, which will be valued for the first time according to the company's perceived growth prospects. Since IPOs almost always have limited market capitalizations—80 percent are under

$60 million, according to Mott—they serve as a litmus test for the small-cap market in general. The volume and quality of deals brought to market in a certain period can signal how hot the small sector is, and how long it's likely to stay that way.

Companies typically do IPOs when they think the market is riding high enough to bring them a good price for their shares. If many issuers start rushing to market, they may be exploiting a window of opportunity before it closes. In other words, small caps may be due for a correction.

In fact, corrections usually do follow an IPO surge, according to a study performed by Mott. Mott looked at the Nasdaq Composite stock index's performance after months during which a large number of offerings were done. She found that during the past 16 years, IPO activity and small-cap prices have peaked at the same time. In addition, as the chart below shows, returns on the Nasdaq have been flat or negative three, six, and even 12 months after months in which more than 50 IPOs came to market.

Just as important as the volume of IPOs are their

AN ACTIVE IPO MARKET IS BAD FOR SMALL CAPS

NUMBER OF IPOs	SUBSEQUENT RETURN (%)		
	3 MONTHS	6 MONTHS	12 MONTHS
<10	11.1	20.4	38.5
11-20	3.4	7.4	11.4
21-30	3.5	5.8	14.3
31-40	2.9	8.0	9.3
41-50	3.7	9.5	16.4
51-60	-0.8	-3.4	-1.2
61-70	-0.4	-1.8	0.0
>71	-1.6	-2.9	-2.7

NOTE: DATA COVER THE PERIOD JANUARY 1979 THROUGH OCTOBER 1995.
RETURNS ARE FOR THE NASDAQ COMPOSITE AND DO NOT INCLUDE DIVIDENDS

SOURCE: SECURITIES DATA CORP., PRUDENTIAL SECURITIES INC.

price levels—specifically, where the actual prices lie within the "price talk," or presale range set by the offerings' underwriters. A large percentage of deals coming in at the high end of the talk, says Heartland's Bill Nasgovitz, "would indicate [a] tremendous amount of speculation and 'froth' in the market-place." And froth signals the end of a rally.

The financial solidity of the companies doing the deals is another factor to watch. "When the portfolio managers I speak to start complaining about the quality of deals," says Mott, "I know we're getting into trouble."

Your broker can help you find out what's been going on in the IPO market.

Ask him or her to check the Equity New Issue Calendar on the shop's Bloomberg terminal. This will show the number and total dollar value of deals done every month this year and last. The brokerage should also be able to determine their position within the price talk.

IPOS SERVE AS A SMALL-CAP early-warning system: A lot of activity means that the small-cap market is over-heated and you might want to put off purchases until it cools down a bit. (If you discover a really attractive small company selling at what looks like a cheap price, though, don't wait.) Heeding the warning could save you money. But can you use these offerings to make money, as well?

Yes, but not the way you're thinking. You're not likely to rack up big profits by buying IPOs, unless you're a pension fund or some other big shot. My for-mer Bloomberg sidekick Matt Wright, who covered the IPO market for Bloomberg News, says that under-writers allocate all the best deals—the ones that go up 40 or 50 percent the first day of trading—to institu-tional and large individual investors. These generally make big profits by flipping—buying stakes in the new offerings and then quickly selling them once trading opens.

Investment banks regard IPOs as "the payback to their best institutional or mutual fund clients, like us or Fidelity," John P. Kinnucan, fund manager at the Crabbe Huson Group in Portland, Oregon, told Bloomberg News in August 1995. "It is a game of mutual back-scratching."

Institutions place orders with a firm's trading desk, paying it tidy commissions, and are rewarded by being let into hot deals at their offering prices. When Netscape came public, for instance, Kinnucan was able to get in early and flip his shares for a profit.

That profit was made possible by us little investors. Like mullets, we listen to the sales hype and place market orders to buy pieces of deals at whatever price is available. As we bid the stock up higher and higher, the institutions unload their stakes. When that drives the price down, we're left holding the bag.

One of the Netscape bag-holders was Blaine Kubesh, who describes himself as just "another sucker." As Kubesh explains it: "I was unfortunate enough to have a pending order to buy Netscape at the market price. By the time I heard it was going to open at over $60, it was too late—I couldn't get my cancel order in quick enough." His order to buy 200 shares was executed at $71. He issued a sell order immediately. It was confirmed at $58.50, landing him a $2,500 loss.

If you can't beat 'em, join 'em: Invest in a mutual fund that does a good job of flipping.

According to Morningstar, Garrett Van Wagoner made a king's ransom for his investors by buying and selling IPOs when he was at Govett. To find other champs, read the financial press, which also praises the IPO acumen of the Kaufman fund. Look small, though: The bigger a fund is, the less bang it can get from flipping the relatively small positions they're allotted.

Be a pilot fish instead of a mullet.

Other companies in the same industry as a new offering often get caught up in the feeding frenzy surrounding it. So when a hot IPO hits, look for solid stocks in the same sector that you can scoop up at reasonable prices.

 Catch 'em later.

Charles Royce, president of Quest Advisory, points out that about a year after their initial offerings, many former high-fliers are lying low: The underwriters have stopped touting them, insiders have cashed in their shares, and many will have had a quarter of weaker earnings. At this point, smart investors can pick up shares of good companies at attractive levels. Waiting also helps you avoid the many one-day wonders. According to Mott, the afterlife of the average IPO is dismal. The most successful—and long-lived—deals have solid fundamentals.

ECONOMIC TRENDS AND CYCLES tell you which sectors and industries should do better than others. To figure out which individual stocks are your best picks, you have to look at the particular, not the general. Cues include company earnings, share-price histories and patterns, and the trades of those in the know. These are the subject of the next six sections.

BEYOND YOUR WILDEST EXPECTATIONS

"Surprise is the great corrector."

— DAVID DREMAN, *founder and manager of the Kemper-Dreman funds*

EVERYONE LOVES A NICE surprise, and Wall Street is no exception. Investing in companies that report earnings above analysts' expectations produces market-beating returns. That's been the consistent conclusion of research dating back 25 years, and it was recently reiterated in a 1996 report by Mott and Melissa Brown,

Prudential's director of quantitative research. The effect of positive surprises, moreover, is enhanced among small companies. These have less analyst coverage and more room to grow, so when one announces better-than-expected earnings, investors listen closely. Mott found that small-cap stocks posting positive surprises generated average three-month returns of 13.7 percent, 10.4 percent better than the S&P 500. By comparison, large-cap surprisers, according to Brown, returned only 5.7 percent on average, or 3.1 percent more than the benchmark.

Mott and Brown also discovered that the positive-surprise effect lasts three months. So you don't have to buy shares the day of an earnings announcement to reap the benefits. That's good news for small investors, who usually get information later than the bigger players and can't act on it as quickly.

 You'll find a list of positive surprises at the Primark Investment Research Center Web site (www.pirc.com), published the day after they are announced.

STILL, YOU'D OBVIOUSLY BE ahead of the game if you took your stakes before the stocks were bid up. And you'd really be sitting pretty if you could scoop the market by anticipating positive surprises. But how can you predict when Wall Street's best and brightest will be wrong? Easy. Remember the cockroach theory I mentioned in Chapter 3? Well, when you see one positive surprise, look for others: In 1993 Mott surveyed small companies that had beaten estimates one quarter and calculated they had a 34 percent better chance of doing so again the next quarter than companies that had merely met or fallen below expectations.

 Put your stockbroker on the case.
The firm's Bloomberg terminal can generate a list of all the

companies that produced positive surprises in the current quarter. But bear in mind one drawback to the roach approach: Companies that have previously sprung positive surprises aren't just likely to repeat; they're probably also more expensive than those that produce surprises out of the blue.

Another, very valuable resource that your broker can put to work for you is I/B/E/S International.

I/B/E/S is a subscription-only service that tracks analysts' earnings expectations and publishes a list of the small-cap stocks it feels will beat them. In the past, three-quarters of the firm's picks have turned in positive surprises, and the list as a whole has regularly beaten the S&P 500.

HOWEVER YOU FIND THEM, you should have plenty of surprising stocks to choose from. According to Brown and Mott, nearly 40 percent of companies reporting in the second quarter of 1996 posted earnings that beat estimates, compared with about 22 percent in 1991. Analysts say the increase may indicate that management has discovered the benefits of caution. If a company is too conservative and actual earnings exceed forecasts, the market usually reacts favorably. In contrast, projections that later prove to be overly optimistic can bring lawsuits from disappointed shareholders. So, again quoting Jim Oberweis's September 1996 *Oberweis Report*, managements "tend to work with analysts to keep estimates low."

The result is somewhat like "gradeflation" in academics: Just as grad schools today often give the same weight to an undergraduate's Bs that they used to accord to Cs, so investors increasingly react negatively to companies that merely meet expectations or whose surprises aren't astounding. In October 1996, for example, both Intel and Sun Micro Systems announced third-quarter earnings above their average estimates. The next day Intel was up 5 percent, but Sun was down 9.8 percent. The difference? Unlike Intel, "Sun didn't beat expectations strongly enough," says Furman Selz analyst Martin Pyykkonen, who removed the stock from his "recommended" list. Investor skepticism may perhaps also explain the fact that the duration of the positive-surprise effect has shrunk from six months to three.

When you have a list of companies most likely to fool the wise guys, what do you do with it? You probably don't have enough money to buy shares in them all; even if you did, it wouldn't be a good idea. Remember, you're looking for stocks to hold, not one-quarter wonders, and some surprises could reflect onetime gains, like the sale of property by a company whose real business is computers.

"Understand where the new earnings growth came from, and then question whether it can be duplicated," recommends Christine Baxter of the PBHG family of funds. Did the surprise result from new sales or from onetime non-operational gains? And what effect will the recent outperformance have on future growth? Baxter says that sometimes a young company overworks employees or forces sales on customers before the end of the quarter so that it will meet or exceed its earnings estimate. This can strain resources and put the company in a hole the next quarter, making growth difficult to sustain.

Your best defense against unrepeatable surprises is good fundamental analysis, like that described in Chapter 3. You can incorporate earnings surprises into the buy-and-hold schema outlined there at either the beginning or the end of the stock-picking process. In the first case, your surprise list will give you ideas to research and analyze; pay special attention to relative strength, since Mott and Coker found that stocks scoring high on this measure were the best performers. In the second case, you'll cull the buy candidates you've already researched for those most likely to surprise analysts with their earnings strength. Either way, if the surprises you expect materialize, you'll be holding solid companies with momentum; if they don't, you're still left with good stocks. I'll take those odds anytime.

This strategy is particularly useful for picking value stocks. David Dreman, of Dreman Value Management, a manager known for producing high risk-adjusted returns, noted in a 1996 talk at the New York Society of Security Analysts that, though out-of-favor stocks carry less risk than highfliers, they don't add much to your returns if they *stay* out of favor. Earnings surprises, he said, add the juice that boosts value returns above growth.

Dreman cited a study of the period between 1973 and 1993 in which he and Michael Berry (now with Heartland Advisors) looked at how companies' shares performed during both the quarter and the year after they posted positive earnings surprises. All the surprising stocks outperformed, but, as you can see from the chart below, the stars were those with the lowest p/e's: They beat the market by 20 percent during the first quarter following an announcement and by 9.39 percent during the first year. The num-

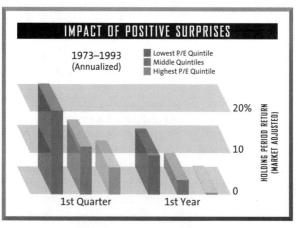

IMPACT OF POSITIVE SURPRISES

1973–1993
(Annualized)

■ Lowest P/E Quintile
■ Middle Quintiles
■ Highest P/E Quintile

HOLDING PERIOD RETURN (MARKET ADJUSTED)

20%

10

0

1st Quarter   1st Year

bers for the stocks with the highest p/e's during the same periods were 6.63 percent and a mere 0.32 percent, respectively.

If you're worried about the effect of negative surprises on your portfolio, take heart—value will see you through. Dreman and Berry's study also found that one year after missing analysts' estimates, the stocks with the lowest p/e still outperformed. Companies with low p/e's that failed to meet expectations underperformed the market during the first quarter by only about 4 percent, compared with 18.4 percent for high-p/e stocks *(see the chart below)*. And once they pass the one-year mark after a negative surprise, the lowest-p/e stocks generally go on to outperform the market by a slim margin.

Earnings surprises may also indicate the general health of the market.

There hasn't been much research on this. On an anecdotal level, though, Bloomberg markets editor Bill Hester and I have found that in recent history the S&P 500 has posted stunning results when twice as many companies in the index produce positive surprises as produce negative ones. When the two groups run neck and neck, the market has

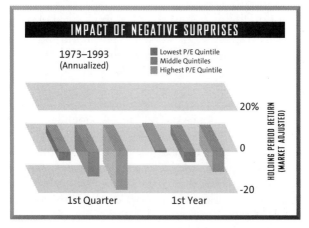

IMPACT OF NEGATIVE SURPRISES

1973–1993
(Annualized)

■ Lowest P/E Quintile
■ Middle Quintiles
■ Highest P/E Quintile

20%

0

-20

HOLDING PERIOD RETURN
(MARKET ADJUSTED)

1st Quarter   1st Year

returned a scanty 0.21 percent per quarter. You can find the index's positive/negative ratio on the Bloomberg Internet page (www.bloomberg.com).

Check interest rates, too. Low rates enhance returns in strong earnings quarters and buoy them in weak ones. But beware of quarters where earnings are coming in weak and rates are rising.

ESTIMATE REVISIONS

"It is rare to find a factor that so consistently defines winners and losers."
—CLAUDIA MOTT *and* DANIEL P. COKER

ESTIMATE REVISIONS ARE LIKE earnings surprises with better timing. Say a dip in the cost of raw materials cuts a manufacturer's costs. If the analysts following the company see this and have time to recrunch their numbers before the earnings announcement, you've got a revision; if they don't, you've got a surprise. Either way, the effect is similar—the stock price rises. It's a matter of math: If a company earning $5 a share is trading at $50, investors must believe the stock is worth 10 times earnings; raise the earnings to $10 a share, and the stock value bounces up to $100.

According to Mott and Coker, buying companies whose estimates have been revised upward is a great small-cap strategy. It works for both growth and value stocks, in up and down markets, and across industries. Pradhuman agrees. He has found that stocks for which analysts keep raising their earnings estimates have, on average, produced annual returns of almost 25 percent. But be careful. He's also found that they generated those returns with a volatility of 20.5 percent—that is, their prices bounced around, with peaks and valleys that diverged 20.5 percent from the mean. My advice here is the same as it is for surprises: Use the revisions as a source for ideas to research or as a final filter for candidates you've already vetted.

You can put together a list of small stocks whose earnings estimates are being raised by checking the Bloomberg Internet page (www.bloomberg.com).

Or ask your broker; if the brokerage has a lot of clout, like Merrill Lynch, it should be able to get you the names. And Zacks Investment Research offers a service on the Internet (www.zacks.com) that will conduct searches like this for $150 a year.

IF THEY GO UP, BUY 'EM!

"The race may not be to the swift nor the victory to the strong, but that's how you bet."
—DAMON RUNYON

MOMENTUM IS A SUPER STRATEGY for a bull market. But at least one Bear has used it, too: Chicago Bear coach Mike Ditka. Ditka made 300-pound William "the Refrigerator" Perry a running back because he figured that bodies in motion tend to stay in motion, and if the body is home-appliance size, watch out! Momentum investors are betting that stocks with a recent history of steadily rising prices are 300-pound backs under a full head of steam.

The investors have a better record than Ditka. Jim O'Shaughnessy, author of *What Works on Wall Street*, has found that since 1954 portfolios composed of the 50 stocks posting the biggest price increases in the previous year have returned about 14.5 percent annually. We've seen the same pattern in the "Bloomberg 100," a list, compiled in January, of the previous year's 100 best performers. The 1994 "100," the first published in *Bloomberg Personal* magazine, went on to trounce the very strong 1995 market.

The companies in that list were almost all small. Merrill's Pradhuman has found that small caps with momentum have returned more than 20 percent a year. There's a catch, though. These stocks have also demonstrated average annual volatility of about 24 percent.

Another caution: Share price may rise for reasons that have little or nothing to do with the quality of the underlying business—the stellar performance of other stocks in the same sector, for example, or rumors that the company is a takeover target. When price increases are not supported by financials, momentum isn't going to carry the stock very far. A refinement of the strategy puts it on a sounder fundamental footing by shifting the focus from price to earnings.

The father of earnings-momentum investing is Richard Driehaus, a Chicago broker who manages over $1 billion in assets. His reasoning is that since earnings drive stock prices, companies with accelerating earnings should outperform. American Century Investors fund managers, who use this approach, explain in a February 1996 *Kiplinger's* article that they apply Driehaus's insight by looking for companies whose profits and revenues are growing at least 30 percent, year over year and quarter over quarter. They then narrow their choices by talking to analysts and managements to determine if the companies' acceleration will continue. For instance, the funds pounced on computer chipmaker Burr-Brown after learning that the company was selling its new higher-margin analog chips as fast as it could produce them. American Century started acquiring the stock at 25 to 30 percent above the previous day's close and kept right on buying.

Gary Pilgrim also looks for accelerating earnings growth—of at least 20 percent—but he requires upward estimate revisions and positive surprises, as well. According to Morningstar, his PBHG Growth ranks among the top five of all funds in 5- and 10-year performance. Pilgrim told *Kiplinger's* in an October 1996 article that he uses a combination of revisions, surprises, and growth, weighted 35, 25, and 40 percent, respectively, to rank the stocks in the PBHG universe: 10 is perfect; 1 means forget it.

In contrast to the American Century managers, Pilgrim prefers not to know too much about the operations of the companies he owns. Instead, he uses statistical measures to calculate each one's underlying long-term growth rate. "My objective is to know how these companies are doing, as opposed to what they are doing," he told *Kiplinger's*. "It's much more important to know that analysts are raising earnings estimates, that competitors aren't gaining ground, that controversies over products are being resolved. In other words, I want my knowledge to be a mile wide and an inch deep."

Both American Century and PBHG agree, though, on pulling the plug when the acceleration that attracted their attention begins to slow. First Team Sports, a maker of in-line roller skates, for example, dropped out of the American Century universe when its annual revenue growth fell from 100 percent to 48 percent and management began painting a less rosy picture of its prospects.

Check historical earnings rates in the S&P 600 guide *(see Chapter 3)* **or the company financial reports.**
Again, use this research either to suggest ideas or to screen your finalists. But remember, one of the momentum managers' most important assets is discipline—they adhere strictly to their criteria for buying and, in particular, selling.

THE EARNINGS MOMENTUM STRATEGY can pay off big: American Century Vista and PBHG Growth returned 47 and 50 percent, respectively, in 1995. But, like price momentum, it can also bomb. Vista and PBHG dropped about 41 and 50 percent at one point in 1987, and 15 and 9 percent in 1990. If you can't stomach this much volatility, try the Aurora approach.

AURORA

"If you want a Ferrari, you gotta pay for a Ferrari."
—GARRETT VAN WAGONER

THE MAIN REASON THE RETURNS of strict momentum investors like Gary Pilgrim and the American Century managers vary so widely is that their models have no value component. "If we can find securities that have a year or two of positive surprises ahead of them, the p/e today doesn't matter," Glen Fogel, manager of the American Century Giftrust fund, told *Kiplinger's*, "because growth overwhelms the current valuation."

That may be true, and Giftrust did return 38.32 percent in 1995. But value criteria can provide a useful safety valve. By looking at p/e and price/book ratios, momentum managers might avoid buying grossly overvalued stocks. Value criteria might also help them discern when a theme has run its course and it's time to jump ship.

Adding a value safety valve is fairly easy. It's also profitable. O'Shaughnessy found that when he pared his list of stocks with good price momentum to just those with price-sales ratios less than 1, average annual returns since 1954 increased to more than 18 percent. You can put O'Shaughnessy's research to work for you by applying it to the "Bloomberg 100," selecting the companies with price-sales ratios less than one.

Aurora is another, more mathematically rigorous approach to tempering a fundamentally emerging-growth style with value. Its designer, Merrill's Satya Pradhuman, uses a model that ranks stocks—from a low of 1 to a high of 100—according to a weighted combination of three factors: the first is relative strength, which is measured by a stock's percentage price increase over the past year. The second is the size of positive earnings-estimate revisions. And the third is a "valuation" component emphasizing low price to cash flow (a measure similar to p/e but less vulnerable to accounting manipulations) relative to the stock's industry sectors.

The Aurora portfolio is composed of the stocks scoring in the top percentile when the strength, earnings, and valuation components are assigned weights of 40, 30, and 30 percent, respectively. From February 1980 through December 1995, this approach returned a whopping 31 percent a year, with 225 basis points less volatility than pure momentum.

In a less bullish market, Pradhuman thought it would be wise to change emphasis, to a basic value style spiced with growth. So he also created the Enhanced Contrarian Portfolio, using fundamentally the same model but changing the weightings to 70 percent value, 15 percent strength, and 15 percent earnings. This approach generated returns of almost 25 percent per year from 1980 to 1995, with volatility of 20.5 percent.

The Aurora and Contrarian portfolios share an Achilles heel, though: If the market really tanks—dropping, say, 8 percent in a month—both will get spanked, perhaps even slightly worse than stocks picked using other methods.

You can create a poor man's version of Pradhuman's portfolios using the Friday edition of *Investor's Business Daily*, which lists stocks' percentile scores for relative strength and earnings momentum.
Pick out the ones with the highest scores and lowest p/e's, and research them. Then apply one of Pradhuman's weighting systems. Finally, choose the high scorers with the best fundamentals.

INSIDER TRADING, THE LEGAL WAY

"Executives have a good insight into an industry, where Wall Street sometimes has a myopic view."

— THOMAS FITZGERALD, *president of T.H. Fitzgerald & Co., which runs the Reserve Informed Investors Growth Fund*

INSIDERS—OFFICERS, MEMBERS of the board—should have a better idea of a company's prospects than any outsider, no matter how talented. They have what Tweedy, Browne Co., in its customer booklet, terms "insight information": firsthand knowledge of new marketing programs, planned cost efficiencies, and price hikes, as well as industry conditions. You can trade on this information indirectly by watching when insiders buy company stock. This tells you that the people who really know the business have enough confidence in its future to stake their own money on it.

"We like to invest alongside the people that run the companies," says Praveen Gottipalli, a principal at Symphony Asset Management, which manages Bear, Stearns & Co.'s Insiders Select Fund.

Buying with the insiders certainly worked for purchasers of Guidant Corp. shares. In late September 1995, roughly a year after it was spun off by Eli Lilly & Co. at 14½, the medical-device maker's chairman, president, and chief financial officer all bought large blocks of its stock. The share price at the time was 26; a year later it had more than doubled, to 55½.

Nejat Seyhun, a professor of finance at the University of Michigan, conducted a study of the one-year performance of companies following a year in which insiders were either net buyers or net sellers of their stock. Seyhun found that companies associated with insider buying beat the market by almost 5 percent, while those associated with insider selling performed worse than the market.

When sorting through your investment ideas, check your prospects' insider-trading histories.

Anyone who owns more than 5 percent of a company's

shares or holds a high position in its management must notify the Securities and Exchange Commission whenever he or she trades the stock. You can find out who's done what by checking form 4 (which must be filed by any insider trading a company's shares) and form 144 (filed by holders of restricted stock); both can be accessed on Edgar (see Chapter 3, page 118).

If purchases accounted for the greatest dollar volume of insider trades during the past year, that's definitely a plus. Selling is a much less perfect indicator: Though people generally buy stock for only one reason—because they think it'll make them money—any number of reasons exist for selling, and some have nothing to do with the company's prospects. An executive may want to diversify his portfolio, for example, or need the cash to pay his daughter's college tuition. Also bear in mind that the absolute number of shares someone sells is less important than the percentage of his or her total stake this number represents. For example, the fact that Microsoft chairman Bill Gates sold 520,955 of his company's shares in August 1996 looks less significant when you realize that he still holds 141 million.

Once you've made your purchases, keep an eye on insider activity. It could tip the balance if you're wavering between holding and selling a stock.

A VARIATION ON INSIDER PURCHASING occurs when the company buys back its own shares on the open market. This is a good sign for several reasons. By reducing the number of shares outstanding, a buyback raises earnings per share and reduces the amount of money that must be paid out in dividends. Perhaps most important, though, it usually indicates that company officers feel the stock is cheap. So if you follow management's lead, you could be picking up a bargain.

Share price does tend to increase after a buyback. According to a 1994 study by Rice University professor David Ikenberry, stocks rise an average of 3 percent the day an announcement is made and then beat the market by 12 percent over the next four years.

With results like that, buybacks should definitely have a role in your stock selection, either as a source of ideas or as a screen. They're a particularly good signal when you're choosing value investments. In the Rice study, buyback stocks that were cheap according to value criteria "returned an average of 45 percent more over a four-year period than similar nonbuyback stocks."

Be a little skeptical, though. Ask yourself why a company is spending its money on its stock rather than on its business. Has it run out of growth opportunities and products to research? Or is the buyback just a quick way to boost share price? Often the announcement itself accomplishes that goal, and the companies never actually follow through. In fact, some analysts estimate that only a third of the shares slated for buybacks get repurchased. Empty talk won't sustain share price long.

If you buy a stock on the basis of an announced buyback, check the next quarterly statement to see if shares outstanding have decreased, indicating that the company is making good on its promise.

Another way to profit from other people's purchases is to jump into stocks just before the big guns discover them.

Many professional investors will look for stocks with very low institutional ownership and hope that new-product launches or earnings surprises will draw fund managers' attention. A tiny stake by institutional standards can be enough to drive a small company's shares sky-high.

You'll find the percentage of institutional ownership among the Key Stock Statistics in the S&P guide reports. If the company isn't in the guide, ask your broker to check Morningstar, Bloomberg, or the charts put out by *IBD* publisher O'Neil & Co. Make a low institutional stake one of your sorting criteria, but not a must-have.

TECHNICAL MARKS

"I use fundamentals and technicals closely. Fundamentals are first, and if you have them, you have a huge advantage. But market conditions change, and you need to have a plan for that. I often use fundamental analysis to determine how much downside a stock might have. The ideal situation is when our fundamental upside is three or more times greater than [the stock's technical support level]—for example, where we see the upside as being 50 percent, but the downside is only 10 percent."

—LISA GRAY, *a Memphis stockbroker*

PRETTY MUCH ALL THE STRATEGIES discussed to this point have involved fundamentals, such as the figures on a company's balance sheet and income statement. Fundamentals were also the focus of Chapter 3. The reason is that they give you a window on how a business is run and what management thinks. Many analysts ignore them, though, and focus not on a company's business but on the stock itself. Technical analysis, as this approach is called, treats a company's shares as commodities subject to market forces that can be traced by charting trade-volume and price trends. Analysts use the patterns revealed in these charts to predict where a stock is headed.

If you want to find out how they do that, read Thomas Dorsey's book, *Point & Figure Charting*. Listening to some tech guys, you'd think the waves and angles they graph were cabalistic symbols with mystic connections to the future. Dorsey brings it all down to earth, invoking the prosaic forces of supply and demand. The idea is to deduce from the patterns of volume and price moves whether sellers or buyers are dominating the market. You want to be holding a stock when buyers outnumber sellers.

To determine who has the upper hand, techies may use bar and line graphs, which plot share price and trade volume against time, or point-and-figure charts. Dorsey favors the latter. These indicate the magnitude and direction of share-price moves, but not the time they occur: Each square represents a specified price unit; when a stock's price moves up a unit, an X is put in the square above the previous point; when it falls, an O is entered one square down. Whenever the direction changes, the marks are made one column over, so each column contains either all Xs or all Os. An example of a point-and-figure chart, for Veterinary Center of America, appears at right.

Charting—whether by bar, line, or point and figure—reveals patterns, which must be interpreted. Interpretation involves a combination of science and art. Some of the signals are pretty clear. When each rising trend reaches a summit higher than the previous one, the buyers (bulls) are riding high; seller (bear) domination is indicated by successively lower falls. When both rises and falls remain within a narrow horizontal band, the stock is said to have stabilized, or based; if this period of stasis was preceded by a rise, it will probably be followed by a further rise; a preceding drop foreshadows a future fall.

Often a chart will show a series of peaks or dips that reach but never pass a particular price. The ceiling to rises is termed a resistance level; the floor to drops, a support level. Similar to these are trend lines, which connect series of declining peaks or rising dips. When a stock's price breaks through a resistance level, it means that investors are willing to buy at higher levels than in the past; a fall through a support level signals willingness to sell at lower prices. Breaching a trend line may presage a change in the direction of price movements.

EXAMPLE OF POINT AND FIGURE CHARTING

Veterinary Center of America (VCAI)
(5/16/94 - 1/8/97)

```
35.0 ┌
34.0 │
33.0 │          *
32.0 │          X *
31.0 │          X O *
30.0 ┼ ···· X ··· X O · * ···········
29.0 │      X O X O      *
28.0 │   X  X O X O        *
27.0 │   X O X O X O    X  *
26.0 │   X O X O   O X  X O  *
25.0 ┼ · X O ···· O X O X O ···· * ····
24.0 │   X        O X O X O      *    *
23.0 │   X        O X O        *  X *
22.0 │   X        O     O       X * X O *
21.0 │   X              O       X O X O  *
20.0 ┼ · X ········· O X ···· X O X O X · * ··
19.5 │   X           O X O X   X O   O X O    *
19.0 ┼ · X ········· O X O X O X ···· O X O X · * ····
18.5 │   X           O X O X O X O   O X O X O   *
18.0 ┼ · X ········· O X O X O X · * O · O X O ···· * ··
17.5 │   X           O X O X O   *      O   O       *
17.0 ┼ · X ········· O X O X ·· * ············· O ······· * ····
16.5 O   X           O X O X *                  O          *
16.0 · O X · X ········· * O X O * ············· O ··········
15.5 O X O X          *   O X *               O
15.0 · O X O X ····· * ··· O * ·············· O ··········
14.5 O X O           *      *                O
14.0 · O X ········ * ···················· O ··········
13.5 O X       *                           O
13.0 · O ····· * ························· O X ··········
12.5 │      *                             O X O
12.0 ┼ · * ······························· O X O ····
11.5 │ *                                 O X O
11.0 ┼ * ································· O X O ····
10.5 *                                  O X O
10.0 ┼ ································· O X O ····
 9.5 │                                  O X
 9.0 ┼ ·································· O X ····
 8.5 │                                  O X
 8.0 ┼ ······························· O ····
 7.5 │
 7.0 ┼
 6.5 │
 6.0 ┼
 5.5 │
 5.0 ┴
```

Opinions are divided on how great a role technical analysis should play in small-cap investing. Charts are most valuable, technicians say, in liquid markets, where information is freely available and which are too large to manipulate. For example, in the huge government bond market, crucial information, such as employment, GDP, and inflation figures, is kept quiet until it can be released to all players simultaneously. So T-bond price and volume movements are good indicators of where other players in the market are willing to buy and sell. In the small-cap sector, in contrast, the prices of the many thinly traded, low-priced stocks are easily manipulated. An unscrupulous investor with a lot of microcap shares to unload might pick up a large block of the stock at a higher price, hoping others would notice the volume and assume the smart money was loading up. With duped investors rushing to buy the stock, the manipulator would be able to sell his stake at a tidy profit.

Ease of manipulation reduces the reliability of small-cap price and volume patterns. Accordingly, many investors in the sector use technicals merely to supplement their basic fundamental analysis. Dorsey, for example, infers from his charts how defensive or aggressive an investor should be. Other managers employ technicals to reduce their risk—to ensure, say, that an undervalued company isn't going to stay that way too long. Bill Nasgovitz is one of those. Though charts aren't a cornerstone of Heartland's stock-picking strategy, Nasgovitz does what technical types call base building. He looks for out-of-favor stocks whose charts resemble "a dead man's heartbeat"—in other words, flat-liners whose prices have based after a period of decline and, he hopes, are poised to take off.

Nasgovitz wants to be the first to discover a story. Jim Oberweis, in contrast, feels that other investors are too smart to get scooped too often. He becomes concerned if nobody else is excited about one of his picks. So he looks at charts like those published by O'Neil & Co., which plot relative strength, for signs of an uptrend and market outperformance.

 Keep technicals in perspective.
Over the long run, fundamentals drive stock prices, period. But if you can check a chart, do it: You'll reduce your risk by looking for good value and growth companies that are emerging from a base.

Some of Tom Dorsey's research appears on the Internet at www.dorseywright.com. Try e-mailing that address for help finding a local brokerage with good research on small stocks that could also chart your holdings.

UP TO NOW, I'VE TALKED ABOUT using economic, fundamental, and technical signals to decide what stocks to buy and sell when. The remaining sections discuss more esoteric trading techniques and instruments, as well as cost-cutters.

GOING SHORT

"We've put together a relatively small short portfolio of about 15 of Wall Street's most overvalued, most overloved securities, which we think are ripe for a fall."
— *Heartland funds'* BILL NASGOVITZ

RULE NUMBER ONE IN SMALL-CAP investing: Beware of froth. When companies become Wall Street sweethearts and institutions own a large percentage of their shares, not enough demand remains in the market to drive their prices higher. Worse, their high p/e's increase the risk that one disappointment will send them tumbling.

Such stocks are poor buys. But they're good candidates for *shorting*—selling shares borrowed from a broker in hopes of replacing them with others bought later at a lower price. Bill Nasgovitz uses this tactic for his Small Cap Contrarian fund, which can have as much as 25 percent of its portfolio in short positions. Nasgovitz improves his odds by looking for frothy stocks that are being sold by company insiders (*see above*).

"When we're buying shares, we like to see insiders expressing their confidence by buying, too," he says. "With shorts, it's just the opposite—we look for high-flying stocks where there's been strong and consistent insider selling, in size."

Nasgovitz probably also limits his shorting to the larger companies within the small-cap sector. The smallest stocks are thinly traded, making it too easy for shorts to get caught in a squeeze—forced to buy scarce shares at high prices to replace the borrowed ones they sold.

Short selling is not for the general public. You need time and patience and—most of all, warns Nasgovitz—a good stomach. "You sell something at 20, it might go to 30 in this market," he says. "It's difficult to do, to handle your emotions."

Here's a less stomach-churning way, also used by Heartland, to make money on short sales. Start with your group of thoroughly researched, solid companies, and buy those with high short interest—your broker can check the stock screens for you, or you can look yourself at the back of *Barron's.*

The key to this strategy is that all the shorts will ultimately need to buy shares to cover their positions. Of course, they could know some deep, dark secret about a company that will keep its price in the dumps despite their purchases. So check what insiders are doing. If the corporate execs, who really know the company, are buying, you can be more confident that the shorts are wrong and that their covering will drive the share price up.

PAIRED TRADING

*"[Trading stocks in pairs] is a way to contain risk
but still play with some of the juicier, riskier types
of securities."*
— ERIC KOBREN, *money manager and publisher of*
FundsNet Insight, *in an interview with Scott Schnipper of*
Bloomberg News

A VARIATION ON SHORT SELLING that Nasgovitz likes to
use in his Contra fund is *paired trading*. It's like betting
the spread in football: What counts is not who beats
who, but by how much. A paired trade is a bet that the
best company in an industry will thump the worst.
The bigger the spread, the more you earn.

It works like this: You take a long position on your
pick to win while shorting your designated loser.
Then if the two companies perform as you expect,
you pocket profits from both ends.

Paired trading also provides protection against bad
bounces. Say you hold complementary positions in an
industry that tanks, as the semiconductor group did
in fall 1995. Your profits from the shorted stock will
offset your losses on your long bet.

In spring 1996 Nasgovitz pulled off a successful
paired trade in the videoconferencing industry. The
laggard of the group, Boca Research, was an ideal
value buy. Despite the fact that its earnings had soared
50 percent the previous year and it had recently
announced plans to bring videoconferencing to personal computers, the company was trading at only
about 13 times estimated earnings. In contrast, Picturetel Corp., whose book value of $6.09 a share was
comparable to Boca's $6.50, was selling at 37 times
earnings, topping the sector.

Nasgovitz bought the first and shorted the second
in early spring. By April, Boca had moved little, but
Picturetel shares had tumbled to 29¾ from a February

peak of almost 45, allowing Contra to cover its position and realize a profit.

Paired trading works best when equities are neither roaring ahead nor going down the chute. A rising market can buoy even the fumblers, and a falling one can sink the best-run companies; either way, there won't be many stocks headed in radically different directions to create the yawning spreads you need to exploit. A stagnant market is also exactly the environment in which you need ingenious ploys like this to spice up bland returns.

In any environment, however, this technique, like straight shorting, is probably best left to the pros. Even they make miscalls. Dallas-based money manager David Tice, for instance, paired Sullivan Dental Products and Patterson Dental, two comparable companies whose market valuations seemed out of line with their fundamentals: Sullivan's too low, at 1.6 times book value, and Patterson's too high, at almost 6 times book. Tice bought the first and shorted the second. Patterson proceeded to rise almost 5 percent, while Sullivan advanced a mere 1 percent.

If you decide to try this at home, start by sorting through your list of researched candidates for the best value prospect. Then enlist your broker's help to find its evil twin—a company in the same business whose fundamentals don't seem to support its share price.

Next check insider activity. You want to see the companies' officers on your side of the trades, buying your long pick and selling your short. Finally, to be certain you're not walking into a squeeze, have your broker pull up your short candidate's *short-interest ratio*. This tells you what percentage of the stock's daily trade volume the total outstanding short positions in it represent. If the percentage is too high, you'll have a lot of competition when you go to cover, which will drive up the price .

CALL OPTIONS AND CONVERTIBLE BONDS

"Be careful with derivatives. Bad judgment and borrowed money can be a dangerous combination."

—WARREN BUFFETT

ANOTHER WAY TO CASH IN on a small company's growth is to invest in its stock without buying any shares. Sounds like a pretty good trick, huh? Actually, it's just derivative business as usual. By purchasing equity call options or convertible bonds instead of the stock itself, you can benefit from a short-term rise in share price with less exposure to a fall.

An *equity call option* is a contract conferring the right (but not the obligation) to buy 100 shares of a company's stock at a specified price, called the *strike price,* on or before a specified expiration date. The option's price, or *premium,* is determined by two factors: its *intrinsic* and *time values.* A call option's intrinsic value is the difference between its strike and the stock's current share price, as long as the latter is higher. If the share price is lower than the strike, the option has no intrinsic value. It still has time value, though, which reflects the market's estimation of the likelihood that the stock price will reach or surpass the strike before the option expires.

For instance, at the end of July 1996, when Intel was selling at 74, or $7,400 for 100 shares, you could have picked up a call option on its stock, expiring January 1999 and with a strike of 100, for $1,000. Since the strike was higher than the current share price, the premium was composed entirely of time value. Say that eight months later Intel stock rose to 146. Your option would then have had an intrinsic value of $46, and its premium would have risen accordingly. You could sell it at this point and realize approximately the same capital gain as if you had bought and sold 100 shares of the stock.

Of course, if the share price fails to rise above the strike before the expiration date, you lose the entire premium. This sum, however, is considerably less than the cost of the 100 shares the option represents—in the example, $1,000 versus $7,400. So a call option effectively gives you the same profit opportunity as 100 shares of stock (though you miss out on any dividends) while putting much less of your principal at risk.

On the other hand, stock ownership has an important advantage over option investing: A stock, unlike an option, always has time value. Most options have lives of less than a year. (*LEAPS,* or *long-term equity anticipation securities,* are options with longer maturities—two to three years—and much higher price tags.) If you own a three-month call and the underlying shares shoot up from nowhere after three months and one day, you're out of luck. If you own the stock, though, you can wait the extra day—or an extra month, or a year—and still profit.

For that reason, options are not good for investing in value stocks, which can languish at low price levels for long periods. Because of the downside protection they afford, they're probably best for investing in the smallest, and most volatile, companies. Few of those, however, issue options. To follow the derivative route here, you'd have to switch markets and look into convertible debt.

A *convertible* is a corporate bond that can be exchanged for shares of the issuing company's stock. Each bond is associated not only with a yield but also with a conversion ratio, which specifies the number of shares per $1,000 of face value the investor is entitled to. For instance, if you bought a $10,000 Pee Wee Corp. convertible bond with a ratio of 250, you could exchange it for 2,500 shares of Pee Wee stock.

Because the conversion feature acts like an equity call option, the market value of the bond rises with that of the stock. It will also fall as the share price falls, but usually not as far. The bond is cushioned by its own investment value (the price at which an identical bond without a conversion feature would trade) and the time value of the option component.

"It's like buying the stock and getting a 7 percent yield while you wait for it to take off," says Eric Miller, an analyst with the Heartland Value Plus Fund, which has about 17 percent of its assets in these bonds.

Convertibles are well suited to value investors like Heartland. The issuers are generally small or obscure companies, which would find straight debt structures prohibitively expensive. The bonds also tend to be thinly traded. All this makes for just the sort of market on which value investors thrive.

"When you consider that the stock is underfollowed and then include the fact that many of these bonds aren't rated and many institutions are excluded from buying them, you have an extra degree of inefficiency," says Miller, who has exploited this inefficiency quite successfully. The Quantum Health Resources convertibles that he bought at 76.90, for instance, surged soon afterward to more than 92, an increase of almost 20 percent.

The same characteristics that make convertibles attractive value plays also make them risky for individual investors.
Because they're often not rated by S&P or Moody's Investors Service, you have to do a lot of digging yourself to find out how likely the issuing companies are to default. The odds of failure may well be higher than you find comfortable. So be careful: Don't buy the convertibles of any company whose stock you wouldn't invest in.

A PENNY SAVED

NO MATTER HOW GOOD your stock picks are and how disciplined you are about selling, you'll always do better if you can keep your transaction costs down. I already outlined a few ways to do this in Chapter 3. Here are some other, more sophisticated, tricks of the trade:

◆ **When you buy a stock, place a limit order between its bid and ask.** Occasionally your order will fill and you'll end up with a price that's better than the one market makers are offering.

◆ **Ask your broker to put your order on Instinet or Bloomberg Tradebook.** These are fast-growing systems used by a number of OTC departments to place offers within the spread for dealers to see and act upon. They are fairly recent innovations; ask if your broker has access to them.

◆ **See if your broker will allow you to match trades within the brokerage or its market maker.** Charles Schwab, through its Assurance Trading program, is one of the few firms that offer this service. If you're allowed to do it, matching can get you a better price than the bid or ask. It may not work too well, though, with small stocks that don't trade heavily, because there won't be many people willing to take the other side.

Small-Cap
RECAP

THIS IS THE END. NOW I've given you every technique and tactic I know for making money in small stocks. The danger is that in all the details, you can lose sight of the fundamental investing process. So here, in summary, are the basic precepts.

Be an investor, not a speculator. This book is about achieving superior returns over a long term with reasonable risk. Small-cap stocks play an integral role in that process, but only as part of a balanced portfolio whose makeup reflects your long- and short-term savings goals.

So, diversify. Invest in both small and large stocks—in domestic and foreign companies—that reflect both growth and value styles. Put enough money in cash and bonds to take care of expenses looming in the near future. Then, with the rest, you can ride the equity market's ups and downs, ultimately reaping its superior long-term returns.

Look for great companies at good prices and good companies at great prices. As Warren Buffett says, growth and value are joined at the hip. A crummy business that can't make money is no bargain, no matter how cheap it is. Even a wonderful business won't make you much money if its market value is hyperinflated.

Exploit your edge. The markets, by and large, are very efficient. Few good companies stay undervalued for long. The guys who make real money are the ones who find out first about whatever it is that drives a stock's price up. Your chances of scooping Wall Street on one of the big companies are almost nil. The odds get better as you go down the scale in size. With small companies, which are not well followed on the Street, special knowledge of a business or acquaintance with management can give you a real edge to exploit.

Tip the odds in your favor. You're searching for companies with great products, whose management you trust and whose financial house is in order. But not every good business is a good buy—you need some indication that the share price is going to increase. Success is more likely if the stock meets the following criteria:

1 earnings yield is higher than corporate bond yields.
2 Its price-to-sales ratio is less than 1.
3 It is priced below book value.
4 Its ROE is greater than 20.
5 It is being bought by insiders or by the company itself.
6 Analysts are raising the company's earnings estimates.
7 Earnings consistently exceed expectations.
8 Sales and earnings are growing faster than 30 percent annually, or quarter over quarter, or both.
9 The company has a strong brand name or dominates an industry or niche.
10 The stock has been outperforming the S&P 600.

Buy to hold. Invest only in companies you feel comfortable living with for a long time. Jumping in and out of stocks costs too much in fees, spreads, and taxes to be profitable, even assuming you could time your trades successfully.

But don't be sentimental about your investments. You'd better have a good reason for holding a stock in the following situations:

1 The company's p/e is greater than 1.5 times a conservative estimate of its long-term earnings growth rate.
2 Insider selling of its shares exceeds insider buying.
3 The company carries more debt than equity.
4 Its management or investor relations officer side-steps your questions.
5 Growth in earnings, revenues, or profit margins has declined in several consecutive quarters.
6 The company posts earnings significantly below analyst expectations.
7 Analysts lower their earnings estimates.
8 Analysts rate the stock a sell.
9 The stock has consistently underperformed the S&P 600, and management has not enunciated a clear plan for turning things around.
10 Everyone loves it.

Enjoy yourself. Some people get a kick out of doing research and playing with numbers; others leave that to the pros by investing in well-managed mutual funds. Whatever your style, you should get a warm feeling watching your savings grow.

RESOURCES

HERE ARE SOME SOURCES you can use to delve more deeply into the topics touched on in the book, as well as to implement the strategies discussed. They're divided into three sections: **READING MATTER**, which lists the books, newsletters, and magazines mentioned in the text, together with some additional ones you might find helpful; **WEB SITES**, containing useful Internet addresses; and **REGIONAL BROKERS**, which provides the names and phone numbers of some brokerages that specialize in companies located in particular areas of the country.

READING MATTER

ENTRIES PROVIDE PUBLISHING or subscription information, but before you shell out a lot of money, you may want to check your local library's holdings.

BOOKS

BOOKS ARE SOME THE GREATEST tools for an investor. By spending about 10 to 50 bucks and a few days studying, you can absorb knowledge that it has taken some smart person years to acquire. Though I mostly advocate bottom-up, buy-and-hold investing, I've included in the list below books on other disciplines and trading, which will give you a broader understanding of how the stock market really works.

The Art of Short Selling, by Kathryn F. Staley [John Wiley & Sons, 1997; $34.95, hardcover].
Well written and thoroughly researched, this book will open your eyes to the perils of investing without doing thorough research, and it will teach you how to be a better analyst.

Classics: An Investor's Anthology [Business One Irwin, 1988, hardcover] and **Classics II: Another Investor's Anthology** [Irwin Professional Publishing, 1991; $50.00, hardcover], by Charles D. Ellis and James R. Vertin.

Though *Classics* is out of print and may be hard to find, it and its sequel, *Classics II,* include some of the finest articles ever written about investing. Reading these books will make you a seasoned veteran.

Common Stocks and Uncommon Profits and Other Writings, by Philip A. Fisher [John Wiley & Sons, 1996; $19.95].

According to press sources, this book had a huge influence on Warren Buffett. Enough said.

A Commonsense Guide to Mutual Funds, by Mary Rowland [Bloomberg Personal Bookshelf, 1996; $19.95, hardcover].

Mary Rowland is one of the few people writing about mutual funds today who has been doing it for more than 10 years. Her guide contains much of the wisdom she's gleaned from meeting hundreds of great and not-so-great investors. It's a quick read that will probably improve your investment results.

The Guide to Understanding Financial Statements, by Geza Szurovy and S.B. Costales [McGraw-Hill, 1993; $14.95].

About as easy to read as accounting books get. It is short, to the point, and has great instructions for creating a spreadsheet to calculate important ratios.

Hoover's Handbook of American Business, edited by Patric J. Spain and James R. Talbot [Hoover's Inc., 1996; $79.95, 2-vol. set, hardcover].

Hoover's provides great descriptions and history on a large number of companies. It should be available in most public libraries.

How to Buy Technology Stocks, by Michael Gianturco [Little Brown & Co., 1996; $13.95].

Gianturco does an excellent job explaining how

investors can make profits in tech stocks without betting the farm.

How to Make Money in Stocks, by William J. O'Neil [McGraw-Hill, 1994; $10.95].
I've told you that *Investor's Business Daily* is one of the best sources for learning about small stocks. O'Neil's book will teach you how to use all of the tables of information in *IBD* to improve your investing.

The Intelligent Investor, by Benjamin Graham [Harper-Collins, 1997; $30.00, hardcover].
One of the greatest investing books of all time. You should read it every five years.

Market Timing for the Nineties, by Stephen Leeb and Roger S. Conrad [HarperCollins, 1994; $12.50].
Offers some commonsense market indicators.

The Market Wizards [HarperCollins, 1993; $15.00] and **The New Market Wizards** [John Wiley & Sons, 1995; $34.95, hardcover], by Jack D. Schwager.
Even if you never intend to be an active trader, you will become a better and more confident investor by reading these books.

Midas Investing, by Jonathan Steinberg [Times Books, 1996; $23.00, hardcover].
This brand-new book from the editor of *Individual Investor* magazine is a good handbook on investing in momentum stocks.

The Money Masters [HarperCollins, 1994; $14.00] and **The New Money Masters** [Harperperennial Library, 1994; $14.00], by John Train.
Interviews with some of the best money managers.

Nelson's Directory of Investment Research [Nelson

Publications, 1995; $535.00].

One Up on Wall Street, by Peter Lynch [Penguin USA, 1990; $12.95].

I recommend this and anything else Lynch writes or has written. The guy is a genius.

Options As a Strategic Investment, by Lawrence G. McMillan [NY Institute of Finance, 1992; $49.95, hard-cover].

If you really want to invest in options, you better read this book first.

Point & Figure Charting, by Thomas J. Dorsey [John Wiley & Sons, 1995; $55.00 hardcover].

If you think technical analysis is a bunch of baloney, you should read Dorsey's book. Dorsey believes that picking the most solid businesses won't necessarily make you money, since about three quarters of the risk in a stock comes from the market and the industry. He reduces his risk by studying supply and demand.

A Random Walk Down Wall Street, by Burton G. Malkiel [W.W. Norton & Co., 1996; $15.95].

Read this book. It tells you everything you'd get from an MBA course in finance, but in a far more lively style. Malkiel also outlines strategies you can put to work.

Security Analysis, by Benjamin Graham and David L. Dodd [McGraw-Hill, 1997; $50.00, hardcover].

The "holy book" of investing. I won't promise that you'll enjoy reading it or that you'll be able to get through it quickly, but it will really teach you to invest like a pro.

Small Cap Stocks, edited by Robert A. Klein and Jess Led-

erman [Probus Publishing Co., 1993; $70.00, hardcover].
This book contains some fantastic research on the
small-cap market. It's a must-read for pros, but it
would bore most amateurs.

Standard & Poor's SmallCap 600 Guide [McGraw-Hill, 1997; $24.95].
A very good source on small-cap stocks.

Value Investing Made Easy, by Janet Lowe [McGraw-Hill, 1996; $22.95, hardcover].
A nice little book about Benjamin Graham's life
and value investing.

Walker's Manual of Unlisted Stocks [Walker's Manual Llc., 1996; $75.00, hardcover].
The manual, which you can order by calling (800)
932-2922, contains four years of financial data on
500 penny stocks. Read it before you put any money
into that market.

What Works on Wall Street, by James P. O'Shaughnessy [McGraw-Hill, 1996; $29.95, hardcover].
A great book that explains which investing strategies beat the market over the long haul.

A Zebra in Lion Country, by Ralph Wanger [Simon &
Schuster, 1997; $25.00, hardcover].
Wanger is one of the great small-cap investors. The
book is not yet in the stores at this writing, but I'm
sure you'll want to read it.

NEWSLETTERS
AND MAGAZINES

Barron's. Many market professionals consider *Barron's* a must-read for information on all the markets
(800-328-6800, ext. 550).

Bloomberg Personal. As an editor, I'm obviously biased toward *Personal*. It contains interviews with and articles by many of the people mentioned in this book. You'll also find stocks that meet some of the investing criteria described here (888-432-5820).

Charles Schwab Mutual Funds Performance Guide. A comprehensive listing of small-cap funds (800-435-4000).

Individual Investor. One of the only magazines that concentrates on small stocks. I like the fact that the editors provide lots of thoroughly researched ideas in each issue. But don't forget that you need to follow up their research with your own (800-383-5901).

Investor's Business Daily. A great source for both stock and fund investors. If you include the paper's special features in your investment analysis and idea generating, your results will improve (800-831-2525).

Kiplinger's Personal Finance Magazine. *Kiplinger's* is a simple, no-nonsense magazine, containing lots of good ideas for managing your finances. Editor Fred Frailey also does great interviews (800-544-0155).

Morningstar Mutual Funds. This loose-leaf binder of 1,600 funds is a great source of mutual fund information. But you pay for what you get. Get your local library to subscribe if it doesn't already. You may be able to get Morningstar reports from your broker or from a fund you are planning to invest in. The company also publishes a monthly newsletter, *Morningstar Investor* (800-876-5005).

Mutual Funds. I started subscribing to this magazine

because the subscription rate was really low, about $10. Now I learn something every time I thumb through (800-442-9000).

The No-Load Fund Investor. Sheldon Jacobs, a long-time observer of the mutual fund industry, covers new funds and provides recommendations and suggested portfolios (914-693-7420).

Oberweis Report. Always one of the top-ranked investment newsletters. Its picks have returned more than 28 percent a year since 1976 (630-801-6000).

The Red Chip Review. Marc Robins and his staff really dig to uncover great small companies that nobody else is following. You wouldn't believe how many pros speak highly of this report. It's also good to see that almost everyone on the staff is working to earn the Chartered Financial Analyst designation (503-241-1265, or 800-RedChip/800-838-9248).

SmartMoney. Here's another one to read on your trips to the library. It carries a regular feature on small-cap stocks once a year but doesn't devote much ink to companies with market caps below $500 million. Features on other areas of finance win lots of industry awards, though (800-444-4204).

Value Line Investment Survey. A compendium of one-page company reports published by Value Line, which ranks stocks according to safety and projected performance (800-833-0046).

Vickers Weekly Insider Report (800-645-5043) and **Insiders' Chronicle** (800-243-2324). Two newsletters that give you a window on insider buying and selling.

WEB SITES

THE INTERNET IS SHAPING UP as an extremely valuable source of investment advice. It seems like a new Web page pops up every day. I'll warn you right away, though, that you can't trust everything you read in print and you really can't trust everything you see on the Net. Some sites—like Bloomberg's and those run by our competitors Dow Jones, Standard & Poor's, and Reuters—should provide reliable information. I can vouch for the quality of Bloomberg's data, which is one of the things I really like about the site. There are other so-called information providers, though, that are merely mouthpieces companies pay to tout their stocks. So watch out for deception or just plain inaccuracy.

You should find helpful information at these addresses:

www.bloomberg.com Run by Bloomberg Financial Markets; provides news along with comprehensive stock and bond info.

www.cda.com CDA Investment publishes information on insider buying and selling.

www.dorseywright.com Dorsey, Wright & Associates' site can fill you in on point-and-figure technical analysis.

www.nasdaq.com Run by Nasdaq; provides price quotes.

www.pirc.com Run by the Primark Investment Research Center; publishes a list of companies announcing positive earnings surprises.

www.quote.com/info/vickers.html Run by Vickers Insider Trade Report Service; tattles on insider trading.

www.russell.com The Frank Russell Co., which compiles the Russell 2000 index, publishes asset allocation and market performance information on this Web site.

www.sec.gov/edgarhp.htm Edgar (Electronic Data

Gathering, Analysis, and Retrieval).

www.stockinfo.standardpoor.com Standard & Poor's Reports-on-Demand service.

www.wsbi.com/spweb Run by Standard & Poor's Investor Center; offers tons of stock info you can download.

www.zacks.com Run by Zacks Investment Research; will conduct stock searches for $150 a year.

REGIONAL BROKERS

REGIONAL FIRMS CAN BE a good source for ideas. Here are the names of some that were highly ranked in *The Wall Street Journal*'s February 1997 survey of investment houses' stock-picking prowess.

Raymond James and Associates, St. Petersburg, FL: (813) 573-3800

A.G. Edwards & Sons, St. Louis, MO: (314) 955-3000

Everen Securities, Chicago, IL: (312) 574-6000

Edward D. Jones, St. Louis, MO: (314) 515-2000

Piper Jaffray, Minneapolis, MN: (612) 342-6000

Wheat First, Richmond, VA: (804) 649-2311

PERMISSIONS CREDITS

GRATEFUL ACKNOWLEDGMENT IS MADE to the following publishers and organizations for permission to reproduce copyrighted material. This page constitutes a continuation of the copyright page.

For the data for the graphics in the Introduction, *"10-Year Rolling Period Returns"* and *"20-Year Rolling Period Returns,"* and, in Chapter 1, *"Returns for Large and Small Caps"*: © Computed using data from *Stocks, Bonds, Bills & Inflation 1996 Yearbook*™, Ibbotson Associates, Chicago (annually updates work by Roger G. Ibbotson and Rex Sinquefield). Used with permission. All rights reserved.

For the graphic reprinted in Chapter 1, *"Typical Recommended Asset Allocations"*: From *A Random Walk Down Wall Street* by Burton G. Malkiel. Copyright © 1990, 1985, 1981, 1975, 1973 by W.W. Norton & Company, Inc. Reprinted by permission of W.W. Norton & Company, Inc.

APPENDIX

TICKER	COMPANY NAME	ADDRESS
AIR	AAR Corp	1111 Nicholas Blvd., Elk Grove Villg., IL 60007
ABM	ABM Indust. Inc	50 Fremont St., San Francisco, CA 94105
AMI	Acme Metals Inc	13500 S. Perry Ave., Riverdale, IL 60627
ACXM	Acxiom Corp	301 Industrial Blvd., Conway, AR 72033
ADAC	ADAC Labs	540 Alder Dr., Milpitas, CA 95035
ATIS	Advanced Tissue Sciences Inc	10933 N. Torrey Pines Rd., La Jolla, CA 92037
AD	ADVO Inc	1 Univac La., P.O. Box 755, Windsor, CT 06095
AG	AGCO Corp	4830 River Green Pkwy., Duluth, GA 30136
AWT	Air & Water Tech	3040 US Hwy. 22 W., Branchburg, NJ 08876
AEIC	Air Express Intl CP	120 Tokeneke Rd., Darien, CT 06820
AB	Alex Brown Inc	1 South St., Baltimore, MD 21202
ALN	Allen Group	25101 Chagrin Blvd., Beachwood, OH 44122
ALLP	Alliance Pharm. CP	3040 Science Pk. Rd., San Diego, CA 92121
ATK	Alliant Techsystems Inc	600 Second St. NE, Hopkins, MN 55343
GRP	Allied Group Inc	701 Fifth Ave., Des Moines, IA 50391
ALW	Allwaste Inc	5151 San Felipe, Houston, TX 77056
ALO	Alpharma Inc	1 Executive Dr., Fort Lee, NJ 07024
AIZ	Amcast Indl Corp	7887 Wash. Village Dr., Dayton, OH 45459
ACOL	AMCOL Intl Corp	1500 West Shure Dr., Arlington Hts., IL 60004
ABIG	Amer. Bankers Insur	11222 Quail Roost Dr., Miami, FL 33157
AFWY	Amer. Freightways	2200 Forward Dr., Harrison, AR 72601
AMSY	Amer. Mgmt. Sys.	4050 Legato Rd., Fairfax, VA 22033
EMT	Amer. Medical Response	2821 South Parker Rd., Aurora, CO 80014
AMMB	Amresco Inc	700 N. Pearl St., Dallas, TX 75201
AMTC	Amtech Corp	17304 Preston Rd., Bldg E100, Dallas, TX 75252
AGL	Angelica Corp	424 S. Woods Mill Rd., Chesterfield, MO 63017

COMPANIES THAT WERE members of the S&P 600
SmallCap Index as of 2/10/97

PHONE	WEB ADDRESS AS OF 2/10/97	INDUSTRY SUBGROUP
847-439-3939		Aerospace/Defense-Equip
415-597-4500	www.abm.com	Building-Maint/Service
708-849-2500		Steel-Producers
501-336-1000	www.acxiom.com	Data Processing/Mgmt
408-321-9100	www.adaclabs.com	Medical Imaging Systems
619-450-5730		Medical-Biomed/Gene
860-285-6100		Direct Mktg
770-813-9200		Machinery-Farm
908-685-4600		Environ Consulting/Eng
203-655-7900	www.aeilogis.com	Transport-Air Freight
410-727-1700	www.alexbrown.com	Finance-Invest Bnkr/Brkr
216-765-5800	www.allengroup.com	Telecomm Equip
619-558-4300	www.allp.com	Medical-Biomed/Gene
612-931-6000	www.atk.com	Firearms/Ammunition
515-280-4211	www.cfonews.com/algr	Property/Casualty Insur
713-623-8777	www.allwaste.com	Hazardous Waste Dispsl
201-947-7774	www.alpharma.com	Medical-Generic Drugs
937-291-7000	www.amcast.com	Metal Proc/Fabrica
847-394-8730	www.amcol.com	Metal-Diversified
305-253-2244	www.abig.com	Multi-line Insurance
501-741-9000		Transport-Truck
703-267-8000	www.amsinc.com	Computer Services
303-614-8500		Commercial Services
214-953-7700	www.amresco.com	Finance-Other Services
972-733-6600		Computers-Intgrtd Syst
314-854-3800		Linen Supply/Rel Items

TICKER	COMPANY NAME	ADDRESS
AXE	Anixter Intl Inc	2 N. Riverside Plz., Chicago, IL 60606
APOG	Apogee Enterprises	7900 Xerxes Ave. S., Minneapolis, MN 55431
APPB	Applebees Intl Inc	4551 W. 107th St., Ste. 100, Overland Park, KS 66207
ATR	AptarGroup Inc	475 W. Terra Cotta Ave., Crystal Lake, IL 60014
WTR	Aquarion Co	835 Main St., Bridgeport, CT 06604
ARBR	Arbor Drugs Inc	3331 W. Big Beaver, Troy, MI 48084
ACAT	Arctic Cat Inc	600 Brooks Ave. S., Thief River Falls, MN 56701
ABFS	Arkansas Best Corp	3801 Old Greenwood Rd., Fort Smith, AR 72903
ASHW	Ashworth Inc	2791 Loker Ave. West, Carlsbad, CA 92008
ASPT	Aspect Telecomm.	1730 Fox Dr., San Jose, CA 95131
ASTE	Astec Industries Inc	4101 Jerome Ave., Chattanooga, TN 37407
ASFC	Astoria Financial	1 Astoria Fed'l Plz., Lake Success, NY 11042
ATO	Atmos Energy Corp	5430 LBJ Freeway, Ste. 160, Dallas, TX 75240
ABPCA	Au Bon Pain Co Inc	19 Fid Kennedy Ave., Boston, MA 02210
ASPX	Auspex Sys. Inc	5200 Grt. Amer. Pkwy., Santa Clara, CA 95054
ASM	Authentic Fitness	6040 Bandini Blvd., Commerce, CA 90040
AZR	Aztar Corp	2390 E. Camelback Rd., Phoenix, AZ 85016
JBAK	Baker (J.) Inc	555 Turnpike St., Canton, MA 02021
BEZ	Baldor Electric	5711 RS Boreham Jr St., Fort Smith, AR 72908
BMP	Ballard Med. Prod.	12050 Lone Peak Pkwy., Draper, UT 84020
BTC	BancTec Inc	4435 Spring Valley Rd., Dallas, TX 75244
BGR	Bangor Hydro-Electr	33 State St., Bangor, ME 04401
BNYN	Banyan Sys. Inc	120 Flanders Rd., Westboro, MA 01581
BRR	Barrett Resources	1515 Arapahoe St.,Tower 3, Denver, CO 80202
BSET	Bassett Furniture Inds	Main St., Bassett, VA 24055
BBN	BBN Corp	150 Cambridge Pk. Dr., Cambridge, MA 02140
BEAV	BE Aerospace Inc	1400 Corp. Cntr. Way, Wellington, FL 33414
BI	Bell Industries Inc	11812 San Vicente Blvd., Los Angeles, CA 90049
BSPT	Bell Sports Corp	15170 N. Hayden, Ste. 1, Scottsdale, AZ 85260
BHE	Benchmark Elctrncs	3000 Technology Dr., Angleton, TX 77515
BNTN	Benton Oil &Gas Co	1145 Eugenia Pl., Carpinteria, CA93013
BERT	Bertucci's, Inc	14 Audubon Rd., Wakefield, MA 01880
BIR	Birmingham Steel	1000 Urban Cntr. Pkwy, Birmingham, AL 35242
BSYS	BISYS Group Inc	150 Clove Rd., Little Falls, NJ 07424
BMC	BMC Inds Inc-Minn	2 Appletree Sq., Minneapolis, MN 55425

PHONE	WEB ADDRESS AS OF 2/10/97	INDUSTRY SUBGROUP
312-902-1515	www.anixter.com	Wire/Cable Products
612-835-1874		Glass Products
913-967-4000	www.applebees.com	Retail-Restaurants
815-477-0424		Containers-Paper/Plastic
203-335-2333		Water
810-643-9420	www.arbordrugs.com	Retail-Drug Store
218-681-8558		Recreational Vehicles
501-785-6000	www.abfs.com	Transport-Truck
619-438-6610	www.golfman.com	Apparel Manufacturers
408-325-2200	www.aspect.com	Telecomm Equip
423-867-4210		Machine-Constr/Mining
516-327-3000		S&L/Thrifts-Eastern US
972-934-9227	www.atmosenergy.com	Gas-Distribution
617-423-2100	www.boston.com/aubonpain	Retail-Restaurants
408-986-2000	www.auspex.com	Networking Products
213-726-1262		Textile-Products
602-381-4100		Casino Hotels
617-828-9300		Retail-Apparel/Shoe
501-646-4711	www.industry.net/baldor	Machinery-Electrical
801-572-6800	www.bmed.com	Medical Products
972-450-7700	www.banc-tec.com	Optical Recognition Soft
207-945-5621		Electric-Integrated
508-898-1000	www.banyan.com	Network Software
303-572-3900		Oil Comp-Explor/Prodtn
540-629-6000	www.bassettfurniture.com	Home Furnishings-Orig
617-873-2000	www.bbn.com	Networking Products
561-791-5000	www.beav.com	Aerospace/Defense-Equip
310-826-2355	www.bellind.com	Electronic Parts Distrib
602-951-0033	www.bellsports.com	Leisure/Rec Products
409-849-6550		Electronic Compo-Misc
805-566-5600	www.bentonoil.com	Oil Comp-Explor/Prodtn
617-246-6700		Retail-Restaurants
205-970-1200		Steel-Producers
201-812-8600	www.bisys.com	Computer Services
612-851-6000		Electronic Compo-Misc

TICKER	COMPANY NAME	ADDRESS
BMCW	BMC West Corp	1475 Tyrell La., Boise, ID 83706
BBA	Bombay Comp. (The)	550 Bailey Ave., Fort Worth, TX 76107
BAMM	Books-A-Million Inc	402 Industrial La., Birmingham, AL 35211
BOOL	Boole & Babbage	3131 Zanker Rd., San Jose, CA 95134
BNE	Bowne & Co Inc	345 Hudson St., New York, NY 10014
BOXXB	Box Energy Corp	8201 Preston Rd., Dallas, TX 75225
BDT	Breed Technologies	5300 Old Tampa Hwy., Lakeland, FL 33811
BBTK	Broadband Technologies Inc	4024 Stirrup Creek Dr., P.O. Box 13737, Durham, NC 27709
BROD	Broderbund Software	500 Redwood Blvd.,Novato, CA 94948
BG	Brown Group Inc	8300 Maryland Ave., St. Louis, MO 63105
BBR	Butler Mfg Co	31st SW Trafficway, Kansas City, MO 64108
BWF	BW/IP Inc	200 Oceangate Blvd., Long Beach, CA 90802
CCBL	C-COR Electronics	60 Decibel Rd., State College, PA 16801
COG	Cabot Oil & Gas	15375 Memorial Dr., Houston, TX 77079
CGNE	Calgene Inc	1920 Fifth St., Davis, CA 95616
CMIC	California Microwave	555 Twin Dolphin Dr., Redwood City, CA 94065
CBM	Cambrex Corp	1 Meadowlands Plz., E. Rutherford, NJ 07073
CAM	Camco Intl Inc	7030 Ardmore, Houston, TX 77054
KRE	Capital RE Corp	1325 Ave. of the Americas, New York, NY 10019
CSAR	Caraustar Ind. Inc	3100 Washington St., Austell, GA 30001
CKE	Carmike Cinemas Inc	1301 First Ave., Columbus, GA 31901
CRP	Carson Pirie Scott	331 W. Wisconsin Ave., Milwaukee, WI 53203
CGC	Cascade Nat.Gas Corp	222 Fairview Ave. N., Seattle, WA 98109
CASY	Casey's Gen'l Stores	1 Convenience Blvd., Ankeny, IA 50021
PWN	Cash America Investments Inc	1600 W. 7th St., Fort Worth, TX 76102
CMAG	Casino Magic Corp	711 Casino Magic Dr., Bay St. Louis, MS 39520
CAS	Castle (A.M.) & Co	3400 N. Wolf Rd., Franklin Park, IL 60131
POS	Catalina Mktg. Corp	11300 Ninth St. N., St. Petersburg, FL 33716
CACOA	Cato Corp	8100 Denmark Rd., Charlotte, NC 28273
CCB	CCB Financial Corp	111 Corcoran St., Durham, NC 27702
CDI	CDI Corp	1717 Arch St., Philadelphia, PA 19103
CPRO	CellPro Inc	22215 26th Ave. SE, Bothell, WA 98021
CGRM	Centigram Comms.	91 E. Tasman Dr., San Jose, CA 95134

PHONE	WEB ADDRESS AS OF 2/10/97	INDUSTRY SUBGROUP
208-331-4410		Bldg Products-Ret/Whsle
817-347-8200	www.bombayco.com	Retail-Home Furnishings
205-942-3737		Retail-Bookstore
408-526-3000	www.boole.com	Computer Software
212-924-5500	www.bowne.com	Printing-Commercial
214-890-8000		Oil Comp-Explor/Prodtn
813-284-6000	www.breedtech.com	Auto/Trk Prts/Equip-Orig
919-544-0015	www.bbt.com	Telecomm Equip
415-382-4400	www.broderbund.com	Computer Software
314-854-4000	www.browngroup.com	Retail-Apparel/Shoe
816-968-3000	www.butlermfg.com	Bldg/Const. Prod-Misc
310-435-3700	www.bwip.com	Instruments-Controls
814-238-2461	www.c-cor.com	Electronic Compo-Misc
713-589-4600	www.cabotog.com	Oil/Gas Drilling
916-753-6313	www.calgene.com	Agricultural Biotech
415-596-9000	www.calmike.com	Telecomm Equip
201-804-3000		Chemicals-Diversified
713-747-4000		Oil Field Mach/Equip
212-974-0100		Financial Guarantee Ins
770-948-3101		Paper/Related Products
706-576-3400		Theaters
414-347-4141	www.carsons.com	Retail-Major Dept Store
206-624-3900		Gas-Distribution
515-965-6100	www.caseys.com	Retail-Convenience Store
817-335-1100		Retail-Pawn Shops
601-467-9257	www.casinomagic.com	Gambling (Non-Hotel)
847-455-7111		Metal Products-Distrib
813-579-5000	www.catalinamktg.com	Direct Mktg
704-554-8510		Retail-Apparel/Shoe
919-683-7777		Commer Banks-So US
215-569-2200		Engineer/R&D Services
206-485-7644	www.cellpro.com	Medical-Biomed/Gene
408-944-0250	www.centigram.com	Telecomm Equip

TICKER	COMPANY NAME	ADDRESS
CNH	Central Hudson Gas & Electric	284 South Ave., Poughkeepsie, NY 12601
CV	Central Vermont Public Service	77 Grove St., Rutland, VT 05701
CBC	Centura Banks Inc	134 N. Church St., Rocky Mount, NC 27804
CEPH	Cephalon Inc	145 Brandywine Pkwy., W. Chester, PA 19380
CERN	Cerner Corp	2800 Rockcreek Pkwy., Kansas City, MO 64117
CHB	Champion Enterprises Inc	2701 University Dr., Ste. 320, Auburn Hills, MI 48326
COFI	Charter One Fin Inc	1215 Superior Ave. NE, Cleveland, OH 44114
CAKE	Cheesecake Factory	26950 Agoura Rd., Calabasas Hills, CA 91301
CHE	Chemed Corp	2600 Chemed Cntr., 255 E. 5th St. Cincinnati, OH 45202
CEM	ChemFirst Inc	700 North St., P.O.B.1249, Jackson, MS 39215
CHPS	Chips & Technols. Inc	2950 Zanker Rd., San Jose, CA 95134
CQB	Chiquita Brands Intl	250 E. Fifth St., Cincinnati, OH 45202
CER	Cilcorp Inc	300 Hamilton Blvd., Ste. 300, Peoria, IL 61602
CPX	Cineplex Odeon Corp	1303 Yonge St., Toronto, Ont. M4T 2Y9, Can.
CCON	Circon Corp	6500 Hollister Ave., Santa Barbara, CA 93117
CKR	CKE Restaurant Inc	1200 N. Harbor Blvd., Anaheim, CA 92801
CLC	Clarcor Inc	2323 Sixth St., P.O.B. 7007, Rockford, IL 61125
CMT	CMAC Invstmnt	1601 Market St., 12 Fl., Philadelphia, PA 19103
CSA	Coast Savings Financial Inc	1000 Wilshire Blvd., Los Angeles, CA 90017
COKE	Coca-Cola Bottling	1900 Rexford Rd., Charlotte, NC 28211
CDE	Coeur d'Alene Mines	505 Front Ave., Coeur d'Alene, ID 83814
CGNX	Cognex Corp	1 Vision Dr., Natick, MA 01760
COHR	Coherent Inc	5100 Patrick Henry Dr., Santa Clara, CA 95054
CGEN	Collagen Corp	2500 Farber Pl., Palo Alto, CA 94303
COFD	Collective Bancorp Inc	158 Philadelphia Ave. Egg Harbor City, NJ 08215
COMR	Comair Holdings Inc	P. O. Box 75021, Cincinnati Intl. Airport, Cincinnati, OH 45275
CFB	Commercial Federal Corp	2120 S. 72nd St., Omaha, NE 68101

PHONE	WEB ADDRESS AS OF 2/10/97	INDUSTRY SUBGROUP
914-452-2000	www.cenhud.com	Electric-Integrated
802-773-2711	www.cvps.com	Electric-Integrated
919-977-4400	www.centura.com	Commer Banks-So US
610-344-0200		Medical-Drugs
816-221-1024	www.cerner.com	Medical Information Sys
810-340-9090		Bldg-Mobil Hm/Mfd Hous
216-566-5300	www.charterone.com	S&L/Thrifts-Central US
818-880-9323		Retail-Restaurants
513-762-6900		Chemicals-Specialty
601-948-7550	www.chemfirst.com	Chemicals-Diversified
408-434-0600	www.chips.com	Elctrnc Compo-Semicon
513-784-8000	www.chiquita.com	Food-Misc/Diversified
309-675-8810	www.cilco.com	Electric-Integrated
416-323-6600		Theaters
805-685-5100	www.circoncorp.com	Medical Instruments
714-774-5796	www.ckr.com	Retail-Restaurants
815-962-8867	www.clarcor.com	Diversified Operations
215-564-6600	www.cmacmi.com	Financial Guarantee Ins
213-362-2000	www.coastfederal.com	S&L/Thrifts-Western US
704-551-4400	www.cocacola.com	Beverages-Non-alcoholic
208-667-3511	www.coeur.com/coeur/	Gold Mining
508-650-3000	www.cognex.com	Computers -Intgrtd Syst
408-764-4000	www.cohr.com	Lasers-Syst/Components
415-856-0200	www.collagen.com	Medical Instruments
609-625-1110		S&L/Thrifts-Eastern US
606-767-2550	www.fly-comair.com	Airlines
402-554-9200	www.comfedbank.com	S&L/Thrifts-Central US

TICKER	COMPANY NAME	ADDRESS
CMC	Commercial Metals Co	7800 Stemmons Freeway, P.O.B. 1046, Dallas, TX 75221
CELS	Commnet Cellular Inc	8350 E. Crescent Pkwy., Ste. 400, Englewood, CO 80111
CALC	Commonwealth Aluminum Corp	1200 Meidinger Tower, Louisville, KY 40202
CES	Commonwealth Energy Sys.	1 Main Street, Cambridge, MA 02142
CPDN	Compdent Corp	8800 Roswell Rd., Ste. 244, Atlanta, GA 30350
CLIX	Compression Labs	350 E. Plumeria Dr., San Jose, CA 95134
CPU	CompUSA Inc	14951 N. Dallas Pkwy., Dallas, TX 75240
CMVT	Comverse Technology	170 Crossways Pk. Dr., Woodbury, NY 11797
COE	Cone Mills Corp	3101 N. Elm St., Greensboro, NC 27415
CNE	Conn. Energy Corp	855 Main St., Bridgeport, CT 06604
CONW	Consumers Water Co	Three Canal Plz., Portland, ME 04101
CON	Continental Homes Holding	7001 N. Scottsdale Rd., Ste. 2050, Scottsdale, AZ 85253
CDAT	Control Data Systems Inc	4201 N. Lexington Ave., Arden Hills, MN 55126
CORR	COR Therapeutics Inc	256 E. Grand Ave., S. San Francisco, CA 94080
CRI	Core Industries Inc	500 N. Woodward Ave., P. O. Box 2000, Bloomfield Hills, MI 48304
CXC	Corrections Corp of America	102 Woodmont Blvd., Nashville, TN 37205
CVTY	Coventry Corp	53 Century Blvd., Ste. 250, Nashville, TN 37214
ATX/A	Cross (A.T.) Company	1 Albion Rd., Lincoln, RI 02865
XTO	Cross Timbers Oil Co	810 Houston St., Ste. 2000, Ft. Worth, TX 76102
CFBI	Cullen/Frost Bankers	100 W. Houston St., San Antonio, TX 78205
CSTM	Custom Chrome Inc	16100 Jacqueline Ct., Morgan Hill, CA 95037
CYGN	Cygnus Inc	400 Penobscot Dr., Redwood City, CA 94063
CYRX	Cyrix Corp	2703 N. Centrl. Expwy., Richardson, TX 75080
CYRK	Cyrk Intl Inc	3 Pond Rd., Gloucester, MA 01930
DS	Dallas Semiconductor	4401 Beltwood Pkwy. S., Dallas, TX 75244
DMRK	Damark Intl Inc	7101 Winnetka Ave. N. Minneapolis, MN 55428
DM	Dames & Moore Inc	911 Wilshire Blvd., Los Angeles, CA 90017

PHONE	WEB ADDRESS AS OF 2/10/97	INDUSTRY SUBGROUP
214-689-4300		Metal Processors/Fabrica
303-694-3234	www.cels.com	Cellular Telecomm
502-589-8100		Metal-Aluminum
617-225-4000	www.comenergy.com	Electric-Integrated
770-998-8936		Life/Health Insurance
408-435-3000	www.clix.com	Telecomm Equip
972-982-4000	www.compusa.com	Retail-Consumer Electron
516-677-7200		Computers-Intgrtd Syst
910-379-6220		Textile-Products
203-579-1732	www.connenergy.com	Gas-Distribution
207-773-6438	www.consumerswater.com	Water
602-483-0006		Bldg-Residential/Commer
612-482-2401	www.cdc.com	Computer Services
415-244-6800		Medical-Biomed/Gene
810-642-3400	www.core-ind.com	Diversified Operations
615-292-3100		Protection-Safety
615-391-2440		Medical-HMO
401-333-1200		Office Supplies/Forms
817-870-2800		Oil Comp-Explor/Prodtn
210-220-4011	www.frostbank.com	Com Banks-Central US
408-778-0500		Leisure/Rec Products
415-369-4300		Drug Delivery Systems
972-968-8387	www.cyrix.com	Elctrnc Compo-Semicon
508-283-5800		Apparel Manufacturers
972-371-4000	www.dalsemi.com	Elctrnc Compo-Semicon
612-531-0066		Retail-Mail Order
213-683-1560		Pollution Control

TICKER	COMPANY NAME	ADDRESS
DAN	Daniel Industries	9753 Pine Lake Dr., Houston, TX 77055
SEEDB	Dekalb Genetics Corp	3100 Sycamore Rd., Dekalb, IL 60115
DLW	Delta Woodside Industries Inc	233 N. Main St., Hammond Sq., Ste. 200, Greenville, SC 29601
DEP	Deposit Guaranty Corp	210 E. Capitol St., P.O.B. 730 Jackson, MS 39205
DESI	Designs Inc	66 B St., Needham, MA 02194
DVN	Devon Energy Corp	20 N. Broadway, Oklahoma City, OK 73102
DV	Devry Inc	1 Tower La., Oakbrook Terrace, IL 60181
DGII	Digi Intl Inc	11001 Bren Rd. E., Minnetonka, MN 55343
DMIC	Digital Microwave	170 Rose Orchard Way, San Jose, CA 95134
DMN	Dimon Inc	512 Bridge St., P.O.B. 681, Danville, VA 24543
DNEX	Dionex Corp	1228 Titan Way, Sunnyvale, CA 94086
DAP	Discount Auto Parts	4900 Frontage Rd. S., Lakeland, FL 33815
DXYN	Dixie Yarns Inc	1100 S. Watkins St., Chattanooga, TN 37404
DSL	Downey Finan. Corp	3501 Jamboree Rd., Newport Beach, CA 92660
DRV	Dravo Corp	3600 One Oliver Plz., Pittsburgh, PA 15222
DBRN	Dress Barn Inc	30 Dunnigan Dr., Suffern, NY 10901
DYT	Dynatech Corp	3 New England Exec. Pk., Burlington, MA 01803
EAGL	Eagle Hrdw. & Grdn.	981 Powell Ave. SW, Renton, WA 98055
EGR	Earthgrains Co	8400 Maryland Ave., St. Louis, MO 63105
EUA	Eastern Utilities Assoc	1 Liberty Sq., Boston, MA 02109
EV	Eaton Vance Corp	24 Federal St., Boston, MA 02110
EGN	Energen Corp	2101 Sixth Ave. N. Birmimgham, AL 35203
EFS	Enhance Finl Svcs Gp.	335 Madison Ave., New York, NY 10017
ENVY	Envoy Corporation	2 Lakeview Pl., 15 Century Blvd., Ste. 600 Nashville, TN 37214
ENZ	Enzo Biochem Inc	60 Executive Blvd., Farmingdale, NY 11735
ETEC	Etec Systems Inc	26460 Corporate Ave., Hayward, CA 94545
ETH	Ethan Allen Interiors	Ethan Allen Dr., Danbury, CT 06811
EXPD	Expeditors Internatl. of Washington Inc	999 Third Ave., Ste. 2500, Seattle, WA 98104
ESRX	Express Scripts Inc	14000 Riverport Dr., Maryland Heights, MO 63043
FCA/A	Fabri-Centers of Amer	5555 Darrow Rd., Hudson, OH 44236
FIC	Fair Isaac & Company	120 N. Redwood Dr., San Rafael, CA 94903
FJC	Fedders Corp	505 Martinsville Rd., Liberty Corner, NJ 07938

PHONE	WEB ADDRESS AS OF 2/10/97	INDUSTRY SUBGROUP
713-467-6000	www.danielind.com	Oil Field Mach/Equip
815-758-3461	www.dekalb.com	Agricultural Operations
864-232-8301		Textile-Apparel
601-354-8497	www.dgb.com	Commer Banks-So US
617-444-7222		Retail-Apparel/Shoe
405-235-3611		Oil Comp-Explor/Prodtn
630-571-7700	www.devry.com	Human Resources
612-912-3444	www.dgii.com	Communication Software
408-943-0777	www.dmcwave.com	Fiber Optics
804-792-7511		Tobacco
408-737-0700	www.dionex.com	Instruments-Scientific
941-687-9226		Auto Parts-Retail/Whsle
423-698-2501		Textile-Products
714-854-0300	www.downeysavings.com	S&L/Thrifts-Western US
412-566-3000		BldgProd-Cement/Aggreg
914-369-4500		Retail-Apparel/Shoe
617-272-6100	www.dytc.com	Electronic Measur Instr
206-227-5740		Bldg Products-Ret/Whsle
314-259-7000		Food-Baking
617-357-9590	www.eua.com	Electric-Integrated
617-482-8260		Invest Mgmnt/Advis Serv
205 326-2700		Gas-Distribution
212-983-3100		Financial Guarantee Ins
615-885-3700	www.neic.com	Computer Services
516-755-5500		Medical-Biomed/Gene
510-783-9210	www.etec.com	Elctrnc Compo-Semicon
203-743-8000	www.ethanallen.com	Retail-Home Furnishings
206-674-3400	www.expd2.com	Transport-Air Freight
314-770-1666	www.expressscripts.com	Medical-HMO
216-656-2600		Retail-Fabric Store
415-472-2211	www.fairissac.com	Computer Services
908-604-8686		Air Conditioning

TICKER	COMPANY NAME	ADDRESS
FBD	Fibreboard Corp	2200 Ross Ave., Ste. 3600, Dallas, TX 75201
FNF	Fidelity Natl Finl Inc	17911 Von Karman Ave., Irvine, CA 92614
FLD	Fieldcrest Cannon	1 Lake Circle Dr., Kannapolis, NC 28081
FIGIA	Figgie Intl	4420 Sherwin Rd., Willoughby, OH 44094
BSMT	Filene's Basmnt Corp	40 Walnut St., Wellesley, MA 02181
FILE	Filenet Corp	3565 Harbor Blvd., Costa Mesa, CA 92626
FAF	First American Finl	114 E. Fifth St., Santa Ana, CA 92701
FCLR	First Commercial Corp	400 W. Capital Ave., P.O.B. 1471, Little Rock, AR 72201
FFHC	First Fin Corp-Wisc	1305 Main St., Stevens Point, WI 54481
FMBC	First Mich. Bank Corp	1 Financial Plz., Holland, MI 49423
FBP	Firstbank Puerto Rico	1519 Ponce de Leon Ave., Stop 23, Santurce, PR 00908
FMER	FirstMerit Corp	3 Cascade Plz., 7th Fl., Akron, OH 44308
FSH	Fisher Scientific Intl	Liberty La., Hampton, NH 03842
FLOW	Flow Intl Corp	23500-64th Ave. S., Kent, WA 98032
FLK	Fluke Corp	6920 Seaway Blvd., Everett, WA 98203
FM	Foodmaker Inc	9330 Balboa Ave., San Diego, CA 92123
FNQ	Franklin Quest Co	2200 W. Pkwy. Blvd., Salt Lake City, UT 84119
FMT	Fremont General Corp	2020 Santa Monica Blvd., Ste. 600, Santa Monica, CA 90404
FRTZ	Fritz Companies Inc	706 Mission St., San Francisco, CA 94103
FTR	Frontier Insur Group	195 Lake Louise Marie Rd., Rock Hill, NY 12775
FFEX	Frozen Food Express Industries	1145 Empire Central Pl., Dallas, TX 75247
GKSRA	G & K Svcs. Inc	5995 Opus Pkwy., Minnetonka, MN 55343
GNL	Galey & Lord Inc	980 Ave. of the Americas, New York, NY 10018
AJG	Gallagher (Arthur J.)	2 Pierce Pl., Itasca, IL 60143
GAL	Galoob Toys Inc	500 Forbes Blvd., S. San Francisco, CA 94080
GCX	GC Companies Inc	27 Boylston St., Chestnut Hill, MA 02167
GHV	Genesis Health Ventures	148 West State St., Kennett Square, PA 19348
GNTX	Gentex Corp	600 N. Centennial St., Zeeland, MI 49464
GON	Geon Company	1 Geon Cntr., Avon Lake, OH 44012
GOTK	Geotek Comms. Inc	20 Craig Rd., Montvale, NJ 07645
GRB	Gerber Scientific Inc	83 Gerber Rd. West, South Windsor, CT 06074

PHONE	WEB ADDRESS AS OF 2/10/97	INDUSTRY SUBGROUP
214-954-9500		Bldg/Construct Prod
714-622-5000	www.fnf.com	Property/Casualty Ins
704-939-2000		Textile-Home Furnishings
216-953-2700		Diversified Operations
617-348-7000	www.interstep.com/basement	Retail-Discount
714-966-3400	www.filenet.com	Computer-Peripher Equip
714-558-3211	www.firstam.com	Property/Casualty Ins
501-371-7000	www.firstcommercial.com	Commer Banks-So. US
715-341-0400		S&L/Thrifts-Central US
616-355-9200	www.fmb.com	Commer Banks-Cntrl US
787-729-8200		Commer Banks-So US
330-996-6300		Commer Banks-Cntrl US
603-926-5911	www.fisher1.com	Instruments-Scientific
206-850-3500	www.flowcorp.com	Mach Tools/Rel Products
206-347-6100	www.fluke.com	Electronic Measur Instr
619-571-2121	www.foodmaker.com	Retail-Restaurants
801-975-1776		Computer Services
310-315-5500		Multi-line Insurance
415-904-8360	www.fritz.com	Transport-Services
914-796-2100		Property/Casualty Ins
214-630-8090	www.ffeinc.com	Transport-Truck
612-912-5500	www.gkcares.com	Linen Supply/Rel Items
212-465-3000		Textile-Products
630-773-3800	www.ajg.com	Insurance Brokers
415-952-1678	www.galoob.com	Toys
617-278-5600		Theaters
610-444-6350		Med-Outptnt/Home Med
616-772-1800	www.gentex.com	Auto/Trk Prts/Equip-Orig
216-930-1000	www.geon.com	Chemicals-Plastics
201-930-9305	www.geotek.com	Telecomm Services
860-644-1551	www.gerberscientific.com	Computer Services

TICKER	COMPANY NAME	ADDRESS
GGO	Getchell Gold Corp	5460 S. Quebec St., Englewood, CO 80111
GLG	Glamis Gold Ltd	3324 Four Bentall Centre 1055 Dunsmuir St., Vancouver, B.C., Canada V7X 1L3
GIX	Global Industrial Technologies Inc	2121 San Jacinto St., Ste. 2500, Dallas, TX 75201
GDMK	Goodmark Foods	6131 Falls of Neuse Rd., Raleigh, NC 27609
GOT	Gottschalks Inc	7 River Park Place. East, Fresno, CA 93720
GC	GranCare Inc	1 Ravinia Dr., Ste. 1500, Atlanta, GA 30346
GND	Grand Casinos Inc	130 Cheshire La., Minnetoka, MN 55305
GMP	Green Mtn. Pwr Corp	P.O.B. 85025, South Burlington, VT 05402
GFII	Greenfield Inds Inc	2743 Perimeter Pkwy., Augusta, GA 30909
GFF	Griffon Corp	100 Jericho Quadrangle, Jericho, NY 11753
GFD	Guilford Mills Inc	4925 W. Market St., Greensboro, NC 27407
HGGR	Haggar Corp	6113 Lemmon Ave., Dallas, TX 75209
HNH	Handy & Harman	250 Park Ave. New York, NY 10177
HRMN	Harmon Industries Inc	1300 Jefferson Ct., Blue Springs, MO 64015
HMX	Hartmarx Corp	101 N. Wacker Dr., Chicago, IL 60606
HAUS	Hauser Inc	5555 Airport Blvd., Boulder, CO 80301
HTLD	Heartland Express Inc	2777 Heartland Dr., Coralville, IA 52241
HECHA	Hechinger Co	1801 McCormick Dr., Largo, MD 20774
HL	Hecla Mining Co	6500 Mineral Dr., Coeur D'Alene, ID 83814
JKHY	Henry (Jack) & Assoc	663 W. Hwy. 60, Monett, MO 65708
HRH	Hilb Rogal&Hamilton	4235 Innslake Dr., Glen Allen, VA 23060
HPRK	Hollywood Park Inc	1050 S. Prairie Ave., Inglewood, CA 90301
HSE	HS Resources Inc	1 Maritime Plz., San Francisco, CA 94111
HUF	Huffy Corp	225 Byers Rd., Miamisburg, OH 45342
HUG	Hughes Supply Inc	20 N. Orange Ave., Orlando, FL 32801
HYSW	Hyperion Software	900 Long Ridge Rd., Stamford, CT 06902
IDXX	IDEXX Labs Inc	1 IDEXX Dr., Westbrook, ME 04092
IHOP	IHOP Corp	525 N. Brand Blvd., Glendale, CA 91203
IMR	IMCO Recycling Inc	5215 N. O'Connor Blvd., Irving, TX 75039
IMUL	ImmuLogic Pharm.	610 Lincoln St., Waltham, MA 02154
IMNR	Immune Response	5935 Darwin Ct., Carlsbad, CA 92008
IMD	IMO Industries Inc	1009 Lenox Dr., Lawrenceville, NJ 08648
IO	Input/Output Inc	11104 W. Airport Blvd., Stafford, TX 77477
INSUA	Insituform Technols.	1770 Kirby Pkwy., Ste. 300, Memphis, TN 38138

PHONE	WEB ADDRESS AS OF 2/10/97	INDUSTRY SUBGROUP
303-771-9000		Precious Metals
604-681-3541	www.glamis.com	Precious Metals
214-953-4500		Mach-Constr/Mining
919-790-9940		Food-Meat Products
209-434-8000	www.gotts.com	Retail-Regnl Dept Store
770-393-0199		Medical-Nursing Homes
612-449-9092	www.grandcasinos.com	Gambling (Non-Hotel)
802-864-5731	www.gmpvt.com	Electric-Integrated
706-863-7708	www.gfii.com	Mach Tools/Rel Products
516-938-5544		Diversified Operations
910-316-4000	www.guilfordmills.com	Textile-Products
214-352-8481		Apparel Manufacturers
212-661-2400		Precious Metals
816-229-3345		Electronic Compo-Misc
312-372-6300		Apparel Manufacturers
303-443-4662	www.hauser.com/hauser	Chemicals-Specialty
319-645-2728	www.heartlandexpress.com	Transp-Truck
301-341-1000		Bldg Products-Ret/Whsle
208-769-4100	www.hecla-mining.com	Precious Metals
417-235-6652	www.jackhenry.com	Computers-Intgrtd Sys
804-747-6500	www.hrh.com	Insurance Brokers
310-419-1500	www.racetech.com	Racetracks
415-433-5795	www.hsresources.com	Oil Comp-Explor/Prodtn
513-866-6251		Bicycle Manufacturing
407-841-4755	www.hughessupply.com	Bldg Products-Ret/Whsle
203-703-3000	www.hysoft.com	Data Processing/Mgmt
207-856-0300	www.idex.com	Medical Instruments
818-240-6055		Retail-Restaurants
972-869-6575		Recycling
617-466-6000		Medical-Biomed/Gene
619-431-7080	www.imnr.com	Medical-Drugs
609-896-7600		Instruments-Controls
281-933-3339	www.i-o.com	Oil Field Mach/Equip
901-759-7473		Building/Construct-Misc

TICKER	COMPANY NAME	ADDRESS
III	Insteel Industries	1373 Boggs Dr., Mount Airy, NC 27030
IAAI	Insur. Auto Auctions	1270 W. Northwest Hwy., Palatine, IL 60067
IN	Integon Corp/Del	500 W. Fifth St., Winston-Salem, NC 27152
ICST	Intgrtd. Circuit Sys.	2435 Blvd. of the Genrls., Valley Forge, PA 19482
IHS	Intgrtd. Health Svcs.	10065 Red Run Blvd., Owings Mills, MD 21117
IFSIA	Interface Inc	2859 Paces Ferry Rd., Atlanta, GA 30339
IS	Interim Svcs. Inc	2050 Spectrum Blvd., Ft. Lauderdale, FL 33309
IMG	Intermagnetics General Corp	450 Old Niskayuna Rd., P.O.B. 461, Latham, NY 12110
INMT	Intermet Corp	5445 Corporate Dr., Ste. 200, Troy, MI 48098
IFG	Interra Financial Inc	Dain Bosworth Plz., 60 S. Sixth St., Minneapolis, MN 55402
IBC	Interstate Bakeries	12 E. Armour Blvd., Kansas City, MO 64111
IPW	Interstate Power Co	1000 Main St., Dubuque, IA 52004
INTV	Intervoice Inc	17811 Waterview Pkwy., Dallas, TX 75252
FAM	Intl Fam. Entertainm.	2877 Guardian La., Virginia Beach, VA 23452
IRF	Intl Rectifier Corp	233 Kansas St., El Segundo, CA 90245
IVCR	Invacare Corp	899 Cleveland St., Elyria, OH 44035
ION	IONICS Inc	65 Grove St., Watertown, MA 02172
ITRI	ITRON Inc	2818 N. Sullivan Rd., Spokane, WA 99216
JJSF	J & J Snack Foods	6000 Central Hwy., Pennsauken, NJ 08109
JBM	Jan Bell Marketing	13801 NW 14th St., Sunrise, FL 33323
JII	Johnston Ind-Del	105 Thirteenth St., Columbus, GA 31901
JSBF	JSB Financial Inc	303 Merrick Rd., Lynbrook, NY 11563
WON	JumboSports Inc	4701 W. Hillsborough Ave., Tampa, FL 33614
JUNO	Juno Lighting Inc	2001 S. Mt. Prospect Rd., Des Plaines, IL 60017
JSTN	Justin Industries	2821 W. 7th St., Fort Worth, TX 76107
KNE	K N Energy Inc	370 Van Gordon St., Lakewood, CO 80228
KSWS	K-Swiss Inc	20664 Bahama St., Chatsworth, CA 91311
KTO	K2 Inc	4900 S. Eastern Ave., Los Angeles, CA 90040
KAMN	Kaman Corp	1332 Blue Hills Ave., Bloomfield, CT 06002
KCS	KCS Energy Inc	379 Thornall St., Edison, NJ 08837
KEA	Keane Inc	Ten City Sq., Boston, MA 02129
KWD	Kellwood Co	600 Kellwood Pkwy., Chesterfield, MO 63017
KMET	Kemet Corp	2835 Kemet Way, Simpsonville, SC 29681
KNT	Kent Electronics Corp	7433 Harwin Dr., Houston, TX 77036

PHONE	WEB ADDRESS AS OF 2/10/97	INDUSTRY SUBGROUP
910-786-2141		Wire/Cable Products
847-705-9550	www.sandiego.sisna.com/iaa	Commercial Services
910-770-2000		Property/Casualty Ins
610-630-5300	www.icst.com	Elctrnc Compo-Semicon
410-998-8400	www.ihs-inc.com	Medical-Hospitals
770-437-6800	www.ifsia.com	Textile-Home Furnishings
954-938-7600	www.interim.com	Human Resources
518-782-1122		Superconductor Prod/Sys
810-952-2500		Auto/Trk Prts/Equip-Orig
612-371-7750		Finance-Invest Bnkr/Brkr
816-502-4000	www.irin.com/ibc	Food-Baking
319-582-5421		Electric-Integrated
972-454-8000	www.intervoice.com	Computers-Voice Recogn
757-459-6000	www.famfun.com	Cable TV
310-726-8000	www.irf.com	Electrnc Compo-Semicon
216-329-6000	www.invacare.com	Hospital Beds/Equipment
617-926-2500	www.ionics.com	Water Treatment Syst
509-924-9900	www.itron.com	Electronic Measur Instr
609-665-9533		Food-Misc/Diversified
954-846-2705		Precious Metals/Jewelry
706-641-3140		Textile-Products
516-887-7000		S&L/Thrifts-Eastern US
813-886-9688		Retail-Sporting Goods
847-827-9880		Bldg Prod-Light Fixtures
817-336-5125	www.justinind.com	Diversified Operations
303-989-1740	www.kne.com	Oil Refining/Mktg
818-998-3388	www.kswiss.com	Athletic Footwear
213-724-2800	www.k2sports.com	Leisure/Rec Products
860-243-7100	www.kaman.com	Aerospace/Defense-Equip
908-632-1770		Oil Comp-Explor/Prodtn
617-241-9200	www.keane.com	Data Processing/Mgmt
314-576-3100		Apparel Manufacturers
864-963-6300	www.kemet.com	Capacitors
713-780-7770	www.kentelec.com	Electronic Parts Distrib

TICKER	COMPANY NAME	ADDRESS
KSTN	Keystone Finl Inc	1 Keystone Plz., Harrisburg, PA 17101
KCLC	KinderCare Lrng. Ctrs	2400 Presidents Dr., Montgomery, AL 36116
KEX	Kirby Corp	1775 St. James Pl., Ste. 300, Houston, TX 77056
KMAG	Komag Inc	275 S. Hillview Dr., Milpitas, CA 95035
KRON	Kronos Inc	400 Fifth Ave., Waltham, MA 02154
KUH	Kuhlman Corp	3 Skidaway Village Sq., Savannah, GA 31411
KZ	Kysor Industrial Corp	1 Madison Ave., Cadillac, MI 49601
LZB	LA-Z-Boy Inc	1284 N. Telegraph Rd., Monroe, MI 48162
LSTR	Landstar System Inc	1000 Bridgeport Ave., Shelton, CT 06484
LSCC	Lattice Semiconduct.	5555 NE Moore Ct., Hillsboro, OR 97124
LECH	Lechters Inc	1 Cape May St., Harrison, NJ 07029
LM	Legg Mason Inc	111 S. Calvert St., Baltimore, MD 21202
LFI	Levitz Furniture Inc	6111 Broken Sound Parkway NW, Boca Raton, FL 33487
LBNA	Liberty Bancorp/Okl.	100 N. Broadway, Oklahoma City, OK 73102
LRE	Life Re Corp	969 High Ridge Rd., Stamford, CT 06905
LVC	Lillian Vernon Corp	543 Main St., New Rochelle, NY 10801
LI	Lilly Industries Inc	733 South West St., Indianapolis, IN 46225
LNCR	Lincare Holdings Inc	19337 US 19 N., Ste. 500, Clearwater, FL 34624
LINZ	Lindsay Manuf Co	East Hwy. 91, Lindsay, NE 68644
LIPO	Liposome Co Inc	1 Resrch. Way, Forrestal Ctr., Princeton, NJ 08540
LCA	Living Cntrs of Amer.	15415 Katy Freeway, Houston, TX 77094
LGN	Logicon Inc	3701 Skypark Dr., Torrance, CA 90505
LCE	Lone Star Industries	300 First Stamford Pl., Stamford, CT 06912
LSB	LSB Industries Inc	16 S. Pennsylvania Ave., Oklahoma City, OK 73107
LUB	Luby's Cafeterias Inc	2211 NE Loop 410, San Antonio, TX 78265
LDL	Lydall Inc	1 Colonial Rd., Manchester, CT 06040
MGL	Magellan Health Svcs	3414 Peachtree Rd. NE, Atlanta, GA 30326
MGR	Magna Group Inc	1401 S. Brentwood Blvd., St. Louis, MO 63144
MAIL	Mail Boxes Etc	6060 Cornerstone Ct. W., San Diego, CA 92121
MTW	Manitowoc Co	500 S. 16th St., Manitowoc, WI 54220
MCS	Marcus Corp	250 E. Wisconsin Ave., Milwaukee, WI 53202
MRNR	Mariner Health Grp	125 Eugene O'Neill Dr., New London, CT 06320
MTB	Mark Twain Bancshares Inc	8820 Ladue Rd., St. Louis, MO 63124
MI	Marshall Industries	9320 Telstar Ave., El Monte, CA 91731

PHONE	WEB ADDRESS AS OF 2/10/97	INDUSTRY SUBGROUP
717-233-1555	www.keyfin.com	Commer Banks-Eastrn US
334-277-5090	www.kindercare.com	Commercial Services
713-629-9370		Transport-Marine
408-946-2300	www.komag.com	Computers-Mem Devices
617-890-3232	www.kronos.com	Computers-Intgrtd Syst
912-598-7809		Machinery-Electric Util
616-779-2200	www.prosonline.com/kysor	Auto/Trk Prts/Equip-Orig
313-241-4414	www.lazyboy.com	Home Furnishings-Orig
203-925-2900	www.landstar.com	Transport-Truck
503-681-0118	www.latticesemi.com	Elctrnc Compo-Semicon
201-481-1100	www.lechters.com	Retail-Cutlery/Cookware
410-539-0000	www.leggmason.com	Finance-Invest Bnkr/Brkr
561-994-6006	www.levitz.com	Retail-Home Furnishings
405-231-6000	www.libertybank.com	Commer Banks-Cntrl US
203-321-3000		Life/Health Insurance
914-576-6400		Retail-Mail Order
317-687-6700	www.lillyindustries.com	Chemicals-Specialty
813-530-7700	www.lincare.com	Med-Outptnt/Home Med
402-428-2131		Machinery-Farm
609-452-7060	www.lipo.com	Medical-Biomed/Gene
281-578-4600		Medical-Nursing Homes
310-373-0220	www.logicon.com	Electronics-Military
203-969-8600		BldgProd-Cement/Aggreg
405-235-4546		Diversified Operations
210-654-9000	www.lubys.com	Retail-Restaurants
860-646-1233		Pollution Control
404-841-9200		Medical-Hospitals
314-963-2500	www.magnabank.com	Commer Banks-Cntrl US
619-455-8800	www.mbe.com	Retail-Misc/Diversified
414-684-4410	www.manitowoc.com	Machine-Constr/Mining
414-272-6020		Hotels/Motels
860-701-2000		Medical-Nursing Homes
314-727-1000	www.marktwain.com	Commer Banks-Cntrl US
818-307-6000	www.marshall.com	Elctrnc Compo-Semicon

TICKER	COMPANY NAME	ADDRESS
MSC	Material Sciences Crp	2300 E. Pratt Blvd., Elk Grove Village, IL 60007
MWT	McWhorter Techns.	400 E. Cottage Pl., Carpentersville, IL 60110
MDC	MDC Holdings Inc	3600 S. Yosemite St., Ste. 900, Denver, CO 80237
MEDI	MedImmune Inc	35 W. Watkins Mill Rd., Gaithersburg, MD 20878
MSA	Medusa Corp	3008 Monticello Blvd., Cleveland Hts., OH 44118
MNTR	Mentor Corp	5425 Hollister Ave., Santa Barbara, CA 93111
MRLL	Merrill Corporation	1 Merrill Cir., St., Paul, MN 55108
MESA	Mesa Air Group Inc	3753 Howard Hughes Pkwy., Ste. 200 Las Vegas, NV 89109
MXP	Mesa Inc	1400 Williams Sq. W., 5205 N. O'Connor Blvd., Irving, TX 75039
METHA	Methode Electronics	7444 W. Wilson Ave., Harwood Hts., IL 60656
MIKE	Michaels Stores Inc	8000 Bent Branch Dr., Irving, TX 75063
MICA	MicroAge Inc	2400 S. MicroAge Way, Tempe, AZ 85282
MCHP	Microchip Technlgy	2355 W. Chandler Blvd., Chandler, AZ 85224
MNPI	Microcom Inc	500 River Ridge Dr., Norwood, MA 02062
GRO	Mississippi Chemical	P.O.B. 388, Yazoo City, MS 39194
MOHK	Mohawk Indust. Inc	160 S. Industrial Blvd., Calhoun, GA 30701
MB	Molecular Biosys. Inc	10030 Barnes Canyon Rd., San Diego, CA 92121
MK	Morrison Knudsen	Morrison Knudsen Plz., Boise, ID 83729
MOSI	Mosinee Paper Corp	1244 Kronenwetter Dr., Mosinee, WI 54455
MSCA	MS Carriers Inc	3171 Directors Row, Memphis, TN 38131
MLI	Mueller Indust. Inc	6799 Great Oaks Rd., Memphis, TN 38138
MM	Mutual Risk Mgmt	44 Church St., Hamilton HM 12, Bermuda
MYCO	Mycogen Corp	5501 Oberlin Dr., San Diego, CA 92121
MYE	Myers Indust. Inc	1293 S. Main St., Akron, OH 44301
NAFC	Nash Finch Co	7600 France Ave. S., Ste. 200, Edina, MN 55435
NSH	Nashua Corp	44 Franklin St., Nashua, NH 03060
NAK	Nat. Auto Credit Inc	30000 Aurora Rd., Solon, OH 44139
NLCS	National Computer Systems Inc	11000 Prairie Lakes Dr., Eden Prairie, MN 55344
NDC	National Data Corp	National Data Plz., Atlanta, GA 30329
NATR	Nature's Sunshine Products Inc	75 E. 1700 South, Provo, UT 84606
NAUT	Nautica Enterprises	40 W. 57th St., New York, NY 10019
NBTY	NBTY Inc	90 Orville Dr., Bohemia, NY 11716

PHONE	WEB ADDRESS AS OF 2/10/97	INDUSTRY SUBGROUP
847-439-8270	www.matsci.com	Steel-Specialty
847-428-2657		Chemicals-Specialty
303-773-1100		Building/Construct-Misc
301-417-0770	www.medimmune.com	Medical-Biomed/Gene
216-371-4000		BldgProd-Cement/Aggreg
805-681-6000		Medical Products
612-646-4501	www.merrillcorp.com	Printing-Commercial
702-892-3773	www.mesa-air.com	Airlines
972-444-9001	www.mesainc.com	Oil Comp-Explor/Prodtn
708-867-9600	www.methode.com	Electronic Compo-Misc
972-409-1300	www.michaels.com	Retail-Arts/Crafts
602-804-2000	www.microage.com	Retail-Whsle Companies
602-786-7200	www.microchip.com	Instruments-Controls
617-551-1000	www.microcom.com	Networking Products
601-746-4131	www.misschem.com	Fertilizers
706-629-7721	www.mohawkcarpet.com	Textile-Home Furnishings
619-452-0681		Medical-Biomed/Gene
208-386-5000		Building-Heavy Construct
715-693-4470		Paper/Related Products
901-332-2500		Transport-Truck
901-753-3200		Metal Processors/Fabrica
441-295-5688	www.mutrisk.com	Property/Casualty Ins
619-453-8030	www.mycogen.com	Medical-Biomed/Gene
330-253-5592		Rubber/Plastics
612-832-0534		Food Items-Wholesale
603-880-2323	www.nashua.mv.com	Office Supplies/Forms
216-349-1000		Finance-Auto Loan Serv
612-829-3000	www.ncs.com	Optical Recognition Soft
404-728-2000		Data Processing/Mgmt
801-342-4300	www.natr.com	Cosmetics/Toiletries
212-541-5990		Apparel Manufacturers
516-567-9500		Cosmetics/Toiletries

TICKER	COMPANY NAME	ADDRESS
NWK	Network Eqpt. Techn	800 Saginaw Dr., Redwood City, CA 94063
NETG	Network General	4200 Bohannon Dr., Menlo Park, CA 94025
NEB	New England Business Svc Inc	500 Main St., Groton, MA 01471
NJR	N J Resources	1415 Wyckoff Rd., Wall, NJ 07719
NFX	Newfield Exploration Co	363 N. Sam Houston Pkwy. E., Ste. 2020, Houston, TX 77060
NFOR	NFO Research Inc	2 Pickwick Plz., Greenwich, CT 06830
NE	Noble Drilling Corp	10370 Richmond Ave., Houston, TX 77042
NRND	Norand Corp	550 Second St. SE Cedar Rapids, IA 52401
NRL	Norrell Corp	3535 Piedmont Rd. NE, Atlanta, GA 30305
NAC	North American Mortgage Co	3883 Airway Dr., Santa Rosa, CA 95403
NVX	North American Vaccine Inc	12103 Indian Creek Ct., Beltsville, MD 20705
NWNG	Northwest Nat. Gas	220 NW Second Ave.,Portland, OR 97209
NWSW	Northwestern Steel & Wire Co	121 Wallace St., Sterling, IL 61081
NVLS	Novellus Sys. Inc	3970 N. First St., San Jose, CA 95134
NOVN	Noven Phamaceutls.	11960 SW 144th St., Miami, FL 33186
NTN	NTN Comms. Inc	5966 La Place Ct., Carlsbad, CA 92008
ORLY	O'Reilly Automotive	233 S. Patterson Ave., Springfield, MO 65802
OSL	O'Sullivan Corp	1944 Valley Ave., Winchester, VA 22601
OAK	Oak Industries Inc	1000 Winter St., Waltham, MA 02154
OH	Oakwood Homes	7800 McCloud Rd., Greensboro, NC 27409
OII	Oceaneering Intl Inc	16001 Pk. Ten Pl., Ste. 600, Houston, TX 77084
OLOG	Offshore Logistics	224 Rue de Jean, Lafayette, LA 70508
OHM	OHM Corp	16406 U.S. Route 224 East, Findlay, OH 45840
OMP	OM Group Inc	50 Public Square, 3800 Terminal Tower, Cleveland, OH 44113
OMEG	Omega Environmental Inc	19805 N. Creek Pkwy., Bothell, WA 98011
OCR	Omnicare Inc	255 E. Fifth St., Cincinnati, OH 45202
ONBK	ONBANCorp Inc	101 S. Salina St., Syracuse, NY 13202
ORU	Orange & Rockland Utilities	1 Blue Hill Plz., Pearl River, NY 10965

PHONE	WEB ADDRESS AS OF 2/10/97	INDUSTRY SUBGROUP
415-366-4400	www.net.com	Telecomm Equip
415-473-2000	www.ngc.com	Network Software
508-448-6111	www.nebs.com	Office Supplies/Forms
908-938-1480	www.njng.com	Gas-Distribution
281-847-6000	www.newfld.com	Oil Comp-Explor/Prodtn
203-629-8888	www.nfor.com	Commercial Services
713-974-3131		Oil/Gas Drilling
319-369-3100	www.norand.com	Computers-Intgrtd Syst
404-240-3000	www.norrell.com	Human Resources
707-523-5000	www.namc.com	Fin-Mtge Loan/Banker
301-470-6100	www.nava.com	Medical-Drugs
503-226-4211	www.nng.com	Gas-Distribution
815-625-2500		Steel-Producers
408-943-9700		Elctrnc Compo-Semicon
305-253-5099		Medical-Drugs
619-438-7400	www.ntn.com	Cable TV
417-862-3333		Auto Parts-Retail/Whsle
540-667-6666	www.osul.com	Rubber/Plastics
617-890-0400		Electronic Compo-Misc
910-664-2400	www.oakwooodhomes.com	Mobil Home/Mfd Hous
281-578-8868	www.oceaneering.com	Oil-Field Services
318-233-1221		Transport-Services
419-423-3529	www.ohm.com	Hazardous Waste Dspsl
216-781-0083	www.omgi.com	Chemicals-Specialty
206-486-4800		Remediation Services
513-762-6666		Pharmacy Services
315-424-4400	www.onbank.com	S&L/Thrifts-Eastern US
914-352-6000	www.oru.com	Electric-Integrated

TICKER	COMPANY NAME	ADDRESS
ORBI	Orbital Sciences Corp	21700 Atlantic Blvd., Dulles, VA 20166
OC	Orion Capital Corp	600 Fifth Ave., New York, NY 10020
GOSHA	Oshkosh B'Gosh Inc	112 Otter Ave., Oshkosh, WI 54901
OM	Outboard Marine	100 Seahorse Dr., Waukegan, IL 60085
OMI	Owens & Minor Inc	4800 Cox Rd., Glen Allen, VA 20360
OXM	Oxford Industries Inc	222 Piedmont Ave. NE, Atlanta, GA 30308
PSX	Pacific Scientific Co	620 Nwprt. Cntr. Dr., Newport Beach, CA 92660
PTB	Paragon Trade Brands Inc	180 Technology Pkwy., Norcross, GA 30092
PKE	Park Electrochemical	5 Dakota Dr., Lake Success, NY 11042
PDCO	Patterson Dental Co	1031 Mendota Heights Rd, St. Paul, MN 55120
PXR	PAXAR Corp	105 Corporate Pk. Dr., White Plains, NY 10604
PCS	Payless Cashways	2300 Main St., Kansas City, MO 64108
PNT	Penn Enterprises Inc	39 Public Sq., Wilkes-Barre, PA 18711
PENW	Penwest Ltd	777-108th Ave. NE, Bellevue, WA 98004
PBIO	PerSeptive Biosystems Inc	500 Old Connecticut. Path, Framingham, MA 01701
PMRX	Pharmaceutical Marketing Svs.	45 Rockefeller Plz., Ste. 912, New York, NY 10111
PRX	Pharmaceutical Resources Inc	1 Ram Ridge Rd., Spring Valley, NY 10977
PSC	Phila. Suburban Corp	762 Lancaster Ave., Bryn Mawr, PA 19010
PVH	Phillips-Van Heusen	1290 Ave. of the Americas, New York, NY 10104
PLAB	Photronics Inc	1061 E. Indiantown Rd., Jupiter, FL 33477
PHYC	PhyCor Inc	30 Burton Hills Blvd, Nashville, TN 37215
PCTL	PictureTel Corp	100 Minuteman Rd., Andover, MA 01810
PNY	Piedmont Nat. Gas	1915 Rexford Rd., Charlotte, NC 28211
PIR	Pier 1 Imports Inc	301 Commerce St., Fort Worth, TX 76102
PTX	Pillowtex Corp	4111 Mint Way, Dallas, TX 75237
PIOG	Pioneer Group Inc	60 State St., Boston, MA 02109
PIOS	Pioneer Standard Electronics	4800 East 131st Street, Cleveland, OH 44105
PJC	Piper Jaffrey Funds	222 S. Ninth St., Minneapolis, MN 55402
PZX	Pittston Burlington	1000 Virginia Cntr. Pkwy., Glen Allen, VA 23060
PLX	Plains Resources Inc	1600 Smith St., Ste. 1500, Houston, TX 77002
PSQL	Platinum Software	195 Technology Dr., Irvine, CA 92618

PHONE	WEB ADDRESS AS OF 2/10/97	INDUSTRY SUBGROUP
703-406-5000	www.orbital.com	Aerospace/Defense-Equip
212-332-8080		Property/Casualty Ins
414-231-8800		Apparel Manufacturers
847-689-6200	www.omc-online.com	Recreational Vehicles
804-747-9794		Medical Products
404-659-2424		Apparel Manufacturers
714-720-1714		Machinery-Electrical
770-300-4000		Paper/Related Products
516-354-4100	www.parkelectro.com	Circuit Boards
612-686-1600	www.pdental.com	Dental Supplies/Equip
914-697-6800	www.paxar.com	Machinery-Generl Indust
816-234-6000	www.payless.cashways.com	Bldg Products Ret/Whsle
717-829-8843		Gas-Distribution
206-462-6000	www.penw.com	Chemicals-Specialty
508-383-7700	www.pbio.com	Instruments-Scientific
212-841-0610		Commercial Services
914-425-7100		Medical-Generic Drugs
610-527-8000	www.suburbanwater.com	Water
212-541-5200		Apparel Manufacturers
561-745-1222	www.photronics.com	Elctrnc Compo-Semicon
615-665-9066	www.phycor.com	Health Care Cost Contain
508-292-5000	www.picturetel.com	Telecomm Equip
704-364-3120	www.piedmontng.com	Gas-Distribution
817-878-8000	www.pier1.com	Retail-Home Furnishings
214-333-3225	www.pillowtex.com	Textile-Home Furnishings
617-742-7825		Finance-Invest Bnkr/Brkr
216-587-3600	www.pios.com	Elctrnc Compo-Semicon
612-342-6000	www.piperjaffray.com	Finance-Invest Bnkr/Brkr
804-553-3600		Transport-Air Freight
713-654-1414		Oil Comp-Explor/Prodtn
714-453-4000	www.platsoft.com	Applications Software

TICKER	COMPANY NAME	ADDRESS
PLAT	Platinum Technlgy	815 S. Meyers Rd., Oakbrook Terr., IL 60181
PLAY	Players Intl Inc	1300 Atlantic Ave., Atlantic City, NJ 08401
PLEN	Plenum Publishing	233 Spring St., New York, NY 10013
PLXS	Plexus Corp	55 Jewelers Park Dr., Neenah, WI 54957
PGI	Ply Gem Industries	777 Third Ave., New York, NY 10017
PPP	Pogo Producing Co	5 Greenway Plz., Houston, TX 77046
PESC	Pool Energy Svcs. Co	10375 Richmond Ave., Houston, TX 77042
POP	Pope & Talbot Inc	1500 SW First Ave., Portland, OR 97201
PMI	Premark Intl Inc	1717 Deerfield Rd., Deerfield, IL 60015
PRDE	Pride Petroleum Svcs	1500 City West Blvd., Houston, TX 77042
PMK	Primark Corp	1000 Winter St., Waltham, MA 02154
PDQ	Prime Hospitality	700 Route 46 East, Fairfield, NJ 07004
PROP	Production Operators Corp	11302 Tanner Rd., Houston, TX 77041
PRFT	Proffitts Inc	115 N. Calderwood St., Alcoa, TN 37701
PRGS	Progress Software	14 Oak Park, Bedford, MA 01730
PL	Protective Life Corp	2801 Hwy. 280 South, Birmingham, AL 35223
PDLI	Protein Design Labs	2375 Garcia Avenue, Mountain View, CA 94043
PRBK	Provident Bancorp	1 E. Fourth St., Cincinnati, OH 45202
PGS	Public Svc. Co of NC	400 Cox Rd., Gastonia, NC 28054
KWR	Quaker Chemical Crp	Elm and Lee Streets, Conshohocken, PA 19428
NX	Quanex Corp	1900 West Loop S., Houston, TX 77027
BQR	Quick & Reilly Group	230 S. County Rd., Palm Beach, FL 33480
RTEX	Railtex Inc	4040 Broadway, San Antonio, TX 78209
RJF	Raymond James Financial Corp	880 Carillon Parkway, St. Petersburg, FL 33716
RCSB	RCSB Financial Inc	235 E. Main St., Rochester, NY 14604
RDM	RDM Sports Group	250 Spring St. NW, Atlanta, GA 30303
RDRT	Read-Rite Corp	345 Los Coches St., Milpitas, CA 95035
RBC	Regal Beloit	200 State St., Beloit, WI 53511
REGL	Regal Cinemas Inc	7132 Commercial Pk. Dr., Knoxville, TN 37918
REGN	Regeneron Pharmaceuticals	777 Old Saw Mill River Rd., Tarrytown, NY 10591
RGIS	Regis Corp	7201 Metro Blvd., Minneapolis, MN 55439
RGC	Republic Gypsum Co	811 E. 30th Ave., Hutchinson, KS 67502
RSND	Resound Corp	220 Saginaw Dr., Redwood City, CA 94063

PHONE	WEB ADDRESS AS OF 2/10/97	INDUSTRY SUBGROUP
630-620-5000	www.platinum.com	Computer Software
609-449-7777		Gambling (Non-Hotel)
212-620-8000		Publishing-Books
414-722-3451	www.plexus.com	Elctrnc Compo-Semicon
212-832-1550	www.plygem.com	Bldg/Construct Prod-Misc
713-297-5000		Oil Comp-Explor/Prodtn
713-954-3000		Oil-Field Services
503-228-9161	www.poptal.com	Paper/Related Products
847-405-6000	www.premarkintl.com	Retail-Cutlery/Cookware
713-789-1400	www.prde.com	Oil-Field Services
617-466-6611	www.primark.com	Computer Services
201-882-1010		Hotels/Motels
713-466-0980		Oil-Field Services
423-983-7000	www.proffitts.com	Retail-Regnl Dept Store
617-280-4000	www.progress.com	Applications Software
205-879-9230	www.protective.com	Life/Health Insurance
415-903-3700	www.pdl.com	Medical-Biomed/Gene
513-345-7102	www.cin.ix.net/provident	Commer Banks-Cntrl US
704-864-6731		Gas-Distribution
610-832-4000		Chemicals-Specialty
713-961-4600		Steel Pipe/Tube
407-655-8000	www.quick-reilly.com	Finance-Invest Bnkr/Brkr
210-841-7600		Transport-Rail
813-573-3800	www.rjf.com	Finance-Invest Bnkr/Brkr
716-423-7270		S&L/Thrifts-Eastern US
404-586-9000		Athletic Equipment
408-262-6700	www.readrite.com	Computers-Mem Devices
608-364-8800		Mach Tools/Rel Products
423-922-1123		Theaters
914-347-7000		Medical-Biomed/Gene
612-947-7777		Retail-Hair Salons
316-727-2700	www.republic-group.com	Bldg/Construct Prod-Misc
415-780-7800	www.resound.com	Medical Products

TICKER	COMPANY NAME	ADDRESS
RESP	Respironics Inc	1001 Murry Ridge Dr, Murrysville, PA 15668
RXL	Rexel Inc	150 Alhambra Cir., Coral Gables, FL 33134
RFH	Richfood Holdings	8258 Richfood Rd., Mechanicsville,VA 23116
RIGS	Riggs National Corp Washington D.C.	1503 Pennsylvania Ave. NW, Washington, DC 20005
RIVL	Rival Co (The)	800 E. 101st Terr., Kansas City, MO 64131
RPCX	Roberts Pharm. Corp	Meridian Cntr. 2, 4 Industrial Way W., Eatontown, NJ 07724
REN	Rollins Environmental Svcs	1 Rollins Plz., Wilmington, DE 19803
RLC	Rollins Truck Leasing	1 Rollins Plz., Wilmington, DE 19803
RFED	Roosevelt Financial Group Inc	900 Roosevelt Parkway, Chesterfield, MO 63017
ROP	Roper Industries Inc	160 Ben Burton Rd., Bogart, GA 30622
ROST	Ross Stores Inc	8333 Central Ave, Newark, CA 94560
RAM	Royal Appliance Mfg	650 Alpha Dr.,Cleveland, OH 44143
RI	Ruby Tuesday Inc	4721 Morrison Dr., Mobile, AL 36609
RUS	Russ Berrie & Co Inc	111 Bauer Dr., Oakland, NJ 07436
RYAN	Ryan's Family Steak Houses Inc	405 Lancaster Avenue., Greer, SC 29650
RYK	Rykoff-Sexton Inc	613 Baltimore Dr., Wilkes-Barre, PA 18702
RYL	Ryland Group Inc	11000 Broken Land Pkwy., Columbia, MD 21044
SIII	S3 Inc	2770 San Tomas Expwy., Santa Clara, CA 95051
SFSK	Safeskin Corp	12671 High Bluff Dr., San Diego, CA 92130
SANM	Sanmina Corp	355 E. Trimble Rd., San Jose, CA 95131
SCIS	SCI Systems Inc	2101 W. Clinton Ave., Huntsville, AL 35801
SCLN	SciClone Pharm. Inc	901 Mariner's Isl. Blvd., San Mateo, CA 94404
SMG	Scotts Co (The)	14111 Scottslawn Rd., Marysville, OH 43041
SEIC	SEI Investments Co	1 Freedom Valley Dr., Oaks, PA 19456
SEI	Seitel Inc	50 Briar Hollow La., W. Bldg., Houston, TX 77027
SIGI	Selective Insur. Grp.	40 Wantage Ave., Branchville, NJ 07826
SEQU	SEQUUS Pharmaceuticals Inc	960 Hamilton Ct., Menlo Park, CA 94025
SHN	Shoney's Inc	1727 Elm Hill Pike, Nashville, TN 37210
SKO	Shopko Stores Inc	700 Pilgrim Way, Green Bay, WI 54304

PHONE	WEB ADDRESS AS OF 2/10/97	INDUSTRY SUBGROUP
412-733-0200	www.respironics.com	Respiratory Products
305-446-8000	www.rexel.com	Electronic Products-Misc
804-746-6000	www.richfood.com	Food Items-Wholesale
301-887-6000		Commer Banks-Eastrn US
816-943-4100	www.rivco.com	Appliances-Household
908-389-1182		Medical-Generic Drugs
302-426-2700		Hazardous Waste Dspsl
302-426-2700	www.rlc-corp.com	Trucking/Leasing
314-532-6200		S&L/Thrifts-Central US
706-369-7170		Miscellan.Manufactur
510-505-4400	www.rossstores.com	Retail-Apparel/Shoe
216-449-6150		Appliances-Household
334-344-3000		Retail-Restaurants
201-337-9000	www.russ-berrie.com	Consumer Products-Misc
864-879-1000		Retail-Restaurants
717-831-7500		Food Items-Wholesale
410-715-7000		Bldg-Residential/Commer
408-980-5400	www.s3.com	Elctrnc Compo-Semicon
619-794-8111		Disposable Medical Prod
408-435-8444	www.sanmina.com	Circuit Boards
205-882-4800	www.sci.com	Electronic Compo-Misc
415-358-3456	www.biospace.com/sciclone	Therapeutics
937-644-0011		Fertilizers
610-676-1000		Investment Companies
713-627-1990		Oil-Field Services
201-948-3000	www.select-ins.com	Property/Casualty Ins
415-323-9011	www.sequus.com	Medical-Drugs
615-391-5201		Retail-Restaurants
414-497-2211		Retail-Discount

TICKER	COMPANY NAME	ADDRESS
SHOR	Shorewood Packaging Corp	277 Park Ave., New York, NY 10172
SHBZ	Showbiz Pizza Time	4441 W. Airport Freeway, rving, TX 75062
SBO	Showboat Inc	2800 Fremont St., Las Vegas, NV 89104
SIE	Sierra Health Svcs.	2724 N. Tenaya Way, Las Vegas, NV 89128
SRP	Sierra Pacif. Resrcs.	6100 Neil Road, Reno, NV 89511
SMPS	Simpson Industries	47603 Halyard Dr., Plymouth, MI 48170
SKY	Skyline Corp	2520 By-Pass Rd., Elkhart, IN 46514
SKYW	Skywest Inc	444 S. River Rd., St. George, UT 84790
AOS	Smith (A.O.) Corp	11270 W. Park Pl., Milwaukee, WI 53224
SFD	Smith's Food & Drug Centers	1550 S. Redwood Road, Salt Lake City, UT 84104
SFDS	Smithfield Foods Inc	999 Waterside Dr., Norfolk, VA 23510
SNY	Snyder Oil Corp	777 Main St., Ste. 2500, Fort Worth, TX 76102
SOL	Sola Intl Inc	2420 Sand Hill Rd., Menlo Park, CA 94025
SONC	Sonic Corp	101 Park Ave., Oklahoma City, OK 73102
SCW	Southern California Water Co	630 East Foothill Blvd., San Dimas, CA 91773
SEHI	Southern Energy Homes Inc	Highway 41 North, Addison, AL 35540
SWX	Southwest Gas Corp	5241 Spring Mountain Rd., Las Vegas, NV 89193
SWN	Southwestern Energy Company	1083 Sain St., P.O.B. 1408, Fayetteville, AR 72702-1408
SVRN	Sovereign Bancorp	1130 Berkshire Blvd., Wyomissing, PA 19610
SLMD	SpaceLabs Medical	15220 NE 40th St., Redmond, WA 98052
SPAR	Spartan Motors Inc	1000 Reynolds Rd., Charlotte, MI 48813
TSA	Sports Authority Inc	3383 N. State Rd. 7, Fort Lauderdale, FL 33319
ST	SPS Technologies	101 Greenwood Ave., Jenkintown, PA 19046
SPW	SPX Corp	700 Terrace Point Dr., Muskegon, MI 49443
SJK	St John Knits Inc	17422 Derian Ave., Irvine, CA 92614
MARY	St Mary Land & Exploration Co	1776 Lincoln St., Ste. 1100, Denver, CO 80203
SPBC	St Paul Bancorp Inc	6700 W. North Ave., Chicago, IL 60707
SMSC	Standard Microsystems Corp	80 Arkay Drive, Hauppauge, NY 11788

PHONE	WEB ADDRESS AS OF 2/10/97	INDUSTRY SUBGROUP
212-371-1500		Containers-Paper/Plastic
972-258-8507		Retail-Restaurants
702-385-9123		Casino Hotels
702-242-7000		Medical-HMO
702-689-3600	www.sierrapacific.com	Electric-Integrated
313-207-6200		Auto/Trk Prts/Equip-Orig
219-294-6521		Bldg-MoblHome/MfHous
801-634-3000	www.skywest-air.com	Airlines
414-359-4000	www.aosmith.com	Auto/Trk Prts/Equip-Orig
801-974-1400		Food-Retail
757-365-3000		Food-Meat Products
817-338-4043		Oil Comp-Explor/Prodtn
415-324-6868	www.sola.com	Optical Supplies
405-280-7654	www.sonicdrivein.com	Retail-Restaurants
909-394-3600		Water
205-747-8589		Bldg-MoblHome/MfHous
702-876-7237		Gas-Distribution
501-521-1141		Gas-Distribution
610-320-8400	www.sovereignbank.com	S&L/Thrifts-Eastern US
206-882-3700	www.spacelabs.com	Patient Monitoring Equip
517-543-6400		Auto/Trk Prts/Equip-Orig
954-735-1701	www.pwr.com/SportsAuthority/	Retail-Sporting Goods
215-517-2000		Diversified Operations
616-724-5000	www.spx.com	Mach Tools/Rel Products
714-863-1171		Apparel Manufacturers
303-861-8140		Oil Comp-Explor/Prodtn
773-622-5000		S&L/Thrifts-Central US
516-435-6000	www.smc.com	Networking Products

TICKER	COMPANY NAME	ADDRESS
SMP	Standard Motor Products	37-18 Northern Blvd., Long Island City, NY 11101
SPD	Standard ProductsCo	2401 S. Gulley Rd., Dearborn, MI 48124
SPF	Standard-Pacific Crp.	1565 W. MacArthur Blvd., Costa Mesa, CA 92626
SXI	Standex Intl Corp	6 Manor Pkwy., Salem, NH 03079
STTX	Steel Technologies	15415 Shelbyville Rd., Louisville, KY 40245
SMRT	Stein Mart Inc	1200 Riverplace Blvd., Jacksonville, FL 32207
STRL	STERIS Corp	5960 Heisley Rd., Mentor, OH 44060
SSW	Sterling Software	8080 N. Central Expwy., Dallas, TX 75206
PGMS	Stillwater Mining Co	536 E. Pike Ave., Columbus, MT 59019
SW	Stone & Webster Inc	250 W. 34th St., New York, NY 10119
RGR	Sturm Ruger & Co Inc	Lacey Pl., Southport, CT 06490
BEAM	Summit Technology	21 Hickory Dr., Waltham, MA 02154
SNDT	Sungard Data Sys.	1285 Drummers La., Wayne, PA 19087
SMD	Sunrise Medical Inc	2382 Faraday Ave., Carlsbad, CA 92008
SABI	Swiss Army Brands	1 Research Dr., Shelton, CT 06484
SYB	Sybron Intl Corp	411 E. Wisconsin Ave., Milwaukee, WI 53202
SYMM	Symmetricom Inc	85 W. Tasman Dr., San Jose, CA 95134
SCOR	Syncor Intl Corp-Del	20001 Prairie St., Chatsworth, CA 91311
SSAX	System Software Associates Inc	500 W. Madison St., 32nd Fl. Chicago, IL 60661
TACO	Taco Cabana	8918 Tesoro Dr., San Antonio, TX 78217
TBCC	TBC Corp	4770 Hickory Hill Rd., Memphis, TN 38141
TBY	TCBY Enterprises Inc	425 W. Capitol Ave., Little Rock, AR 72201
TCB	TCF Financial Corp	801 Marquette Ave., Minneapolis, MN 55402
TCS	TCSI Corporation	1080 Marina Village Pkwy., Alameda, CA 94501
TECD	Tech Data Corp	5350 Tech Data Dr., Clearwater, FL 34620
TCNL	TECHNOL Medical Products Inc	7201 Industrial Park Blvd., Fort Worth, TX 76180
TLXN	Telxon Corp	3330 W. Market St., Akron, OH 44333
TNCR	Tencor Instruments	1 Technology Dr., Milpitas, CA 95035
TTRA	Tetra Technologies	25025 I-45 N., The Woodlands, TX 77380
TXI	Texas Industries Inc	1341 W. Mockingbird La., Dallas, TX 75247
THRT	Theratech Inc/Utah	417 Wakara Way, Salt Lake City, UT 84108
TII	Thomas Industries	4360 Brownsboro Rd., Louisville, KY 40207
TNM	Thomas Nelson Inc	501 Nelson Pl., Nashville, TN 37214

PHONE	WEB ADDRESS AS OF 2/10/97	INDUSTRY SUBGROUP
718-392-0200		Auto/Trk Prts/Equip-Repl
313-561-1100		Auto/Trk Prts/Equip-Orig
714-668-4300		Bldg-Residential/Commer
603-893-9701	www.standex.com	Diversified Operations
502-245-2110		Metal Processors/Fabrica
904-346-1500		Retail-Apparel/Shoe
216-354-2600		Medical Steriliz Product
214-891-8600	www.sterling.com/	Data Processing/Mgmt
303-978-2525		Precious Metals
212-290-7500	www.stoneweb.com	Building-Heavy Construct
203-259-7843	www.ruger-firearms.com	Firearms/Ammunition
617-890-1234	.	Medical Laser Systems
610-341-8700	www.sungard.com	Computer Services
619-930-1500	www.sunrisemedical.com	Hospital Beds/Equipment
203-929-6391		Consumer Products-Misc
414-274-6600	www.sybron.com	Dental Supplies/Equip
408-943-9403	www.symmetricom.com	Telecomm Equip
818-886-7400		Medical-Whsle Drug Dist
312-258-6000	www.ssax.com	Applications Software
210-804-0990		Retail-Restaurants
901-363-8030		Auto/Trk Prts/Equip-Repl
501-688-8229		Retail-Restaurants
612-661-6500		S&L/Thrifts-Central US
510-749-8500	www.tcsi.com	Communicatns Software
813-539-7429	www.techdata.com	Retail-Whsle Companies
817-581-6424		Disposable Medical Prod
330-664-1000	www.telxon.com	Computers-Micro
408-970-9500	www.tencor.com	Electric Products-Misc
281-367-1983	www.tetratec.com	Water Treatmnt Systems
972-647-6700	www.txi.com	BldgProd-Cement/Aggreg
801-588-6200	www.thrt.com	Drug Delivery Systems
502-893-4600	www.thomasind.com	Bldg Prod-Light Fixtures
615-889-9000		Publishing-Books

TICKER	COMPANY NAME	ADDRESS
THO	Thor Industries Inc	419 W. Pike St., Jackson Cntr., OH 45334
TFS	Three-Five Sys. Inc	1600 N. Desert Dr., Tempe, AZ 85281
TBL	Timberland Co	200 Domain Dr., Stratham, NH 03885
TWI	Titan Wheel Intl Inc	2701 Spruce St., Quincy, IL 62301
TJCO	TJ Intl Inc	200 E. Mallard Dr., Boise, Idaho 83706
TNP	TNP Enterprises Inc	4100 Intl. Plz., P.O.B. 2943, Fort Worth, TX 76113
TOL	Toll Brothers Inc	3103 Philmont, Huntington Valley, PA 19006
TTC	Toro Co	8111 Lyndale Ave. S., Bloomington, MN 55420
TG	Tredegar Industries	1100 Boulders Pkwy., Richmond, VA 23225
TREN	Trenwick Group Inc	Metro Cntr., 1 Station Pl., Stamford, CT 06902
TRY	Triarc Companies	280 Park Ave., New York, NY 10017
TRMB	Trimble Navigation	645 N. Mary Ave. Sunnyvale, CA 94088
TNO	True North Comms.	FCB Cntr., 101 E. Erie St., Chicago, IL 60611
TSNG	Tseng Laboratories	6 Terry Dr. Newtown, PA 18940
TUBO	Tuboscope Vetco	2835 Holmes Rd., Houston, TX 77051
TTX	Tultex Corp	101 Commonwealth Blvd, P.O.B. 5191, Martinsville, VA 24115
TTI	Tyco Toys Inc	6000 Midlantic Dr., Mt. Laurel, NJ 08054
UH	U S Home Corp	1800 West Loop S., Houston, TX 77027
UNC	UNC Inc	175 Adm. Cochrane Dr., Annapolis, MD 21401
UPC	Union Planters Corp	6200 Poplar Ave., Memphis TN 38119
UCIT	United Cities Gas Co	5300 Maryland Way, Brentwood, TN 37027
UIL	United Illuminating	157 Church St., New Haven, CT 06506
UMC	United Meridian Crp.	1201 Louisiana, Ste. 1400, Houston, TX 77002
UFPI	Universal Forest Products Inc	2801 East. Beltline NE, Grand Rapids, MI 49505
UHS	Universal Health Services	367 South Gulph Road, King of Prussia, PA 19406
UBS	US Bioscience Inc	1 Tower Bridge, 100 Front St., Ste. 24, West Conshohocken, PA 19428
USF	US Filter Corp	40-004 Cook St., Palm Desert, CA 92211
USTC	US Trust Corp	114 W. 47th St., New York, NY 10036
USAD	USA Detergents Inc	1735 Jersey Ave., North Brunswick, NJ 08902
USFC	USFreightways Corp	9700 Higgins Rd., Ste. 570, Rosemont, IL 60018
VCI	Valassis Comms. Inc	36111 Schoolcraft Rd., Livonia, MI 48150
VLNC	Valence Technology	301 Conestoga Way, Henderson, NV 89015

PHONE	WEB ADDRESS AS OF 2/10/97	INDUSTRY SUBGROUP
937-596-6849		BldgMoblHom/MfgHous
602-389-8600		Computers-Intgrtd Sys
603-772-9500		Footwear/RelatedApparel
217-228-6011		Auto/Trk Prts/Equip-Orig
208-364-3300		Bldg/Constrct Prod-Misc
817-731-0099	www.tnpe.com	Electric-Integrated
215-938-8000	www.tollbrothers.com	Bldg-Residential/Commer
612-888-8801	www.toro.com	Home Furnishings-Orig
804-330-1000	www.tredegar.com	Chemicals-Plastics
203-353-5500		Property/Casualty Ins
212-451-3000		Diversified Operations
408-481-8000	www.trimble.com	Instruments-Controls
312-751-7227		Advertising Agencies
215-968-0502	www.tseng.com	Elctrnc Compo-Semicon
713-799-5100		Oil-Field Services./Intrnatl
540-632-2961		Apparel Manufacturers
609-234-7400		Toys
713-877-1211	www.ushome.com	Bldg-Residential/Commer
410-266-7333		Aerospace/Defense-Equip
901-580-6000	www.unionplanters.com	Commer Banks-So US
615-373-5310		Gas-Distribution
203-499-2000	www.uinet.com	Electric-Integrated
713-654-9110		Oil Comp-Explor/Prodtn
616-364-6161		Bldg Prod-Wood
610-768-3300		Medical-Hospitals
610-832-0570	www.usbio.com	Therapeutics
619-340-0098	www.usfilter.com	Water Treatment Systms
212-852-1000	www.ustrust.com	Commer Banks-Eastrn US
908-828-1800		Soap/Cleaning Prepar
847-696-0200		Transport-Truck
313-591-3000		Printing-Commercial
702-558-1000		Batteries/Battery Sys

TICKER	COMPANY NAME	ADDRESS
VALM	Valmont Industries	P.O.B. 358, Valley, NE 68064
VEN	Venture Stores Inc	2001 E. Terra La., O'Fallon, MO 63366
VRTX	Vertex Pharmaceuts.	130 Waverly St., Cambridge, MA 02139
VICR	Vicor Corp	23 Frontage Rd., Andover, MA 01810
VIEW	Viewlogic Sys. Inc	293 Boston Post Rd. W, Marlboro, MA 01752
VPI	Vintage Petroleum	4200 One Williams Cntr., Tulsa, OK 74172
VISX	VISX Inc	3400 Central Expwy., Santa Clara, CA 95051
VITL	Vital Signs Inc	20 Campus Rd., Totawa, NJ 07512
VTSS	Vitesse Semicond	741 Calle Plano, Camarillo, CA 93012
V	Vivra Inc	1850 Gateway Dr., San Mateo, CA 94404
VLSI	VLSI Technology Inc	1109 McKay Dr., San Jose, CA 95131
WNC	Wabash Natl Corp	1000 Sagamore Pkwy. S., Lafayette, IN 47905
WALB	Walbro Corp	6242 Garfield St., Cass City, MI 48726
WALL	Wall Data Inc	11332 NE 122nd Way, Kirkland, WA 98034
WEG	Washington Energy	815 Mercer St., Seattle, WA 98109
WNT	Washington Natl	300 Tower Pkwy., Lincolnshire, IL 60069
WJ	Watkins-Johnson Co	3333 Hillview Ave., Palo Alto, CA 94304
WDFC	WD-40 Co	1061 Cudahy Pl., San Diego, CA 92110
WERN	Werner Enterprises Inc	14507 Frontier Road., I-80 and Highway 50, Omaha, NE 68138
WTNY	Whitney Holding Crp.	228 St. Charles Ave., New Orleans, LA 70130
WKR	Whittaker Corp	1955 N. Surveyor Ave., Simi Valley, CA 93063
WFMI	Whole Foods Mkt	601 N. Lamar, Ste. 300, Austin, TX 78703
WHX	WHX Corporation	110 E. 59th St., New York, NY 10022
WIC	Wicor Inc	626 E. Wisconsin Ave., Milwaukee, WI 53202
WSGC	Williams-Sonoma	3250 Van Ness Ave., San Francisco, CA 94109
WGO	Winnebago Industries Inc	605 West Crystal Lake Road, Forest City, IA 50436
WZR	Wiser Oil Co	8115 Preston Rd., Ste. 400, Dallas, TX 75225
WMS	WMS	3401 N. California Ave., Chicago, IL 60618
WLV	Wolverine Tube Inc	1525 Perimeter Pkwy., Huntsville, AL 35806
WWW	Wolverine World Wide Inc	9341 Courtland Dr. Rockford, MI 49351
WYL	Wyle Electronics	15370 Barranca Pkwy., Irvine, CA 92718
WN	Wynn's International	500 N. State College Blvd., Orange, CA 92868
XRIT	X-Rite Inc	3100 44th St. SW, Grandville, MI 49418

PHONE	WEB ADDRESS AS OF 2/10/97	INDUSTRY SUBGROUP
402-359-2201	www.valmont.com	Steel Pipe/Tube
314-281-5500	www.venturestores.com	Retail-Discount
617-577-6000	www.vpharm.com	Medical-Biomed/Gene
508-470-2900	www.vicr.com	Power Conv/Supply Equip
508-480-0881	www.viewlogic.com	Computer Software
918-592-0101		Oil Comp-Explor Prodtn
408-733-2020	www.visx.com	Medical Laser Systems
201-790-1330		Medical Products
805-388-3700	www.vitesse.com	Elctrnc Compo-Semicon
415-577-5700		Dialysis Centers
408-434-3000	www.vlsi.com	Elctrnc Compo-Semicon
765-448-1591	www.nlci.com/wabash	Auto-Truck Trailers
517-872-2131		Auto/Trk Prts/Equip-Orig
206-814-9255	www.walldata.com	Network Software
206-622-6767		Gas-Distribution
847-793-3000		Life/Health Insurance
415-493-4141	www.wj.com	Elctrnc Compo-Semicon
619-275-1400		Paint/Related Products
402-895-6640	www.werner.com	Transport-Truck
504-586-7117		Commer Banks-So US
805-526-5700	www.whittaker.com	Electric Products-Misc
512-477-4455	www.wholefoods.com	Food-Retail
212-355-5200		Steel-Producers
414-291-7026		Gas-Distribution
415-421-7900		Retail-Mail Order
515-582-3535	www.winnebagoind.com	Bldg-MoblHome/MfHous
214-265-0080		Oil Comp- Explor/Prodtn
773-961-1111	www.wms.com/williams/	Leisure/Rec/ Gaming
205-353-1310		Metal Processors/Fabrica
616-866-5500		Footwear/RelatedApparel
714-753-9953	www.wyle.com	Electronic Parts Distrib
714-938-3700		Auto/Trk Prts/Equip-Repl
616-534-7663	www.xrite.com	Instruments-Controls

TICKER	COMPANY NAME	ADDRESS
XIRC	Xircom Inc	2300 Corp. Cntr. Dr., Thousand Oaks, CA 91320
YELL	Yellow Corp	10990 Roe Ave., Overland Park, KS 66211
ZBRA	Zebra Technologies	333 Corp. Woods Pkwy., Vernon Hills, IL 60061
ZNT	Zenith Nat. Insur. Cp	21255 Califa St., Woodland Hills, CA 91367
ZRO	Zero Corp-Del	444 S. Flower St., Los Angeles, CA 90071
ZLG	Zilog Inc	210 E. Hacienda Ave, Campbell, CA 95008
ZION	Zions Bancorporation	1 S. Main St., Salt Lake City, UT 84111
ZOLL	Zoll Medical Corp	32 Second Ave., Burlington, MA 01803

PHONE	WEB ADDRESS AS OF 2/10/97	INDUSTRY SUBGROUP
805-376-9300	www.xircom.com	Networking Products
913-696-6100	www.yellowfreight.com/	Transport-Truck
847-634-6700	www.zebra.com	Printers/Related Prod
818-713-1000	www.zic.com	Multi-line Insurance
213-629-7000	www.zerocorp.com	Containers- Metal/Glass
408-370-8000	www.zilog.com	Elctrnc Compo-Semicond
801-524-4787	www.zionsbank.com	Commer Banks-WestrnUS
617-229-0020		Medical Instruments

SMALL-CAPS
State by State

HERE IS A STATE BY STATE directory to the companies in the first part of this Appendix.

ALABAMA

Birmingham Steel Corp
Books-A-Million Inc
Energen Corp
Kinder-Care Learning Centers
Protective Life Corp
Ruby Tuesday Inc
SCI Systems Inc
Southern Energy Homes Inc
Wolverine Tube Inc

ARIZONA

Aztar Corp
Bell Sports Corp
Continental Homes Holding
MicroAge Inc
Microchip Technology Inc
Three-Five Systems Inc

ARKANSAS

Acxiom Corp
American Freightways Corp
Arkansas Best Corp
Baldor Electric
First Commercial Corp

Southwestern Energy Company
TCBY Enterprises Inc

BERMUDA

Mutual Risk Management LTD

CALIFORNIA

ABM Industries Inc
ADAC Laboratories
Advanced Tissue Sciences Inc
Alliance Pharmaceutical Cp
Ashworth Inc
Aspect Telecommunications
Auspex Systems Inc
Authentic Fitness Corp
Bell Industries Inc
Benton Oil & Gas Co
Boole & Babbage Inc
Broderbund Software Inc
BW/IP Inc
Calgene Inc
California Microwave
Centigram Communications
Cheesecake Factory (The)
Chips & Technologies Inc

Circon Corp

CKE Restaurant Inc

Coast Savings Financial Inc

Coherent Inc

Collagen Corp

Compression Labs

COR Therapeutics Inc

Custom Chrome Inc

Cygnus Inc

Dames & Moore Inc

Digital Microwave Corp

Dionex Corp

Downey Financial Corp

Etec Systems Inc

Fair Issac & Company Inc

Fidelity National Finl Inc

Filenet Corp

First American Finl

Foodmaker Inc

Fremont General Corp

Fritz Companies Inc

Galoob Toys Inc

Gottschalks Inc

Hollywood Park Inc

HS Resources Inc

IHOP Corp

Immune Response Corp/Del

Intl Rectifier Corp

K-Swiss Inc

K2 Inc

Komag Inc

Logicon Inc

Mail Boxes Etc

Marshall Industries

Mentor Corp

Molecular Biosystems Inc

Mycogen Corp

Network Equipment Tech Inc

Network General Corp

North American Mortgage

Novellus Systems Inc

NTN Communications Inc

Pacific Scientific Co

Platinum Software Corp

Protein Design Labs Inc

Read-Rite Corp

Resound Corp

Ross Stores Inc

S3 Inc

Safeskin Corp

Sanmina Corp

SciClone Pharmaceuticals Inc

SEQUUS Pharmaceuticals Inc

Sola International Inc

Southern California Water Co

St John Knits Inc

Standard-Pacific Corp

Sunrise Medical Inc

Symmetricom Inc

Syncor Intl Corp-Del

TCSI Corporation

Tencor Instruments

Trimble Navigation Ltd

US Filter Corp

VISX Inc

Vitesse Semiconductor Corp

Vivra Inc

VLSI Technology Inc

Watkins-Johnson Company

WD-40 Co

Whittaker Corp

Williams-Sonoma Inc

Wyle Electronics

Wynn's International Inc

CALIFORNIA (cont.)

Xircom Inc
Zenith National Insurance Cp
Zero Corp-Del
Zilog Inc

CANADA

Cineplex Odeon Corporation
Glamis Gold Ltd

COLORADO

American Medical Response
Barrett Resources Corp
Commnet Cellular Inc
Getchell Gold Corp
Hauser Inc
K N Energy Inc
MDC Holdings Inc
St Mary Land & Exploration

CONNECTICUT

ADVO Inc
Air Express International Cp
Aquarion Co
Connecticut Energy Corp
Ethan Allen Interiors Inc
Gerber Scientific Inc
Hyperion Software Corp
Kaman Corp
Landstar System Inc
Life Re Corp
Lone Star Industries
Lydall Inc
Mariner Health Group Inc
NFO Research Inc
Sturm Ruger & Co Inc
Swiss Army Brands Inc

Trenwick Group Inc
United Illuminating Co

DELAWARE

Rollins Environmental Svcs
Rollins Truck Leasing Corp

WASHINGTON DC

Riggs Natl Corp Wash D C

FLORIDA

American Bankers Insur Group
BE Aerospace Inc
Breed Technologies Inc
Catalina Marketing Corp
Discount Auto Parts
Hughes Supply Inc
Interim Services Inc
Jan Bell Marketing Inc
Jumbosports Inc
Levitz Furniture Inc
Lincare Holdings Inc
Noven Pharmaceuticals Inc
Photronics Inc
Quick & Reilly Group Inc
Raymond James Financial Corp
Rexel Inc
Sports Authority Inc
Stein Mart Inc
Tech Data Corp

GEORGIA

AGCO Corp
Caraustar Industries Inc
Carmike Cinemas Inc
Compdent Corporation
GranCare Inc

Greenfield Industries Inc
Interface Inc
Johnston Ind-Del
Kuhlman Corp
Magellan Health Services
Mohawk Industries Inc
National Data Corp
Norrell Corp
Oxford Industries Inc
Paragon Trade Brands Inc
RDM Sports Group Inc
Roper Industries Inc

IDAHO

BMC West Corp
Coeur D'alene Mines Corp
Hecla Mining Co
Morrison Knudsen Corp
TJ International Inc

ILLINOIS

Aar Corp
Acme Metals Inc
Amcol International Corp
Anixter International Inc
Aptargroup Inc
Castle (A.M.) & Co
Cilcorp Inc
Clarcor Inc
Dekalb Genetics Corp
Devry Inc
Gallagher (Arthur J.) & Co
Hartmarx Corp
Insurance Auto Auctions Inc
Juno Lighting Inc
Material Sciences Corp
McWhorter Technologies Inc

Methode Electronics
Northwestern Steel & Wire Co
Outboard Marine Corp
Platinum Technology Inc
Premark International Inc
St Paul Bancorp Inc
System Software Assoc Inc
Titan Wheel Intl Inc
True North Communications
USFreightways Corporation
Washington Natl Corp
WMS Industries Inc
Zebra Technologies Corp

INDIANA

Lilly Industries Inc
Skyline Corp
Wabash National Corp

IOWA

Allied Group Inc
Casey's General Stores Inc
Heartland Express Inc
Interstate Power Co
Norand Corp
Winnebago Industries

KANSAS

Angelica Corp
Applebees Intl Inc
Republic Gypsum Co
Yellow Corporation

KENTUCKY

Commonwealth Aluminum Corp
Steel Technologies Inc
Thomas Industries Inc

LOUISIANA

Offshore Logistics

MAINE

Bangor Hydro-Electric Co

Consumers Water Co

IDEXX Laboratories Inc

MARYLAND

Alex Brown Inc

Hechinger Co

Integrated Health Services

Legg Mason Inc

MedImmune Inc

North American Vaccine Inc

Ryland Group Inc

UNC Inc

MASSACHUSETTS

Au Bon Pain Co Inc

Baker (J.) Inc

Banyan Systems Inc

BBN Corp

Bertucci's, Inc

Cognex Corp

Commonwealth Energy System

Cyrk International Inc

Designs Inc

Dynatech Corp

Eastern Utilities Assoc

Eaton Vance Corp

Filene's Basement Corp

GC Companies Inc

Immulogic Pharmaceutical

Ionics Inc

Keane Inc

Kronos Inc

Microcom Inc

New England Business Svc Inc

Oak Industries Inc.

PerSeptive Biosystems Inc

PictureTel Corp

Pioneer Group Inc

Primark Corp

Progress Software Corp

Summit Technology Inc

Vertex Pharmaceuticals Inc

Vicor Corp

Viewlogic Systems Inc

Zoll Medical Corp

MICHIGAN

Arbor Drugs Inc

Champion Enterprises Inc

Core Industries Inc

First Michigan Bank Corp

Gentex Corp

Intermet Corp

Kysor Industrial Corp

La-Z-Boy Inc

Simpson Industries

Spartan Motors Inc

SPX Corp

Standard Products Co

Universal Forest Products

Valassis Communications Inc

Walbro Corp

Wolverine World Wide

X-Rite Inc

MINNESOTA

Alliant Techsystems Inc

Apogee Enterprises Inc

Arctic Cat Inc

BMC Industries Inc-Minn
Control Data Systems Inc
Damark International Inc -A
Digi International Inc
G & K Services Inc
Grand Casinos Inc
Interra Financial Inc
Merrill Corporation
Nash Finch Co
National Computer Sys Inc
Patterson Dental Company
Piper Jaffrey Funds
Regis Corp
TCF Financial Corp
Toro Co

MISSISSIPPI

Casino Magic Corp
Chem First Inc
Deposit Guaranty Corp
Mississippi Chemical Corp

MISSOURI

Brown Group Inc
Butler Mfg Co
Cerner Corp
Earthgrains Company
Express Scripts Inc
Harmon Industries Inc
Henry (Jack) & Associates
Interstate Bakeries
Kellwood Co
Magna Group Inc
Mark Twain Bancshares Inc
O'Reilly Automotive Inc
Payless Cashways Inc
Rival Co (The)

Roosevelt Financial Grp Inc
Venture Stores Inc

MONTANA

Stillwater Mining Company

NEBRASKA

Commercial Federal Corp
Lindsay Manufacturing Co
Valmont Industries
Werner Enterprises Inc

NEVADA

Mesa Air Group Inc
Showboat Inc
Sierra Health Services
Sierra Pacific Resources
Southwest Gas Corp
Valence Technology Inc

NEW HAMPSHIRE

Fisher Scientific Intl
Nashua Corp
Standex International Corp
Timberland Company

NEW JERSEY

Air & Water Tech
Alpharma Inc
BISYS Group Inc
Cambrex Corp
Collective Bancorp Inc
Fedders Corp
Geotek Communications Inc
IMO Industries Inc
J & J Snack Foods Corp
KCS Energy Inc

NEW JERSEY (cont.)

Lechters Inc

Liposome Company Inc

New Jersey Resources

Players International Inc

Prime Hospitality Corp

Roberts Pharmaceutical Corp

Russ Berrie & Co Inc

Selective Insurance Group

Tyco Toys Inc

USA Detergents Inc

Vital Signs Inc

NEW YORK

Astoria Financial Corp

Bowne & Co Inc

Capital Re Corp

Central Hudson Gas & Elec

Comverse Technology Inc

Dress Barn Inc

Enhance Financial Svcs Group

Enzo Biochem Inc

Frontier Insurance Group Inc

Galey & Lord Inc

Griffon Corporation

Handy & Harman

Intermagnetics General Corp

JSB Financial Inc

Lillian Vernon Corp

Nautica Enterprises Inc

NBTY Inc

ONBANCorp Inc

Orange & Rockland Utilities

Orion Capital Corp

Park Electrochemical Corp

PAXAR Corp

Pharmaceutical Marketing Svs

Pharmaceutical Resources Inc

Phillips-Van Heusen

Plenum Publishing Corp

PLY GEM Industries

RCSB Financial Inc

Regeneron Pharmaceutical

Shorewood Packaging Corp

Standard Microsystems Corp

Standard Motor Prods

Stone & Webster Inc

Triarc Companies

US Trust Corp

WHX Corporation

NORTH CAROLINA

Broadband Technologies Inc

Cato Corp

CCB Financial Corp

Centura Banks Inc

Coca-Cola Bottling

Cone Mills Corp

Fieldcrest Cannon

Goodmark Foods

Guilford Mills Inc

Insteel Industries

Integon Corp/Del

Oakwood Homes

Piedmont Natural Gas Co

Public Service Co Of N C

OHIO

Allen Group

Amcast Indl Corp

Charter One Fin Inc

Chemed Corp

Chiquita Brands Intl

Comair Holdings Inc

Fabri-Centers Of America

Figgie International

FirstMerit Corporation

Geon Company

Huffy Corp

Invacare Corp

Medusa Corp

Myers Industries Inc

National Auto Credit Inc

OHM Corp

OM Group Inc

Omnicare Inc

Pioneer Standard Electronics

Provident Bancorp Inc

Royal Appliance Mfg Co

Scotts Company (The)

STERIS Corp

Telxon Corp

Thor Industries Inc

OKLAHOMA

Devon Energy Corporation

Liberty Bancorp Inc/Oklahoma

LSB Industries Inc

Sonic Corp

Vintage Petroleum Inc

Whitney Holding Corp

OREGON

Lattice Semiconductor Corp

Northwest Natural Gas Co

Pope & Talbot Inc

PENNSYLVANIA

C-COR Electronics

CDI Corp

Cephalon Inc

CMAC Investment Corp

Dravo Corp

Genesis Health Ventures

Integrated Circuit Systems

Keystone Fin Inc

Penn Enterprises Inc

Philadelphia Suburban Corp

Quaker Chemical Corp

Respironics Inc

Rykoff-Sexton Inc

SEI Investments Co

Sovereign Bancorp Inc

SPS Technologies Inc

Sungard Data Systems Inc

Toll Brothers Inc

Tseng Laboratories Inc

Universal Health Services

US Bioscience Inc

PUERTO RICO

FirstBank Puerto Rico

RHODE ISLAND

Cross (A.T.) Company

SOUTH CAROLINA

Delta Woodside Inds Inc

KEMET Corp

Ryan's Family Stk Houses Inc

TENNESSEE

Astec Industries Inc

Corrections Corp Of America

Coventry Corporation

Dixie Yarns Inc

Envoy Corporation

Insituform Technologies Inc

TENNESSEE (cont.)

MS Carriers Inc
Mueller Industries Inc
PhyCor Inc
Proffitts Inc
Regal Cinemas Inc
Shoney's Inc
TBC Corp
Thomas Nelson Inc
Union Planters Corp
United Cities Gas Co

TEXAS

Allwaste Inc
Amresco Inc
Amtech Corp
Atmos Energy Corp
BancTec Inc
Benchmark Electronics Inc
Bombay Company Inc (The)
Box Energy Corp
Cabot Oil & Gas Corp
Camco International Inc
Cash America Investments Inc
Commercial Metals Co
CompUSA Inc
Cross Timbers Oil Co
Cullen/Frost Bankers Inc
Cyrix Corp
Dallas Semiconductor Corp
Daniel Industries
Fibreboard Corp
Frozen Food Express Inds
Global Industries Tech Inc
Haggar Corp
IMCO Recycling Inc
Input/Output Inc

Intervoice Inc
Justin Industries
Kent Electronics Corp
Kirby Corp
Living Centers of America
Luby's Cafeterias Inc
Mesa Inc
Michaels Stores Inc
Newfield Exploration Company
Noble Drilling Corp
Oceaneering Intl Inc
Pier 1 Imports Inc-Del
Pillowtex Corp
Plains Resources Inc
Pogo Producing Co
Pool Energy Services Co
Pride Petroleum Svcs Inc
Production Operators Corp
Quanex Corp
Railtex Inc
Seitel Inc
Showbiz Pizza Time Inc
Snyder Oil Corp
Sterling Software Inc
Taco Cabana
Tetra Technologies Inc
Texas Industries Inc
TNP Enterprises Inc
Tuboscope Vetco Intl Corp
U S Home Corp
United Meridian Corp
Whole Foods Market Inc
Wiser Oil Co
Tecnol Medical Products Inc

UTAH

Ballard Medical Products

Franklin Quest Co

Natures Sunshine Prods Inc

Skywest Inc

Smith's Food & Drug Ctrs

Theratech Inc/Utah

Zions Bancorporation

VERMONT

Central Vermont Pub Serv

Green Mountain Power Corp

VIRGINIA

American Management Systems

Bassett Furniture Inds

Dimon Inc

Hilb, Rogal & Hamilton Co

Intl Family Entertainment

O'Sullivan Corp

Orbital Sciences Corp

Owens & Minor Inc Hldg Co

Pittston Burlington Group

Richfood Holdings Inc

Smithfield Foods Inc

Tredegar Industries Inc

Tultex Corp

WASHINGTON

Cascade Natural Gas Corp

CellPro Inc

Eagle Hardware & Garden

Expeditors Intl Wash Inc

Flow Intl Corp

Fluke Corp

Itron Inc

Omega Environmental Inc

Penwest Ltd

SpaceLabs Medical Inc

Wall Data Inc

Washington Energy Co

WISCONSIN

Carson Pirie Scott & Co

First Fin Corp -Wisc

Manitowoc Co

Marcus Corp

Mosinee Paper Corp

Oshkosh B'gosh Inc

Plexus Corp

Regal Beloit

Shopko Stores Inc

Smith (A.O.) Corp

Sybron Intl Corp

Wicor Inc

INDEX

ABOUT BLOOMBERG

Bloomberg Financial Markets is a global, multimedia-based distributor of information services, combining news, data, and analysis for financial markets and businesses. Bloomberg carries real-time pricing, data, history, analytics, and electronic communications that is available 24 hours a day and is currently accessed by 200,000 financial professionals in 91 countries.

Bloomberg covers all key global securities markets, including equities, money markets, currencies, municipals, corporate/euro/sovereign bonds, commodities, mortgage-backed securities, derivative products, and governments. The company also delivers access to Bloomberg News, whose more than 400 reporters and editors in 70 bureaus worldwide provide around-the-clock coverage of economic, financial, and political events.

The company information in the Appendix of this book was provided by Bloomberg's Equity Department, which maintains detailed current data and analytic functions on over 60,000 companies in 80 countries.

To learn more about Bloomberg—one of the world's fastest-growing real-time financial information networks—call a sales representative at:

Frankfurt:	49-69-920-410
Hong Kong:	852-2521-3000
London:	44-171-330-7500
New York:	1-212-318-2000
Princeton:	1-609-279-3000
São Paulo:	5511-3048-4500
Singapore:	65-226-3000
Sydney:	61-29-777-8600
Tokyo:	81-3-3201-8900

ABOUT THE AUTHORS

Christopher Graja is senior markets editor for *Bloomberg: A Magazine for Market Professionals* and *Bloomberg Personal* magazine. He holds an MBA from Rutgers University and was the director of training and a senior researcher for Bloomberg L.P.'s research division.

Mr. Graja welcomes reader comments and suggestions for future editions of this book. He may be reached by mail in care of Bloomberg Press, P.O. Box 888, Princeton, NJ 08542-0888, or via email at smallcap@bloomberg.com.

Elizabeth Ungar, Ph.D., is author of *Swap Literacy: A Comprehensible Guide,* published by Bloomberg Press. She has taught at Trinity College, Dublin, and is a senior editor of both *Bloomberg Personal* and *Bloomberg: A Magazine for Market Professionals,* in which she regularly converts highly technical subjects into highly readable prose. She has worked for *Business Month; Manhattan, inc.; Institutional Investor;* and *American Banker.* Ms. Ungar edited *An Introduction to Option-Adjusted Spread Analysis,* by Tom Windas, published by Bloomberg Professional Library, and is currently editing *Trading Electricity in the New Era of Deregulation,* to be published in the autumn of 1997 by Bloomberg Professional Library.